WARRIORS

WARRIORS

An Epic Battle for Olympic Rowing Victory

Danielle Brittain

BOOK**STORM**

RMB's partnership with Rowing South Africa
not only helps national athletes compete internationally,
but aims to help grow the sport at all levels. Through this
collaboration RMB has helped bring this remarkable story to life.

First edition, first impression 2021

Published by Bookstorm (Pty) Ltd
PO Box 4532
Northcliff 2115
Johannesburg
South Africa
www.bookstorm.co.za

ISBN: 978-1-928257-90-5
e-ISBN: 978-1-928257-91-2

Edited by Angela Voges
Proofread by Tracey Hawthorne
Cover design by mr design
Front cover images:
Top: Sizwe Ndlovu, John Smith, Matthew Brittain and James Thompson
afterw inning gold on Day 6 of the London 2012 Olympics.
Image © Damien Meyer/IOPP Pool/Getty Images
Bottom: Lawrence Brittain and Shaun Keeling on Day 1 of the Rio 2016 Olympics. Image
© Cameron Spencer/Getty Images
Back cover image: *From left* James, Matthew, Charles and Lawrence Brittain, Buffalo
Regatta, 2017. Image courtesy of Nicola Brittain.
Book design and typesetting by Triple M Design
Printed in the USA

For the men in my life,
David, Matthew, Lawrence, James, Charles.
The path with heart – always

For my parents,
Bertie and Doreen,
for being outstanding role models.
My mother, taken tragically and far too early
14.12.1935 – 17.12.1989

Danielle Brittain is the team doctor for the South African rowing team. She has been involved in rowing since 1980 and has followed the sport closely from that time, as her husband and four sons have all rowed for South Africa. Brittain became the team doctor in 2011 and works full time with the national team.

Brittain qualified from the University of the Witwatersrand in 1989 and worked in Rheumatology and Endocrinology at Baragwanath Hospital before becoming a Palliative Consultant. She has a Masters in Palliative Medicine from the University of Cape Town. She is married to David Brittain and currently lives in Pretoria, South Africa.

CONTENTS

It's about being a warrior. It doesn't matter about the cause necessarily. This is your path, and you will pursue it with excellence. You face your fear because your goal demands it. That is the goddamned warrior spirit. I think that the free solo mentality is pretty close to warrior culture: when you give something with 100 per cent focus, because your life depends on it.

– ALEX HONNOLD, FREE SOLO

PROLOGUE

When I began this story, I thought I would be writing about my son, who had cancer, and how he fought to race at the Olympic Games. I was at the Rio Olympic Games when the idea of writing the story entered my head.

I was right, but I was also wrong.

I was right because my son, Lawrence Brittain, had been diagnosed with Stage 4 Hodgkin lymphoma. To be told you have fourth-stage cancer is without doubt one of the most devastating diagnoses for anyone, but for a young athlete preparing to take on the world it was especially hard. Yet the diagnosis gave meaning to why things had been going badly for him from a performance point of view.

I wanted to write his story because it was both extraordinary and inspirational as he battled his way through deteriorating performance, diagnosis and treatment. His story is about fighting on, despite hardships and setbacks. His story is about believing and never giving up. As his mother and the doctor to the South African rowing team, I felt compelled to write it.

I was wrong because the story is so much more than that. In his story are other stories. His family, his brothers, the lightweight four Olympic gold medal, South African rowing. The stories unfold themselves.

I was wrong because this story is, in essence, my story. It is a large part of my journey and how I became the mother of four extraordinary sons.

1

When I started writing, I thought this was a warrior's story.

Again, I was both right and wrong.

It *is* a warrior's story. But not one warrior. It is about *warriors*, that dogged and tenacious spirit in all of us. The warrior who fights on and never gives up.

This is how it all happened.

* * *

London, 2012

There are great lessons to be learnt in pushing ourselves,
physically and mentally, to the edge.
– PETER VAN KETS, *THE EIGHTH SUMMIT*

On 2 August 2012, a mild summer's day with some wind and some cloud, the South African men's lightweight four rowing team lined up at the start on Lake Dorney in Eton, England. They were ready to fight the race of their lives, the final of the Lightweight Four at the London Olympic Games.

In that boat was my eldest son, Matthew Brittain.

On the grandstand watching their brother, shouting and screaming their support, willing him on, wishing that their deep and heartfelt roars could propel him faster, were his three younger brothers Lawrence, James and Charles.

Lawrence had failed to qualify the South African heavyweight men's pair for the London Olympics, suffering a brutal defeat at the Olympic Qualification World Championship Regatta the year before and an equally gutting defeat at the more recent Late Qualification Regatta in Lucerne,

Switzerland. As a consequence, Lawrence did not make it to the 2012 Olympics and was relegated instead to the grandstand where he bravely and resolutely supported his brother as he waved the South African flag, secretly wishing he was representing South Africa and himself at the level of which he knew he was capable.

South African national coach Roger Barrow sent me a message during the competition: 'I am upset Lawrence is not racing here. He should be racing. It must be so tough for him watching this. He will race at the Olympics one day as he is so good. Trust me on this.' I believed the disappointment would make him stronger and more determined. It did. But it did not happen immediately. Lawrence still had a journey ahead of him and he had to sink a lot lower before he could show the world what he could become.

At that time, unbeknown to us, for some deeply inexplicable reason Lawrence's body was changing. His lymphoid cells had begun their oncological change under a mysterious and potentially deadly challenge, silently invading and destroying as they began their stealthy journey to discovery.

Alicia Enslin, Matthew's girlfriend, had come to the Olympics to support him. All the partners of the lightweight four had come, donning special supporter T-shirts they'd had made. Alicia had walked the path with him, slowly building her understanding of this Olympic enigma. She stood with us, the tension pumping around her, watching the racing, screaming out her support, urging Matthew and his crew on.

I stood with my husband David, my father Bertie, and the South African supporters, tension and excitement surging as the race unfolded before us.

For the world's top lightweight crews who faced the biggest six minutes of their lives, this was the moment they had spent years working and striving for.

Their Olympic dream was about to become reality.

* * *

Rio de Janeiro, 2016

If you can do something with joy, you can do it forever.
– STEPHEN KING, *ON WRITING*

Four years later, almost to the day, in a city 9 000 kilometres away from Dorney Lake, the South African men's heavyweight pair lined their boat up on Rodrigo de Freitas Lagoon in the middle of Rio de Janeiro, ready to race their final at the Rio Olympic Games.

In that boat was my second son, Lawrence Brittain.

On the grandstand, cheering and crying for his brother, willing him on stroke by agonising stroke, was Lawrence's elder brother, Matthew. No one knew better than Matthew the indescribable enormity of what Lawrence and his partner Shaun Keeling faced.

Lawrence's girlfriend Nicky Mundell clutched her South African flag, feeling helpless as she watched the race unfold before her. Large, graphic chunks of her journey with Lawrence rolled through her mind. She screamed him on, all the tension, fear and excitement within and around her reaching a staggering crescendo of emotion.

I stood resolutely, tucked in among my family, David, Nicky, Matthew and his wife Alicia. With Shaun's family, his girlfriend Kate Johnstone and her parents, and all the South African supporters, I gathered myself tightly together as I held my breath, bracing myself to urge them on, screaming out my hope for them.

Back in South Africa, watching the race on a TV screen somewhere in Tzaneen, Limpopo, where they were on a rowing training camp, were my youngest sons, James and Charles. As the wave of cheering ebbed and flowed according to the position of the boat, the boys bore witness to the drama. As the race progressed, their roars would become more deafening,

4

a deep reflex action to bring the rowers home, victorious.

Lawrence and Shaun lined their boat up, moving into the starting blocks, tension high. They had come through a long, tough battle to get to this point, and they faced the race of their lives. Everything came down to this moment, the moment of their Olympic dream.

1

OUR WATER

London, 2012

Reach high, for stars lie hidden in you. Dream deep,
for every dream precedes the goal.
– RABINDRANATH TAGORE

A large crowd milled around OR Tambo International Airport. It was the afternoon of 20 July 2012 and the South African Olympic team was preparing to leave for London Heathrow. It was a proud moment for South Africa. Tucked in among the 125 athletes making up the South African delegation were six young athletes hoping to row their way to glory in England.

Sizwe Ndlovu, John Smith, James Thompson and Matthew Brittain made up the crew known as the lightweight men's four. Naydene Smith and Lee-Ann Persse would race as the heavyweight women's pair.

I stood with my sons Lawrence, James and Charles, and my sister Claudine and her four children. Together with the crowd, we flanked a cordoned-off walkway, a long red carpet, and waited for the athletes and teams to walk past on their way to the departure lounge.

I felt overwhelming pride as I watched my eldest son Matthew cross the red carpet, pushing his trolley towards us. He stopped to talk to us, savouring the moment. It was an emotional farewell, the excitement palpable, pumping. I hugged him close, wishing him the best, letting him go. His tenacity and hunger had materialised in a long sought-after dream.

Since being accepted back into international competition in 1992, South Africa had done well in rowing at the Olympics. The best result had been the bronze-medal win by the heavyweight men's pair at the Athens Olympics in 2004, the highly successful and long-standing combination of Ramon di Clemente and Donovan Cech. The same combination had raced to sixth place at the 2000 Sydney Olympics. The next-best South African results at Olympic level were a fifth place in the heavyweight men's pair at the 2008 Beijing Olympics when Ramon teamed up with 21-year-old Shaun Keeling, and two fifth places at the 2000 Sydney Olympics from the men's lightweight four and women's heavyweight pair. Both of these crews had raced at the 1996 Atlanta Olympics, where the women achieved eleventh place and the lightweights had raced to ninth. Since 2000, lightweight rowing had faced some problems. The lightweights had not qualified for either the Beijing or the Athens Olympics.

The lightweight four about to race in London was a formidable team, disciplined and hard-working, determined to perfect every aspect of their training, preparation and mental approach to the Olympic Games. They had an impressive rowing pedigree as individuals. Between the four of them they had achieved one bronze medal, eight silver medals and one gold medal at international level. They had represented South Africa 53 times on the international stage: Matthew and James 13 each, John 8 and Sizwe 19 times. They had the potential of a world-class crew in terms of quality and experience. From the very first time they rowed together, there had been something special in the boat. In their book *The Kiwi Pair*, Eric Murray and Hamish Bond speak of the chemistry in a boat. This is the unmeasurable and unique quality that can exist between crew members, the quality that can give a crew the deciding edge.

Chemistry.

John Smith described what he felt when they rowed together. 'The first time we rowed that combination, we were fast. Our raw speed was good. The crew had magic from the beginning, we felt we had a winning combination.'

One of their coaches, Paul Jackson, affectionately known as Jacko, told me, 'It is not often that a team gels like that, both technically and interpersonally. It was luck that brought them together at that stage. They were an exceptional bunch of guys and it was a privilege to be part of it. They were not scared to dream big.'

The head coach of South Africa, Roger Barrow, put it like this: 'When you see a boat go like that, you can dream.'

On the eve of their leaving for the Games, I asked Matthew, 'How is the boat feeling?' Our family had not seen much of him that year as he had been on two tours and three long camps away from home. He had just completed a pre-Olympic training camp in Tzaneen in Limpopo province, South Africa. His answer was simple, 'We have some speed.' He was not one to give too much away, or be arrogant. He tended to be cautious about what he said, so I felt this was a significant admission.

Once in London, South Africa prepared for battle under the guidance of their two coaches, Paul Jackson and Roger Barrow. There had been a third coach back in South Africa who had worked with the women and the lightweight four and played an important role in the development of these crews in the earlier years. Dustyn Butler was not at the Olympics; there were limits set by SASCOC, the South African Sports Confederation and Olympic Committee. Dustyn's work had been done before the Olympics and proved to be invaluable in the development of the women's pair and the four. According to Jacko, 'Dustyn was technically and naturally gifted. He had the ability to communicate with the athletes on their level, displaying enormous patience, time and care in his work with the crew.'

Dustyn had worked his magic on the crews. He worked with the women up to the Olympic Qualification Regatta in 2011, after which Roger took over their coaching. He then worked with the lightweight four in the year leading up to the Olympics, collaborating well with Paul, setting the team up in the best way possible.

I flew to London with my family a few days before the Games began. This was an experience of a lifetime. At 82, my father Bertie had no intention of missing the chance to see his eldest grandchild perform at the highest sporting level. My father is one of the most disciplined and energetic people I know, and is generally game for anything. He has never let his age stop him from enjoying life to the full. Alicia, Matthew's girlfriend, arrived with the other three partners of the lightweight four. We were all caught up in the last few frantic days of Olympic build-up, joining in the excitement and expectation that descended on London as the city prepared for the Games to begin.

The two South African crews faced heats on the first day of the Games, the day after the opening ceremony. The women's heavyweight pair, Lee-Ann Persse and Naydene Smith, came fourth in their heat, sending them into a second heat known as a repechage two days later. A repechage is a second heat in a competition, giving athletes a second chance to qualify if they do not qualify in the first heat. It comes from the French word 'pêcher', 'to fish'. They had come sixth in the A final two months earlier in Lucerne and sixth the year before in Bled, Slovenia, at the qualification regatta, qualifying easily for the Olympics.

Naydene had only started rowing at university. A skilled swimmer and water polo player at school, she joined the University of Johannesburg as a water polo player, planning on making the Olympics in that discipline. Once at university she had friends who rowed and casually joined them. She rapidly realised she was able to row, took an opening that came her way to go to the World Student Games, and from there decided there was more of a chance of going to the Games in a rowing boat than with a water polo team. There are not many athletes who can choose more than one sport. She joined the rowing squad and trialled for the women's heavyweight pair, earning her place in 2010.

Naydene joined Lee-Ann Persse, who was the anchor of that boat. Lee-Ann had returned to South Africa from the USA after a couple of years of rowing for Boston University and had gone straight into the women's pair. Lee-Ann was an impressive athlete, who brought focus and determination into the boat. They were a striking combination, powerful and determined.

They raced the repechage hoping to make it into the A final. But it was not to be; they came fifth. The top three places sent crews into the A final, and the bottom three into the B final. Their dream of making the A final blew up for them. 'In reality, our regatta was over,' said Lee-Ann. They were shattered.

There was nowhere for them to hide; they had to pick up the pieces and go on. Two days later they raced the B final, coming second, which placed them eighth overall.

Years later, when speaking to me, their memories of this time are still poignant and filled with emotion. 'We were just not prepared enough for the enormity of the Olympic Games, for the pressure of one of the biggest events in the world and performing on such a big stage,' Lee-Ann explained. 'We lacked experience and I needed better tools to deal with my anxiety. My stress and nervousness was overwhelming and I was unable to control this which affected my performance.'

At the same time, however, they were proud to be carrying the rowing flag for South African women. Bearing the hurt, Lee-Ann and Naydene gathered themselves into the moment and supported the four with all the passion and hunger for the team, for rowing and racing, but inside they were in their own harsh world of pain, loss and disappointment. It brought home to me, again, just how savage the world of high-level sport can be.

The lightweight four raced their heat against a formidable line-up of Denmark, Switzerland, Italy and the USA. The Danish were particularly dangerous, famous for winning this event. Denmark had a sublime record, having won gold in the 1996, 2000 and 2004 Olympics and placing third in 2008. They were regarded as one of the most successful teams ever and were captained by Eskild Ebbesen, a superb 40-year-old athlete who was representing Denmark in this Olympic event for the fifth consecutive time.

In a rowing heat, progression to the next round is not standard and depends on the number of entries into that particular event. In the case of the lightweights in London, the first two boats to finish progressed straight through to the semi-final and the rest had to fight it out again in the repechage.

South Africa came second in their heat, losing to Switzerland but beating the dangerous and experienced Denmark. They were tired and lacked the speed of which they knew they were capable. The coaches were concerned that they had overdone it, taken the athletes too far, trained them too hard and for too long prior to racing. The athletes felt they had come out of the start of the race rating too high. They could not bring on the speed at the end as they had overdone the start, which had taken the edge off their performance. Fortunately, as they approached the finish they were in a safe position to progress to the semi-final, so they had not needed to sprint.

Coming second meant the South Africans bypassed the repechage and went straight into the semi-final. Missing the repechage is better for any crew as it saves them from an extra race, so their recovery is just so much better.

Things were beginning to line up positively for the South African crew but they knew they would have to improve their race in the semi-final if they wanted to be fully competitive.

The four faced Denmark, Australia, France, Italy and China in their semi-final. China had beaten them at the World Cup in Lucerne two months earlier, so South Africa had a score to settle, and Denmark remained a dangerous concern. In addition, the French had been the fastest boat through the heats. The South African four had more speed in this race and came second to the Danish, making it comfortably into the A final. They rowed a good race.

'We did not sprint at the end,' Matthew recalled. 'I did not make the call to sprint; I knew we had a big race the next day and needed some reserve.'

One of Matthew's roles in the boat was to make the calls. He needed to decide when to do what. It was a key role in the boat.

The Chinese, French and Italians did not feature in the top three positions and went into the B final. The second semi-final saw Great Britain, Switzerland and the Netherlands going through to the A final.

The final was set, there was no going back. Coming second in the semi-final meant there was a likely chance they could place in the top four in the final.

I knew that the four young men were facing the toughest time ahead, the time before the race. 'In all our hearts we knew we could medal. We even thought of gold. But we did not say it, we did not talk about it. We focused our chats on racing hard, and executing a good race. We knew that if we raced well it would be enough to secure a top finish,' said Matthew.

They needed to recover, rest and gather themselves in their preparation to deliver the final blow, the knockout punch. As lightweights they had the added burden of having to weigh in at the correct weight two hours before they raced.

Lightweight men are restricted to weighing no more than 70 kg, and women 57 kg. There is no weight restriction for heavyweights, the more traditional division of rowing. Lightweight rowing only came into existence in 1996 for the Atlanta Olympics. Because there are fewer lightweight events at the Olympics, it is extremely competitive; every lightweight in the world tries to make it into the events at the Olympic Games. I always feel that, for any lightweight rower, just making it to the Olympics alone is a huge achievement, even before racing has started. They then have the added task of making the weight, of getting themselves to the perfect number as they step onto the scale. Making the prescribed weight can be difficult, easier for some than for others; each athlete tends to have his or her own unique way of making weight.

The four were no exception. They each had their somewhat secretive, not always scientific, sometimes positively crazy and perfectly timed combination of food and fluid restriction and sweating to be on their weight target when they stepped onto the scale the following morning. The four began the final work and the countdown to the weigh-in, when they would be given the go-ahead to race at 70 kg. It is never the easiest time for a lightweight rower.

The cap in weight in lightweight rowing eliminates weight advantage, which is prevalent in heavyweight rowing. The margins are reduced; the race often comes down to technical ability and agility, as well as fitness and the ability to handle more than one race.

The South African lightweight four were not seen as favourites to win. I felt they were not taken seriously. They were hovering in the wings, despite their second place in Lucerne in July and now coming through the heat and semi-final in second place. I felt that no one believed the quality and speed they were harbouring. All eyes were on Denmark and Great Britain.

I knew that something special could happen. I spoke to Matthew after the semi-final. 'How are you guys doing?'

'We are feeling strong. We have beaten the Dutch and the Danish. We can beat the Swiss. I don't think Australia has the legs for a strong finish and may fade towards the end of the race. I am not sure about Great Britain and what they can do. We will have to fight to the death.'

By my reckoning, this effectively put them in the top three crews, which meant a bronze medal was possible. It was very likely that South Africa could medal. Tension, excitement, even expectation was mounting daily.

Within every mother's heart is a wounded and scarred place that holds all the pain and hurt and insecurities her children have suffered over the years. For a mother, one of the strongest and most intense instincts is to protect her children against harm, no matter their age or personality, or what has gone before. It is the closest I have come to pure, unconditional love. I was now about to watch my son take on the world, open himself up and expose to everyone the extent of his ability. I wanted more than anything to shield him from the physical and mental enormity of what he had to do, as well as the profound disappointment if things did not work out. I felt afraid for him but I also knew there was nothing I could do to protect him from the pain of racing. This was something he needed to do without me. It was one more inevitable step in that uneasy, aching process of letting my children go.

The excitement and tension were growing, a deep awful sensation in the core of my being, of fear, of knowing just how hard and painful the race

14

was going to be. But no matter what I was feeling, I knew the crew themselves were grappling with the same fear but on a scale far, far greater than
mine. Their tension and anxiety would be multiplied a thousand times.
The important thing in a team is to feel the nerves but not allow panic
to set in. Feeling nervous is a good thing: it sharpens the blade of performance. If things are too comfortable and relaxed before the race, the
blade is not sharpened enough and will fail to slice its way through stroke
after deadly stroke. If there is too much anxiety and panic, the blade flails
around, hacking away ineffectively without clean, decisive power.

As time draws closer to racing, voices inside the athlete's head reach
a crescendo. Conflicting voices of negativity and fear as well as voices of
belief and affirmation start to battle it out in the athlete's mind. The athlete has to overcome the negative voice, and trust the affirming, positive
voice, giving it space to grow. The mind of the athlete has to be bigger than
the fear. They have to stand up to the fear with all their power. 'You need
the right amount of nervousness; a narrow band of anxiety is important,'
Matthew says. 'The nervousness sharpens you and gets you ready. If the
body is strong, the mind will overcome the negative voices. You have to
control and prevent the negativity.'

A few days earlier, South African swimmers Chad le Clos and Cameron
van der Burgh had claimed gold medals. Chad won the 200-metre butter-
fly event and Cameron the 100-metre breaststroke. The rowing four were
inspired and motivated by these results.

I have watched enough rowing races to have an inkling that racing to
2 000 metres at maximum effort is one of the ultimate tests of speed and
endurance. It requires enormous reserves of physical power, fitness and
conditioning, as well as mental strength and belief. There are few sports
that race to this level of intensity over such a long period. The racing causes
excruciating physical pain, as the legs and lungs start burning from the
first few strokes into the race. Every muscle fibre in the body screams out
for the pain to stop. But the athletes are trained to handle the pain, to bear
the unbearable.

The night before the final, Matthew thrashed around, drifting in and out of a restless sleep. His mind was distracted, thinking ahead to the finish. What if they won? What if they medalled? 'Stay in the moment. All we have to do is focus on a good race,' he tried to calm himself in his waking moments.

Sizwe's memories of that time are similar. 'The night before the race I did not sleep. I told no one the next day, I kept it to myself. I could not control the nerves. That was the most nervous I had ever been before a race.'

On the morning of the final I awoke feeling remarkably calm. It felt weird and unnatural to be that calm. Normally, before racing I was hardly able to bear the anxiety. I was not sure if I felt confident in their ability or whether I had just gone beyond my threshold of tolerance to the stress of the racing and pushed it far away from myself. I think somewhere deep within me, in some secret intuitive place, I knew they were going to do well. I knew Matthew best of all, and how capable he was. He is an extraordinarily sharp, focused person and I knew he had the ability to win; he is a deadly combination of intuition, intelligence and brutal hardness. When he was younger he used to tell me how one day he wanted to race and win a medal at the Olympic Games and then ride the Tour de France. He was that competitive and driven. I am sure many had been subjected to his brutal honesty. They would know what he could do in a battle. He was now teamed with three equally ferocious athletes.

I woke early that morning after a restless night. We set about donning all manner of South African paraphernalia, painting South African flags on our faces, giving ourselves plenty of time. We drove to Windsor where we parked, queued and caught official transport to Dorney Lake. Our family was quiet, nervous yet calm. My dad had a cold that day and was not feeling great. Nothing, however, was going to keep him away from this race. We had hours of waiting ahead of us. I could not sit still, jumping up and down, walking outside the grandstand, trying to contain a rising sense of anxiety and fear. There was a buzz among the South African supporters, an extreme sense of anticipation and expectation, a deep fear that pervades that territory of expecting too much and not hoping enough.

As the time grew closer, I knew when they would be getting on the water, which warm-up drills they would be doing, how they would be following their routine, trying to calm themselves. They knew this was just another race and had done so many before it. They knew what they had to do. They needed to let it happen.

The four athletes, with Roger and Paul, arrived at the venue, tense and quiet. Matthew felt a wall of nausea hit him as he saw the rowing course and the flags flying high on either side. Roger and Paul disappeared to check the boat, leaving the athletes to their routine: find their tent, set themselves up, go for their weight-control jog, weigh in, eat something, drink plenty.

And wait. So much time. There was nothing they could say to one another to ease the tension. Matthew started shivering with nerves, putting on as much kit as he could to stay warm and stop the ice-cold nervousness. As he spoke to me of this time years later, that same tension replicated itself. He was ice cold and shaking as he relived those moments.

They had built extra time into their preparation in case things went wrong, a mistake, a forgotten item.

But that day, nothing went wrong. Everything took less time, not more.

After an interminable wait, they could start moving. They stretched and warmed up, moving to their boat.

Paul spoke to them, keeping it simple, not wanting to distract them too much. 'John, keep your length in the water. Sizwe, make sure you get the catch spot-on. Matthew, bring on the power, don't look out the boat too much. And James, pull as fucking hard as you can.' In this way he gave them key points, but not too much advice, which would increase their risk of achieving nothing. He spoke just as he always did. No sudden dramatic words like 'this is the moment' or 'this is the biggest day of your lives'.

The boat was magnificent. Paul and Roger had washed and polished it to perfection, a spotless, gleaming work of art. It was a joy for the athletes to touch it.

The time had come. This was the point of no return. As they put their hands on the boat and lifted it to carry it down to the water, the tension fell away. 'It was the most calming moment for us. We let familiarity take over. This was what we knew. This was what we did,' Matthew tells me.

Their warm-up routine was standard and they flowed through it, easily, moving well; everything felt good. The warm-up canal was separate from the course, running behind the grandstand, and at any time would be filled with boats rowing up and down, performing their drills, mechanically, reassuringly, as they prepared for the race of their lives. As they completed their warm-up, they would approach the course. Boats are required to be at the start line ten minutes before their race.

The four emerged from the warm-up area onto the course, and as they moved into their lane, lane five, they practised a start. They needed to feel the water move beneath them, the familiarity taking over, the subconscious, the known. They manoeuvred their boat into the starting gate. 'The start is a weird place,' says Matthew. 'It is both calming and tense.' They fiddled around, restless, shifting in their seats, moving up and down in the boat, slapping their legs, adjusting their blades. They gripped each other's hands, a gesture of solidarity.

It went quiet. The umpire called one minute. The time had come to claim the race. At that moment, it comes down to which team wants to win more than anyone else, which team wants it badly enough to overpower the doubt and fear that lurks in their minds. It is all about winning. The athletes strive to win; it is not just about racing.

Matthew kept focusing his mind, repeating, 'Just five good strokes out the start. Don't think further than that.'

Two kilometres away from them, I stood on the grandstand with a bank of South African supporters wedged tightly together, a terrible gnawing fear overwhelming me as I waited in agony. I could barely look at the massive screens in front of me, projecting what was happening at the start.

They were primed and ready. The starting umpire called the boats to attention. The silence was deathly. The umpire's voice called them by country in order of the lanes: 'Netherlands, Switzerland, Great Britain, Denmark, South Africa, Australia.'

The bell rang. The green light flashed.

Six boats powered out the starting gates, slicing through the water with a clear 2 000-metre line ahead of them. With surgical precision, the crews attacked from the beginning. South Africa had a good start, second out of the blocks. Their start was hard and aggressive, building as much speed as possible in the first 250 metres. The Danish were fastest out the blocks and took the lead from the beginning.

Two thousand metres is a long way. The race is rarely won at the start. South Africa knew they needed to pace themselves. They were finding their rhythm and trying to be efficient in the first five hundred metres. They had felt incredible out the start and knew they could attack at this point, but they held back. It was more important to conserve some of that energy for later; now was the time to concentrate on moving with the boat, building a comfortable rhythm.

They had slipped into third by the 500-metre mark and then fourth at 1 000 metres, with Australia and Great Britain in second and third. The Netherlands had fallen into sixth place early in the race and the Swiss were slipping back too. They were out of contention.

Matthew explains, 'You cannot be too emotional in the first half of the race or you risk burning out quickly. It's important to focus on your race rather than on your position, as that can cause panic and too much energy wasted on emotion. Once we passed the thousand-metre mark, the time had come to work on our position. We could allow emotion in and start thinking of racing these guys.'

He knew the time had come to begin their assault. He called out in the boat, 'Our water,' a simple, powerful call of ownership, almost a rite of passage. His call refocused everyone in a second. They knew this called them to race *now*, that this was the time to fight to win. 'This is where we fuck everyone up!' Matthew shouted. The 1 000-metre mark was an important mark for the crew. They were in excruciating pain, the burn stinging their legs. For an athlete this is a dangerous time as the agonising pain allows any demons of self-doubt that may be lurking to take control. This can cause massive damage to the race. 'Your mind has to take over and remind the body it is not going to die of pain,' says Matthew. Once they passed the thousand-metre mark, they refocused. Instantly it became easier to force their bodies to finish. They could do it. The end was in sight.

The Danish continued to dominate the race until the last 500 metres. But after that, Australia, Great Britain and South Africa began to catch them. With Denmark dominating the race, the three crews were lining up behind them, ready to fight for the next two places. At that stage I was aware of thinking, *They can get bronze. They can take Australia.*

The success of the crew depended on trust – a deep, unwavering faith in one another. Trust that no one would back off, no one would stop pulling, no one would succumb to the pain and the desperate need to stop it. The crew trusted Sizwe to set up the rate, they trusted John to follow Sizwe's rate and rhythm and transmit it to the two behind him, and they trusted Matthew and James to pull hard and deliver the power they needed. The crew also trusted Matthew to call, give specific instructions at specific times. He had never lied to them, never pretended the finish was closer than it actually was.

They were used to him calling from around the 400-metre mark. This was normally their time to start sprinting, to wind up the power, pull out all the stops. After the semi-final, Matthew knew that to have a chance at a medal, they would have to do something special, something different. He had already decided to call the sprint earlier than 400 metres. He wanted to call it with 600 metres to go.

As they approached 600 metres, Matthew called them to a sprint. No one had ever heard him call it early but the unfailing trust and belief just took over naturally. They delivered ten massive strokes and suddenly they were right back at the top, fighting for third place.

As they moved into the last 500 metres, James later reflected, 'We weren't hanging on, we were stepping forward.'

The four started to wind it up. They found their hidden gear. They had not sprinted for the finish in their heat or semi-final. No one had seen their sprint, or even knew if they *could* sprint at the end.

And sprint they could. I had seen them sprint before. I knew they were fast, deadly fast, in the sprint to the finish line.

How do you watch your son rowing in an Olympic final? How do you manage to witness it stroke for stroke, metre by metre? The answer is that I suffered with them. I felt every inch of the race. I screamed it out, the pain, the fear, the hope, the glory, I just screamed it all out there, where it was swallowed up in the thundering roar of the crowd. Fifty thousand people screaming out their hopes and fears is a deafening noise and in that moment every part of me, every fibre, realised, in a moment of clarity, 300 metres from the finish, that they could win because their boat was moving faster than those of the British and the Danish.

At 400 metres to go Matthew called for another ten strokes. They could not hear him. His calls were drowned out by the roar of the crowd. Without a clear instruction from Matthew, Sizwe, who stroked the boat, looked out, first right then left, immediately assessed the situation and started a massive last push to the end. The rhythm and pace of rowing is set by the stroke, the oarsman who sits at the stern of the boat. The crew saw Sizwe look out, they felt the rate and power increase as he started to push. They needed no other prompting. They went with him. James screamed out to himself, 'Ten big strokes and you can do this. You can win.'

I witnessed the unimaginable unfolding before my eyes as the South Africans started to come through, with utmost precision, power and speed, faster and faster. Their legs were on fire, but Sizwe kept winding up the rate. At 300 metres to go, they were moving at greater speed than the other crews, at 19.8 kilometres per hour. They were flying past the Australians, and closing in on the British and Danish. Not one of those crews could respond. With 100 metres to go they moved into second place, behind the Danes. The Australians fell back into fourth place and South Africa, Britain and Denmark were in medal positions. South Africa continued their relentless and ruthless attack, moving through the Danish and British, powering their way past the finish line to win gold in an indescribably glorious finish.

As the world's top three lightweight crews crossed the finish line, there was a moment's hesitation in the release of the result as the judges called for a photo finish. For five to ten seconds, the judges reviewed the result. It seemed interminably long for the four young men who had just fought the toughest battle of their lives.

The result was unequivocal.

Gold.

In that moment, they became Olympic champions, a golden measure of what they had put together to deliver the race of a lifetime.

'South Africa came from absolutely nowhere to win gold!' blared the British commentator, mistaking South Africa for Australia in the last quarter of the race. He went on quickly to correct the mistake, shouting out to the world, 'It's a sensational win, one of the most exciting finishes of all time. South Africa claim gold! It's one of the stories of the Games.'

Great Britain claimed silver and the Danish bronze.

There was a deep, guttural roar from the South African crowd as we witnessed the result. The four in the boat were momentarily unsure of their position; Matthew opened his arms wide in question, all four of them looking around for confirmation, feeling they had won, but too afraid to let out the blood-curdling shrieks of victory. As the result flashed onto the screen in front of them, James's face told the story as he grabbed Matthew's arms, letting out a roar of joy and relief, hitting the water with his hands. Sizwe beat the water with his fists, then stood up in the boat in celebration to collapse onto and hug all his team members. John Smith hit the water over and over with his right hand and then bent both his arms into the traditional biceps curl, triumphantly acknowledging to the world that he was the strongest, the best.

Matthew fell backwards in the boat, screaming out the victory, his arms in the air, a gesture of exhaustion and exhilaration, joy and acknowledgement of the sheer guts and determination it had taken to overcome the pain.

It was an awe-inspiring result, neither completely unexpected nor unprecedented. This was no lucky break, no fluke. This was hard-core, bitter fighting to the end, to the ultimate victory in world rowing. A victory earned fairly on the battlefield by four spectacular warriors.

Roger and Paul watched the race from the coach's bicycle track that runs parallel to the course, which allows coaches to watch the entire race with ease. They were both on bicycles. Paul recalls, 'I cycled to the start half an hour before the race began and lay on the grass watching the clouds. I felt extraordinarily disconnected at the start of the race and felt I was riding in a *dwaal* [daze]. At the halfway mark I realised they could medal and I watched them come through to win gold in the last ten strokes.' He let out a deep visceral roar, and dropped his bicycle. Roger and he embraced and Paul continued to roar with passion, almost grunting with shock and joy.

Roger and Paul had had coffee together earlier in the week, and discussed the result. They were confident the four would medal. But neither of them spoke of the gold. This was beyond their expectations and hopes.

Nine thousand kilometres away, two significant people watched the race – Dustyn Butler and Shaun Keeling.

Dustyn watched with fellow coach Andrew (AJ) Grant and AJ's wife Tracy in Pretoria. They screamed through the race, becoming less and less coherent as the race progressed. Dustyn knew they were winning and started crying before they crossed the line, sobbing uncontrollably after the winning finish. His emotion was complex. 'I sobbed for a whole range of reasons. Joy for the four with whom I had worked closely, joy for Jacko for pulling it off in the final, and a tremendous sadness that I was not there to experience it first-hand,' he later told me.

Shaun Keeling, a brawny rowing athlete, watched the race with his girlfriend Kate Johnstone and her family and some friends in a pub in Bryanston, Johannesburg. He exploded with joy and excitement as he watched his friends and colleagues win gold. But mixed in with the jubilation was his own deep pain, bitterness and disappointment that he was not there, racing for South Africa. He had his own story of difficulties, but through the feelings the win evoked, he felt a deep resolve growing within him. It was time to let the anger and frustration go; the next cycle would be his time. He felt he deserved to be at the Games, that he was good enough, that he had raced and trained with all these athletes and it was possible that he too could win.

Matthew's girlfriend Alicia watched from the grandstand, fully invested in the tension and frenzy. She had walked this journey with Matthew since 2006 when she first met him at university and they became friends. Later, in 2010, they became a couple and the journey took on a greater intensity as she witnessed the depth of his commitment, drive and passion to succeed. Alicia herself is impressive, beautiful, disciplined and ferociously organised in her life, setting her own formidable path of becoming an actuary. They matched each other in drive, ability and commitment. Before she met Matthew, high-level competitive sport and the Olympics had not been part of her life. She found herself involved with a man for whom the Olympics were central; she had had to sacrifice time with him while he trained relentlessly, preparing his body for the dream. She witnessed a profound mental focus and unique loyalty in Matthew and she embraced it all.

Now, six years after meeting Matthew, Alicia's journey with him had reached the point for which he had long strived. She stood on the enormous grandstand at Dorney Lake, surrounded by Matthew's family and many South African supporters, proudly dressed in South African kit, waving her flag and screaming out her support. At 300 metres to go, Lawrence was yelling next to her, 'They're going to win,' and in that moment it all made sense, it became the culmination of the journey, the release, the realisation of the dream, the hard, jagged pieces falling perfectly into place. A deep sense of gratitude and pride flooded through her as she acknowledged Matthew, all he had gone through, his previous injury and surgery, the massive journey behind the win.

Lawrence revelled in the glory of the moment, his secret agony of not being there in a boat apparent to no one but himself, swept away as he rejoiced in the win. As brothers, nothing could have been better and he felt pride, respect and an intense energy. There was no secret to their training

24

and preparation, no unknown. He had been part of that programme. If they could do it, so could he. Secretly he vowed to himself that he would race at the next Olympic Games. Their result made him even hungrier and more determined to succeed.

James and Charles rejoiced equally in the moment, an outpouring of joy and pride in their brother and what the four had managed to pull off. Matthew's achievement resonated deeply with them both, lighting a fire of hope. Unintentionally but inevitably, from that moment onwards the bar was set a little higher in our family.

David watched the four cross the line with pure joy and elation. At that moment he felt profound respect for the four. He knew more than anyone what it had taken to win the race and how much they had believed in themselves. Their win surpassed his expectations, his own dreams, his own story. I knew David's journey and the difficulties rowing had thrown at him.

I was standing in the row behind David, holding on to him. I jumped up and down in a wild frenzy as I watched the four take control of the race. The instant they won, I screamed in joy and burst into a flood of tears, the incomprehension of what I had just witnessed flooding through me. At that moment, David turned and I jumped straight into his arms from the row above. Thankfully, he caught me and we hugged each other, laughing and crying at the same time with delight, gratitude and infinite pride. We hugged the boys, hugged everyone, dissolved into one uncontrollable mass of tears.

Moments like these are unforgettable.

A short while later, I watched the four young men stand proudly to attention on the podium as the South African flag slowly rose to the winning position and they sang the words of the fiercely evocative South African anthem, 'Nkosi Sikelel' iAfrika', with the supporters and all of South Africa back home. They stood locked together, arms around one another, medals around their necks, heads held high.

They had done it.

My phone started beeping and ringing as messages and calls poured in. Stories and messages flooded in from all over South Africa. Friends, family, colleagues, casual acquaintances, all manner of people spilled out their congratulations and happiness. They felt part of the win, it was their success too. There was an ecstatic and tumultuous reaction to the win back in South Africa, like the shockwave after an explosion.

It was a time for South Africans to realise that South African rowing was a reality. We were not nobodies; we were neither insignificant nor unremarkable. South Africans have a tendency to have a flawed outlook on themselves, a giant inferiority complex laid down firmly by the injustices of the past. South Africans often believe they are not good enough to win. The gold medal gave South Africa further confirmation that they could win. Winning and succeeding grows confidence faster than anything else.

The four lightweight rowers had achieved what no other rowing team had previously done in South Africa. 'We let it happen,' said John later. This was the first South African rowing gold medal at Olympic level.

A few minutes later David and I were being interviewed by the iconic and imposing figure of Sir Matthew Pinsent, winner of four consecutive Olympic gold medals for Great Britain. He had won three of these medals with the even more esteemed British oarsman Sir Stephen Redgrave, who won five consecutive Olympic gold medals. Matthew Pinsent was roaming the stands for the BBC, hoping for glimpses of the emotional effects of the racing on the spectators.

The win was an incredibly proud moment for our Matthew and our family. It somehow validated some of the difficulties and hardships we had experienced in our lives, as well as the hard work and devotion he had applied to rowing.

Winning makes many things worthwhile.

Later, all the South African supporters met at a pub in Eton, where we rejoiced and celebrated long into the night, each person taking pride in, and some small ownership of, the fabulous achievement of the four.

Days, weeks, months later, every person I met had a story to tell, revealing where they had watched the race, who they had been with, how they had screamed and wept and how exciting it had been. That is what makes sport so important in a community, a country, a nation. It has the powerful and unique ability to cross barriers and bind people. It gathers people together as a common bond, a pure, single goal – to win. Nothing but performance matters. The country will unite behind the excellence and thrive in the glory. 'Sport has the power to inspire and unite people,' said one of the most famous men in history, Nelson Mandela.

Winning a gold medal is unique, and instantly puts the team into the top echelon of sporting achievements. The silver and the bronze medals are great achievements; the gold is exceptional.

But, like any success in life, this win did not happen on the day.

It had been a long journey.

2

GOLDEN BOYS

South Africa, 2012

We trust the process. We crush the body; it will adapt.
— SOUTH AFRICAN LIGHTWEIGHT FOUR, 2012

Winning gold in London was an inspiration to the South African public and created an unprecedented interest in rowing. The dramatic victory catapulted rowing closer to the forefront of South African sport. People suddenly took notice of rowing and began to understand the complexity and demands of this relatively unknown sport.

After their win, the four became known as 'the Golden Boys' and the 'Oarsome Foursome'. But as with any success story, the journey of the lightweight four had not been smooth.

It never is.

Our family witnessed most of this journey with Matthew in the years preceding the Olympics. I felt every moment of that journey, the excitement and elation, the hardships and heartache. A part of me walked many steps with him on that path.

The concept of a lightweight four had been shelved for a few years after 2007 when South Africa failed to qualify a lightweight four for both the Athens (2004) and the Beijing (2008) Olympics.

Two years later, however, in 2009, the situation had changed. At that time, the framework and structure of South African rowing was busy being created by the young national coach, Roger Barrow. In 2009, Roger took over the leadership of South African rowing as the National Head Coach and began the process of building a squad with better funding and a more competitive, integrated environment and programme. He succeeded Christian Felkel, who left the position after the 2008 Beijing Olympics. There was a financial crisis in South African rowing and it was no longer sustainable for him. Christian had coached South African rowing since 1995 and became the head coach in 2001, taking crews to three Olympics in 2000, 2004 and 2008. Christian joined British Rowing and went on to coach the senior British squad, coaching some of the top British crews over the next eight years. He is still with British Rowing; he coached the British men's eight to a bronze medal at the London Olympics and a gold medal at the Rio Olympics.

Shortly after taking over from Christian, Roger was joined by two assistant coaches, Andrew Grant (AJ) and Dustyn Butler, and the three of them put their energy into building elite-level rowing. It was a difficult time as there was little financial backing and the climb seemed steep. Roger was young, but he had worked with Christian for more than four years and had taken a lightweight women's double to the Beijing Olympics. He brought a determined energy and organisation to the sport. He worked hard, had the ability to coach, and had exemplary administrative skills, making him a formidable leader in a ruthless sport. He rapidly made his mark.

From the athletes' side, a growing pool of potential lightweight athletes had come up through the ranks, hungry and keen. Roger had coached Matthew and James Thompson to two silver medals at the Under-23 World Championships in the lightweight pair in 2007 and 2008, and he knew he had athletes with potential. Sizwe Ndlovu reappeared after having retired in 2007, a young John Smith appeared on the scene and, among others, two older athletes, Anthony (Tony) Paladin and Andrew (Polly) Polasek, continued to train, hoping to make it into a potential four.

Lightweight rowing had suddenly become feasible again.

Roger set about developing a lightweight four. He focused on the coaching, and knew he needed help, so he approached Paul (Jacko) Jackson. Jacko had a long history of coaching lightweights but had retired from coaching after the Sydney Olympics and had not coached for ten years. Roger could see the benefit of having an experienced master coaching the lightweight rowers. Despite the ten years that had passed since the Sydney Olympics, the thought of coming back to help coach his favourite boat, a lightweight four, made the decision easy for Jacko. He agreed.

Over the years I have got to know Roger well. He is gifted in his ability to see what is needed, what will ultimately make the boat move faster. He used to speak about the team being on a train, a high-speed train moving rapidly on towards the London Olympic Games.

The start of the new season saw the new squad of lightweights gather momentum. From 2009 to 2011 the coaches relentlessly rotated the athletes to select the fastest. They tried a number of combinations with the seven athletes.

The lightweight squad was growing in strength and the build-up to the London Olympics was underway.

Matthew, James, Polly and Sizwe were selected into a lightweight four and rowed at the Munich and Lucerne World Cups in 2010. Their results were average. The lightweight squad stayed in Europe between the World Cups, training in Athens on the Olympic Course. Matthew comments, 'We were not great and got crushed in the racing. The vibe in the team was going badly. We were too cocky but at the same time insecure. We were immature and there was a lot of teasing and picking on each other.'

They came back to South Africa and things began to improve. John Smith was put into the four and he brought a positive influence to the boat. For the next two weeks the crew that would ultimately become the Olympic four rowed together. John and Matthew referred to it as 'the Dream Team' as undoubtedly there was some magic, some chemistry in the boat. They were fast.

Before being formally selected into that four later in 2012, these were the only two weeks during which they ever rowed together as a four. Matthew felt he took more of a leadership role in the crew after their return from Europe and they started to grow the culture of being a team. Unfortunately, the lightweights were fraught with health problems. Those injured or ill were taken out the boat and 'mixed and matched' with those who were left. The lightweight squad now comprised Sizwe, John, Matthew, James, Polly and Tony.

There is no doubt the Olympic lightweight four would not have made it without all six athletes training hard for the four positions and filling in at different times when injuries and illness prevailed. Having six athletes allowed the coaches to maintain a constant pressure on the selection of the crew. The athletes never felt safe. They constantly had to prove to the coaches why they should be in the boat.

In 2011, Tony, Polly, Matthew and James raced at the second World Cup in Hamburg and a few months later, with one change to the crew, Tony, John, Matthew and James raced at the annual Lucerne World Cup. I was unable to travel to Lucerne that year to watch the racing. David's father, John, was ill and we were visiting him at his home in East London.

The lightweight four made it into the A final. This was a big step up for them. I spoke to Matthew the night before the final. 'It feels like a mountain ahead of us, the competition is so high,' he said, sounding almost overwhelmed. I felt a crushing heaviness settle on me as I visualised what he was telling me.

They came sixth in that race. But they proved they had potential.

Two months after Lucerne, in August 2011, the lightweight four faced the most stressful racing of their careers: the Olympic Qualification Regatta in Bled, Slovenia.

The crew that raced Lucerne was unchanged. Tony, John, Matthew and James prepared themselves to race like never before.

David and I travelled to Bled to watch the championships. We had two sons, Matthew and Lawrence, racing but were torn in other directions too. David's father remained ill and we were worried about him. James celebrated his eighteenth birthday while we were away and Charles was in Grade 9 at school. We were spread thinly. We left my father Bertie in charge at home and headed overseas to support Matthew and Lawrence.

The four came second in their heat, a good start, but not enough to go straight through to the semi-finals. They faced a second heat, the repechage, and made it through in first place, which qualified them for the A/B semi-final. The pressure was mounting.

At that time, for a boat to qualify for the Olympics through the World Championships it had to place in the top eleven positions. An A final would automatically qualify a boat for a spot in the Olympics. The South Africans came sixth in their semi-final, which pushed them into the B final. If they found the pressure high before this race, it was insignificant compared to the pressure they now faced in the B final. Six of the eleven Olympic spots had been bagged by those who had made it into the A final. The last five spots were up for the remaining six crews.

Only one of those crews would not make it.

In what can only be described as one of the most terrifying and stressful races I had ever watched, the lightweights made it, literally just scraping in, edging themselves into the ultimate world of Olympic racing. They beat Serbia into 12th by 59 milliseconds. There were under two seconds between the crew that won and the crew that came sixth. The South Africans were ecstatic. Tony, who stroked the boat, stood up and dived into the beautiful Lake Bled in celebration.

It was one of the most euphoric moments of their journey.

When the squad reconvened after their September break, the training and selection pressures continued. Selection was by no means over, and the coaches continued to rotate the positions between the group of lightweights. When a crew qualifies for the Olympics, it is the boat class that has been qualified, not the crew. The crew who qualified may not be the crew who ends up racing at the Olympics. During that time Polly decided to retire, feeling that he needed to apply himself to his engineering work and develop his career in that direction. Tony continued to fight hard with the other four, Matthew, James, Sizwe and John.

There is nothing kind and empathic about selection. It does not matter how fast you have been or how many medals you have won. It comes down to being the fastest at the time of selection, and the differences can be minute.

In February 2012, Sizwe, John, Matthew and James were selected to race the Grand Challenge race on the Buffalo River in East London. The Grand Challenge is one of the most famous races on the South African rowing calendar, a coveted event in which the top senior fours in the country fight it out to win the magnificent silver Grand Challenge trophy. The chemistry and potential in that crew felt exciting.

But the magical feeling was not enough. They lost.

They came second to a heavier crew comprising Matthew's brother Lawrence, Shaun Keeling, Pete Lambert and Tony, who had jumped into this crew when he was not selected for the lightweight four.

Losing that race was a turning point for the lightweights. They needed work. John said, 'We realised we needed to work harder, we were not there yet, we needed to step things up and make improvements.' They proceeded to put their minds to that process, training harder than before, committing to changes and focusing on building speed.

The training rolled on, the pressure built and, in April 2012, the coaches and selectors made the final crew selection. John, Matthew and James were selected into their positions and Sizwe Ndlovu was chosen for the stroke seat in place of Tony, who had qualified the boat in Bled in 2011. Sizwe had been injured in 2011 and had not been included in the lightweight four at Bled.

The final selection for the Olympics was painful for Tony. He had stroked the four to qualification the year before and been replaced by someone else for the actual Olympic racing. It sounds unfair, but it is the reality of how the sport works. Sport is brutal; it is only about who is the fastest at that moment. The truth is that without Tony, they would never have got to the gold medal. The athlete who has been dropped needs to remember the triumphs and victories along the way; it is dangerous to allow the final

33

selection to overshadow all the good work that has gone before. From what I have seen, selection remains one of the most painful things for any athlete to bear if it goes against them.

Just after the lightweights won their gold medal in London, I sent Tony a message acknowledging his role in their result and how important he had been. I could only imagine his feelings at that moment.

Despite the inevitable selection heartache and difficulties, the decision to go with Sizwe seemed correct. Sizwe just got better and better that year. The crew started to fly. The chemistry seemed to bring out the best in the four men. They were strong and focused, hungry for a result. They believed in themselves because they knew they were fast and there was something special in their boat.

They were coached by Paul Jackson, Dustyn Butler and Roger Barrow. Dustyn had superb technical prowess and the unique ability to focus deeply on the crew, giving everything he could to the movement of the boat. 'He was a gifted coach and added magic to the four,' says Paul. Paul brought the crew together and worked hard on the dynamic energy and spirit between the athletes, managing the complexities of their relationships. He was a master at managing interpersonal relationships and the conflict that inevitably creeps into any team. Roger devised the training programmes, ensured the system worked and held the entire process together. He had clear vision and could see what needed to be done to build boat speed. He let nothing hold back what he thought would help the team.

In 2011, South Africa brought in an international coach, Italian Gianni Postiglione, to help coach the South African team on an impact basis. Gianni came with an impressive pedigree: he was the FISA Rowing Coach of the Year on two occasions and had a number of medal-winning performances, including two silver medals at previous Olympics, to his credit. FISA, the Fédération Internationale des Sociétés d'Aviron, is the governing body of the sport of rowing, setting its rules and regulations. Gianni made a huge impact on the training and development of the athletes as well as the coaches. He had experience and had devoted his entire life to rowing.

Gianni has a philosophical outlook on coaching: 'Perfection is not possible but I try to find the champion in the athlete. The simple approach is better; it must not be too complicated.' Matthew speaks of the time Gianni worked with them: 'He helped us mentally to embrace change. He gave us the ability to take risks, try things and not be scared. Gianni gave us confidence to make changes.' Roger speaks of adjusting to his coaching being fully exposed and of Gianni cutting him down to size on numerous occasions, at the same time as building him up and teaching him. He was open enough to allow Gianni to both challenge and mentor him. Gianni helped each facet of the coaching team and played a significant role in the development of South African rowing.

The coaches' endeavours paid off.

In June 2012 the lightweight four – Sizwe, John, Matthew and James – once again lined up at the start line on the famous rowing water, the Rotsee in Lucerne, ready to race the final of one of the World Cups. This time, there was no feeling of being at the bottom of the mountain. It was no longer overwhelming. They were much, much faster. They raced to second place, claiming the silver medal. They beat the favourites, Great Britain and Denmark. Only the Chinese beat them.

I watched them from the forested pathway that lines the Rotsee and, as they came through the 1 700-metre mark, I realised they were fighting back from fourth position. I started to scream and jump around in excitement as they blitzed through the pack, beating the favourites and narrowly missing out on gold to an impressive Chinese crew.

Their result was proof that their work was paying dividends. They were becoming a world-class crew.

The South African lightweights were almost ready to race at the Olympics.

I knew they were fast. I had become involved with the team over the previous year as the team doctor, and I knew they were capable of a medal. I began to tell family and friends that it was possible they could medal at the Olympics. I told people to watch out for the South African rowers at

35

the Games. I knew they were capable of something special.

Two months later, they proved me right.

Each of the four lightweight rowers showed the calibre of athlete coming up through the ranks of South African rowing. They believed that fundamentally it was the trust within the crew that would underpin their speed, and worked towards earning one another's trust. They achieved this, believing that each of them would fight to the bitter end, to the proverbial death. No one would stop fighting when the pain got too much to bear. They were warriors of the highest degree. With their coaches, they managed to deal with points of conflict, issues that most people do not want to confront, the things that are inevitably pushed aside in many teams, hoping for the best. Jacko used to say, 'Put it on the table.' They forced themselves to confront the toughest and most uncomfortable things. This habit and ability made them strong.

Matthew says, 'It was a great crew. Things came together for us and went in our favour. We had huge respect for each other and were able to attack issues aggressively. None of us felt we were better than anyone else.'

They had a few mottos that shaped their work ethic and pushed them on. 'We don't count days, we make the days count' were strong words that defined their mindset. 'There is always more' is another key phrase they adopted.

All four of the lightweights who rowed in London had begun rowing at school, working their way up to senior-level school rowing in Grades 11 and 12. They were all passionate and, most of all, highly competitive. With the exception of John, they had all rowed at Junior World Championships during their senior school years and then progressed to under-23 level. John came straight into under-23 level. It was this process of slowly coming up through the ranks of junior selection, junior racing, followed by under-23 selection and racing that taught them the invaluable lessons of racing to win – and, more often, racing to lose.

Sizwe Ndlovu was the oldest of the four at 32. His path in life to this point was a humbling story showing the most extraordinary and indefatigable resolve imaginable. Born during apartheid, he had to overcome one relentless hardship after another. Faced with poverty, living in townships in Volksrust and Newcastle without electricity or running water, with chores to complete, a 15-kilometre walk to and from school every day and a stepmother who did not support him, Sizwe's young life could not have been more difficult. He saw his mother four times a year during school holidays when he went to Johannesburg to visit her. She was a domestic worker and had worked for the same family for years. When he was 14, he went up to see her as always. But this time he refused to go back to Newcastle. His life had become intolerable. This was a turning point for him, a key moment. It coincided with the dismantling of apartheid. As a result, he was given a place in a well-known high school in Johannesburg, Mondeor High. His mother could not afford the fees, so Sizwe found himself two part-time jobs. He delivered newspapers in his neighbourhood and he worked as a packer in a small local supermarket.

As I listened intently to his story, my heart went out to him and I felt profound respect for his resolve.

At school, he played water polo and was only introduced to rowing at the age of 16. He was taken under the wing of the late Tom Price, the headmaster of Mondeor High who recognised that Sizwe had the potential to become a good athlete. Mr Price was passionate about rowing and wanted to give athletes from disadvantaged backgrounds a chance to row. He supported and mentored Sizwe as much as possible, ensuring him a scholarship and lifting him to and from rowing training. 'He was a father figure to me,' says Sizwe. This nurturing role paid off and Sizwe was selected to row for South Africa at the Junior World Championships in 1998 and 1999, coming last and 11th respectively.

After matriculating, Sizwe attended the University of Johannesburg (at that stage known as the Rand Afrikaans University, or RAU) and, with ongoing support from Mr Price as well as Rowing South Africa (RowSA), the university and a host of good people, he was able to continue rowing and to represent South Africa at a number of international competitions.

He was part of the lightweight men's four that unfortunately failed to qualify for the 2004 Athens Olympics. As if his road had not been difficult enough already, it became further complicated by health issues and injuries. Once again he failed to qualify the lightweight men's four for the 2008 Beijing Olympics. This marked one of the lowest points in his personal life, as well as his rowing journey. He lost both his parents at this time. This, coupled with the bitter disappointment of not making the 2008 Olympics, pushed him away. He took an extended break from rowing.

The lightweight squad fell apart. It was only a few years later when younger athletes emerged that lightweight rowing took off again and Sizwe's dream of going to the Olympics was reignited. Once again, injury dealt him a blow and he was not in the lightweight four when it qualified at the World Championships at Bled in 2011. He only made it into the Olympic lightweight four at the final selection in 2012.

When South Africa became democratic and was reinstated into the Olympic fold, the government established a quota system to help address the injustices of the apartheid regime and help athletes who had been disadvantaged through race or poverty, and usually both. The quota system was widely criticised but its rationale was clear and without a doubt it helped develop many athletes who had been disadvantaged through no fault of their own. Rowing, however, was not a mainstream sport in South Africa. There was no quota involved. Any athlete who made it into the rowing squad got there by working their way up through the ranks. Sizwe was one of these athletes. He was that good. Tall, strong, perfectly proportioned, Sizwe was the ultimate athlete. According to Jacko, 'Sizwe was a natural athlete, highly gifted, balanced and pragmatic.'

Like Sizwe, the youngest of the four, John Smith, did not start rowing at under-14 level. Tall and thin, he was affectionately known as Bean – he resembled a string bean. He attended St Alban's College, a well-known private boys' school in Pretoria. Like Sizwe, he was a water polo player until a kick to his ear ruptured his eardrum when he was in Grade 9. This required surgery to repair the tympanic membrane. As part of his rehabilitation, the coach suggested he row until his ear was completely healed. Until that point John had always mocked the rowing team, so it was a strange and somewhat belittling experience for him to join the St Alban's rowing training programme.

It proved to be a life-changing experience for him. Unexpectedly, he loved it. A natural oarsman, he had found what he wanted to do. But like the story of any elite rower, he had some disappointment along the way. He was not selected for Junior World Championships in 2008 and he lost the coveted Schools Single Sculls at the South African Schools Championships in his matric year to a relatively unknown athlete in the sculling division – Lawrence Brittain. Both of these losses had the profound effect of making him hungrier than ever.

After leaving school in 2008, John joined the University of Pretoria (UP), also known as Tuks, with a plan to take rowing as far as he could. In 2009 he raced to fourth place in the Under-23 World Championships in Račice, Prague, when he teamed up with Matthew in the lightweight pair. They lost in the final after an extremely promising start to the regatta. This was a further blow for John, as there had been an expectation that he and Matthew would medal. John believed he could do better and became more determined to succeed. The following year, 2010, he was paired with Lawrence in a heavyweight pair and they went on to win a gold medal at the Under-23 World Championships in Belarus, the first gold medal South Africa had achieved at World Championship level.

John finally had a firm foothold in the rowing hierarchy.

On his return from Belarus, a decision was made to select a lightweight four to row at the Senior World Championships in New Zealand later that year. John was selected for this boat as he was now physically much stronger from the time rowing with heavyweight Lawrence, and was suddenly in a favourable position despite his young age. 'Bean was technically gifted, an exceptional boat mover,' comments Paul Jackson. John had an inherent understanding of what it took to move a boat.

The four selected for the 2010 World Rowing Championships to be held on Lake Karapiro in New Zealand were the four who would race two years later at the London Olympics. Unfortunately, just before the World Championships Matthew had to pull out as a result of a back injury and was replaced with Tony Paladin, who had fortuitously decided to come out of retirement six months earlier to be part of the lightweight squad. Tony was in the perfect position to take Matthew's place. Tony also later substituted for Sizwe, who needed surgery to his wrist prior to the World Championships in 2011. During this time of injuries to the crew, John continued to mature and develop.

James Thompson had started rowing in Grade 7 at his school, St Andrew's College in Grahamstown. Beset with learning difficulties that made academics a nightmare for him, he was determined to find a sport to help him achieve what he knew he could achieve outside of a classroom. He was good at rowing and loved it. He made his school's First Eight at the end of his Grade 9 year. He was selected to represent South Africa at the Junior World Championships in 2003 and 2004 in a junior coxed four, and achieved fourth place in 2003 and a bronze medal the following year. James wanted to take rowing further and had no doubt in his mind that Tuks was the right place to do this.

When Matthew arrived at Tuks a year later, in 2006, the two teamed up and rowed together. James was impressed by Matthew's ability to make a plan and carry it through. In 2007 and 2008 they won silver medals in the lightweight pair event at the Under-23 World Championships in Strathclyde, Scotland, and again a year later in Brandenburg, Germany. They were narrowly beaten by Italy by 0.3 seconds in Scotland. Matt and James were a solid pair, dedicated, passionate and hardworking. James has always been a feisty oarsman with a good overall understanding and knowledge about the sport. 'James was blessed with very good physiology and brought great strength and energy to the boat,' Paul Jackson recalls. He has a deep intelligence and natural confidence, with an innate understanding of rowing and the system it needs to function well.

James and Matthew got on well and complemented each other in the boat. 'They had a very special relationship and pushed the boundaries all the way through. Nothing was too much for them,' says Paul. At Matthew's 21st birthday party James made a speech and said, 'There is no one else in the world I would rather row down a course with right now than Matthew.' It was this relationship that set the foundation for the exceptional teamwork that would later prevail in the lightweight four.

Teamwork differentiates rowing from most other sports on a physical and mental level. Physically, the entire crew has to be moving in perfect unison for the boat to move swiftly through the water. Anyone who is out of time will upset the rhythm and unbalance the boat. An unbalanced boat creates drag and the boat slows down with each stroke. Rowers cannot do their own thing in the boat – they have to work as one. Mentally, the crew needs to be relaxed and trust one another. Any irritations will cause tension, which may affect the rhythm and flow of each stroke. Each member brings strengths and weaknesses to the crew. A winning crew will effectively play to each individual's strengths and compensate for the weaknesses. A winning crew needs at least one person to be a facilitator, the catalyst who brings it all together. That is genuine teamwork.

Matthew is a clear, logical thinker with an ability to assess situations quickly and accurately. He is intense and intelligent. I call the intelligence of a rowing athlete savviness, and I believe its presence or absence in a crew can make or break the result. He could pull a crew together in an instant when things were not going well. He brought a hardness and toughness to the crew. 'He had a hunger for criticism and learning,' says Jacko. He expected a lot and was ruthless. In many ways, things were never good enough for Matthew. He always wanted more and expected things to be better. He was also the most volatile of the four, especially in his younger days. He could explode easily and was not afraid to say things directly, which often caused some tension. Roger says, 'Matthew was intelligent and as hard as nails.'

Matthew's route to London had its own set of difficulties. The most serious obstacle was a back operation he had to undergo in September 2010 which, at the time, threatened to stop him rowing.

He had complained of back pain on and off for years but had always managed to settle it down with physiotherapy and the standard, conservative approach to musculoskeletal pain and injury: ice, rest, physiotherapy, cross-training and medication. I was not involved with the team at this time and was living in Johannesburg. Matthew was rowing with the squad and attending UP, where he was studying for his BCom degree. He would tell me about his back but it always seemed to get better, so I left it in the hands of the physiotherapists. Rowing places a high level of strain on the lower back and it is common in rowing to have back pain.

In 2010 the World Championships in New Zealand were to be held later in the year, towards the end of October, so the squad was training later than usual. Early in September, Matthew complained of back pain. He started with the standard treatment and management.

This time, it did not settle.

On the morning of 7 September 2010, he got out the car to train with the lightweight four and could hardly move as he was in so much pain. He broke down at that point – he felt that nothing was helping him and he could no longer continue without improvement. Lawrence phoned me later. 'Mom, you need to help Matthew. He is in serious trouble. His back is really worrying him and today he was unable to row.'

That call shocked me. I had not realised how bad things were. It galvanised me into action and for the first time I realised that Matthew had a potentially serious problem. Things moved rapidly after that. He had an MRI scan, which showed severe lumbar disc degeneration and a prolapsed intervertebral disc between the fifth lumbar vertebra and the sacrum, in layman's terms the proverbial 'slipped disc'. The prolapsed disc had already attached to the outer layer of the spinal cord. His back was in trouble. Had he been 70 years of age he may have accepted it, but at the tender age of 23, with dreams of rowing at the Olympics, this was devastating.

It was a crushing blow for both Matthew and the lightweight four with whom he was training in preparation for the World Championships. All his dreams and hopes were shattered. He was moved out of the lightweight four boat and immediately replaced with Tony Paladin, who had been training with the squad. The injury put Matthew out of the prestigious Senior World Championships and the Tuks Boat Race crew, training at the time for the annual Boat Race. The future that had appeared so promising and exciting was suddenly unclear and uncertain.

It was a grim time for Matthew, and for us, his family, seeing his distress. It was intolerable for me to see Matthew's dreams disintegrate. It has and always will be profoundly painful for me to see the boys suffer in any way and witness the despair and fear that inevitably come when the river of life causes pain and unexpected change.

In the squad system, an injured or ill athlete is immediately replaced. The train moves on at high speed and the injured athlete is left behind, feeling virtually forgotten. The lightweight four moved on. Our family rallied to support him through the dark time.

The university crew lost their stroke man and Matthew's brother, Lawrence, stepped into the stroke seat. When they raced Boat Race in Port Alfred later that month, they all wore bands around their heads or arms saying 'Matt' as a gesture of solidarity.

We consulted four neurosurgeons and each was unequivocal in recommending surgery to remove the disc. They were positive that, with this treatment and the correct rehabilitation, he would have the best chance of training further and making it to the Olympics. Without the operation, he would be unlikely to make it to Olympic level. Either way, there was a risk that he would not row again. We needed to give him the best chance of realising his dream.

Matthew chose to have the surgery. Despite his disappointment and depression, he committed himself completely to the process of surgery, rehabilitation and returning to training. He focused on what needed to be done to get the best outcome. He made the decision that he would survive the setback and that, with hard work and perseverance, he would overcome the obstacle. He was not ready to leave rowing.

On 14 September 2010, Matthew underwent surgery to remove the part of the intervertebral disc that had leaked out and caused so much pain. He did not have a fusion at the time of the surgery as that would reduce mobility in the lumbar spine. As he planned to return to rowing, he would need as much mobility in that area as possible. I paced anxiously in the waiting room. David worked at that hospital so he continued with work, popping in and out during the day. Matthew had to be nursed flat on his back for three days. The monitor alarms kept going off because his heart rate was so low. On day three he was moved into the ward and from that moment the rehabilitation began in earnest.

After a week he was home and together we faced the mountain. He was outstanding in his systematic approach to climbing that mountain. Within a few days he was walking and I accompanied him on these walks. We walked around the neighbourhood, building distance quickly so that within a few days we were doing about 12 kilometres. Matthew was never one to take an easy line or waste time. He was hard on himself. He quietly set himself the target of rowing the single scull at the Buffalo Regatta in February 2011, and moved steadily and resolutely towards that goal.

The Buffalo Regatta is a famous regatta in South African rowing. The single scull and the coxless four events are probably the most prestigious races in South Africa, known respectively as the Silver Sculls and the Grand Challenge. Matthew was determined he would make his comeback at this event and planned to win the Silver Sculls.

I worked with Nicola Macleod, the South African team's biokineticist, and physiotherapists Andri Smit and Garreth Bruni, and together we set about rehabilitating him until he was able to row again. I believe he came right more through his own private determination and tenacity than anything else. He mirrored some key traits prevalent in our family. We are not short on toughness, courage and sheer grittiness. He committed to each level of rehabilitation, working smartly and consistently until he was ready to tackle the next level. The improvements came quickly: within two months he was back in a boat and starting to train with intent.

Five months after his operation he succeeded in racing the Silver Sculls at the Buffalo Regatta. He won the coveted award and at that moment of winning he knew he was going to make it back again. Matthew was back in full contention for the lightweight four. He proved that he could not only get over surgery, but also race at the top level again and have a chance at winning.

He was now back into the pressure of selection for the lightweight four and, with Sizwe, Tony, James and John, he started training and preparation for the all-important Olympic Qualification Regatta in Bled in late August 2011.

But really, this part of the story is the middle and would not have started without a beginning. Where does a story begin, though? The beginning and the end can never be defined. Life simply rolls on, in an endless continuum. All things happen because of what has gone before, and the moments are just part of the never-ending flow in the unbroken, curving river of life. The events that follow the course of life are just a small part of a greater story: something always went before, and will always happen afterwards.

Just as a seed needs the right blend of soil, nutrients, sunlight and water for its roots to take hold and nurture the growth of a strong, hardy plant that can withstand natural hardships, so a young warrior requires an environment that favours their development to handle the harshness of a battleground. But despite its environment, a plant is always going to become a plant, just as a warrior will become a warrior. In the end, it comes down to who survives best.

This story, then, is about survival.

3

⚞⚞⚞⚞

BEGINNINGS

Johannesburg, 1984

It wasn't the first or last time I went with the river inside …
Sometimes the river of life takes you to the rocks.
– GREGORY DAVID ROBERTS, *THE MOUNTAIN SHADOW*

I met my future husband David Brittain in 1984, during my second year at university. We were both studying medicine at the University of the Witwatersrand, Johannesburg, colloquially known as Wits. I met him in the dissection halls over a cadaver, a unique start to an extraordinary life together.

I had decided to study medicine primarily because at the age of 15 I had been completely unexpectedly diagnosed with Hodgkin lymphoma and had undergone intensive radiotherapy treatment. Hodgkin lymphoma is a cancer of the lymphatic system that attacks the lymph glands, spleen, liver, bone marrow and bones. It can also spread to the lungs and brain.

The diagnosis was a cataclysmic shock for my family and for me. It was my first real experience of illness and mortal danger, and I remember being afraid, but I was young and resilient and there was never any doubt in my mind that I would recover. It was my first glimmer of understanding of what was curable and what was not. I felt confronted by an aspect of life that not many see at that age.

In many ways it was the necessary staging of the disease and the subsequent treatment that made me far more ill than the actual disease. To stage cancer, you need to know how big the primary cancer or tumour is, and where it has spread to. It was before computerised scanning and magnetic resonance imaging, so I had to undergo a horrible X-ray procedure called a lymphangiogram and an operation known as an exploratory laparotomy. The lymphangiogram is an X-ray of the lymphatic system that involves injecting a radiocontrast dye into the system. And the laparotomy included the removal of my spleen and various lymph nodes, as well as a liver and bone marrow biopsy. Both were highly traumatic and painful, and I have never forgotten them.

Fortunately, the disease had been caught early. I was Stage 1, so I was assured of a complete recovery. Hodgkin lymphoma is a cancer that responds favourably to treatment. The three months of radiation treatment that followed made me sick. I lost weight and struggled to eat. My hair fell out in chunks where the deadly cobalt rays penetrated my tissue, and my skin burnt as if I had bad sunburn. I had long-term side effects, some of which only manifested many, many years later. I was given a far larger dose of radiation than would be given today, but that was what was known and understood at the time.

I was vulnerable and my family did what families do when they are threatened: they cared for and protected me. They prayed to God that I would be healed and resume a normal life with as few problems as possible. We placed our faith and trust in the doctors caring for me and went forward with every belief and hope that everything would work out for the best.

It did.

I completed the treatment and bounced back from the illness. I went on to complete the year at school and, following a five-year period of close observation, I was declared cured of the disease, with an almost zero risk of recurrence.

At 15 I was in remission from cancer and by 20 I had become a survivor.

There is something inordinately powerful about that word. Survivorship.

I was cured. The biggest worry at that stage was whether I would be able to have children.

Little did I know how insignificant that worry would be in the future.

The illness was a profound experience that altered me significantly. I had grown up. From that point in my life I had more compassion, empathy and understanding of what it felt like to be ill and to suffer. Unknowingly, I was already set on a path towards studying medicine. It was also my first real glimpse of myself, and of learning who I was. It toughened me, but did not blunt me against the hardships of life. I realised that I was strong and resilient, and that hardship could be faced head-on. It was a powerful lesson in moving on and not giving up.

The medical degree programme was tough and required long hours of hard work. The second-year anatomy course had an intense dissection programme. We dissected in small groups of four, spending hours poring over the cadaver as we battled our way through, using the manual *Man's Anatomy* written by our professor of anatomy, the late and highly esteemed anatomist and palaeo-anthropologist Phillip Tobias. It was an extraordinary task. That year of dissection brought home to me how privileged I was to have been chosen to study medicine. My dissection group included Verena Ballhausen who, much, much later, was to play a key role in my son Lawrence's life, and Neil Martinson, who rowed for the Wits Boat Club.

In 1984, David Brittain was a third-year medical student who also rowed for the university. He frequently came down to the dissection hall to visit Neil and talk to him about rowing, as they were equally passionate about the sport. Until that time, I had never heard of rowing. My two brothers, Stephen and Marc, had played the more conventional South African school sports, rugby and cricket. I had never even seen a rowing boat.

On his many visits to speak to Neil, David and I would eye each other out. Without a doubt there was an attraction between us. We were both involved with other people at the time and for me relationships had become complicated. I was finding the territory unmanageable. I was also recovering from a broken heart after saying goodbye to a close friend who emigrated to the USA. It had shattered me, but I resigned myself to the truth and forced myself to settle into a life without him.

Despite all these complications, David and I felt drawn to each other, an attraction that sort of fizzed on for a few years.

In many ways we were ideally suited, and in others poles apart. He was extroverted, tactless, exuberant. I was shy, awkward, the queen of tact and keeping the peace. He was the elder in a family of two boys, I was the middle child in a family of five children, with an elder brother and sister and a younger brother and sister. He was completely comfortable with himself, I was struggling even to know who I was. He asked questions that made me cringe; I avoided asking questions because I sensed they caused discomfort. He was very intelligent, grasping and remembering concepts easily and impressively. I had to slog for long hours, drumming facts into my brain. He was the optimist, I was the realist.

But that all came later. Right then, our lives were involved with others, our schedules were busy, and David was training hard for rowing, so our relationship did not progress. We passed and acknowledged each other in corridors, in the canteen, aware of each other but too busy to give each other much more. We did not see much of each other as we were in different years and life has a way of simply continuing.

David was a passionate oarsman who had rowed for his school, General Smuts High School in Vereeniging. He began rowing at under-14 level, following in what he thought were the footsteps of his father, John, who told him he had rowed Boat Race during his years at the University of Oxford. It later transpired that this had not meant rowing a race in a boat. He had actually played rugby at Oxford; every year, the rugby team would travel to the famous Henley Royal Regatta with a large keg of beer and proceed to drink themselves into oblivion. This drinking game was known as Boat Race; John had never put his big toe into a rowing boat.

Despite having no footsteps in which to follow, David forged his own path. He joined the Wits Rowing Club, known as the Wits University Boat Club, as soon as he started at the university. He had aspirations to represent

49

South Africa in rowing. At that stage, however, South Africa had a sport-ing embargo against it as a result of its deplorable apartheid policies, so it was not possible to row internationally as a Springbok. The springbok was the national animal of South Africa, and the green-and-gold Springbok colours were the highest sporting award of the country. Any serious ath-lete had aspirations to become a Springbok, and David was serious about rowing. He travelled to Germany and England in 1983 as part of the Wits University crew, rowing in Schweinfurt, Hamburg, and the famous Henley Royal Regatta. In 1984, he was selected for and represented South Africa as a Trident rower. Trident rowing was the name used by the national rowing team when it travelled overseas. On his return to South Africa, he received Springbok colours for his representation.

Ten years later, when South Africa finally became a democracy, the Springbok fell away as the emblem of most South African sports, being reserved only for the national rugby team, whose members to this day are known as the Springboks. For the rest of South African athletes, the pro-tea became the new emblem of the highest sporting achievement in the country. The protea is a magnificent flower species, proudly indigenous to South Africa. The king protea is South Africa's national flower and, with the exception of the rugby Springboks, all athletes representing South Africa are now awarded Protea colours.

Unfortunately, David paid a high price for his passion. He did not pass his third year at medical school. The training and travelling took its toll; he had put too much time and energy into rowing and not nearly enough into his studies. I was dissecting with my group when David appeared and told us his grim news. The faculty took a serious view of this and did not accept his rowing as a reason for his failure. They wanted to exclude him from the faculty, as was policy at that time.

Sometimes, though, life has a way of working inexplicably. Professor Duncan Moyes, who was the head of the Department of Anaesthetics, vetoed this decision. He had a son, Justin, who also rowed for Wits, and Moyes understood the demands and complexities of the sport. As professor, he had a say in academic decisions and managed to convince the faculty to give David a second chance. He changed the course of David's life. Effectively, he changed the course of my life too.

It was a key moment, one in which a decision set a path, but could just as easily have set one so completely different that its outcome would have been worlds apart. The faculty allowed David back, with one strict proviso. He was not allowed to represent the Tridents, the Springboks or South Africa in any way while he was studying at the university. He was only allowed to represent the university if he chose to continue rowing. It was a bitter blow, but he wanted to complete his medical degree, so he agreed. It was an important but tough lesson, which taught him much about taking responsibility and recognising that sometimes life offers hard choices.

This was later to become a major theme in our family – of accepting responsibility and using opportunities when they came. This was not always possible. There were times when it was inevitable that the pain of lost chances would be keenly felt.

David and I were now in the same class. The inexplicable attraction grew and gathered itself, moving us slowly and inexorably closer together. We were falling in love. As much as we fought it, we simply flowed along until we realised our destinies were bound, as if our very oppositeness drew us together. It was messy for me. I did not handle break-ups easily and effectively broke the heart of someone special to me in this process. It is not something I am proud of, and it still weighs heavily on me that I was unable to deal effectively with ending one relationship before start-ing another. I did not have the confidence to deal with it openly. It would not be the first time in my life that I did not deal effectively with a difficult situation. I found confrontation almost impossible, and it has taken me my entire life to begin to master this.

Is it ever easy as we negotiate our way through the awkwardness and heartache of those youthful years?

David continued to row for the university. I was learning about rowing as I spent more time with him. He was the stroke of the Wits First Eight, a boat that had an impressive record. I have learnt through the years that the stroke of the boat needs to be technically skilled and have a good feeling for the way the boat feels and moves. They need to respond to calls made in the boat by adjusting the rate and intensity of the work done by the crew. David also stroked the Wits Coxless Four that included Robin McCall, Craig Fussel and Stephen Leigh. At that time, Wits was the dominant university in South Africa with respect to rowing, and held this position for a number of years.

David wanted me to try rowing and was always teasing and trying to casually manipulate me into a boat. I eventually agreed and tried some coxing, and found that I enjoyed it. The coxswain, or cox, is the smallest person in the boat, and is responsible for steering some of the larger crew boats. The cox does not actually row, but is an integral part of the crew. I was a shy, introverted, somewhat awkward person, lacking self-confidence, and was relieved to be placed with novice crews or those lower down in the ranks. I never coxed David's crew as they were an intimidating group who took rowing very seriously. It would have made me awkward and embarrassed, and frankly I was not yet skilled enough. I have never felt skilled enough in most things I have undertaken and have always been hard on myself, expecting so much more. Years later, my heart went out to the young coxes who coxed my own sons in the eights they rowed in. I hoped for their sakes that they had more confidence than I'd had.

In 1986 I was selected to cox the University of the Witwatersrand Women's Eight for the annual Boat Race in Port Alfred. We had a cracker of a heat and won convincingly. Unfortunately, during the final against the University of Cape Town, our boat sank in the notorious Bay of Biscay, a well-known part of the course on the Kowie River. To this day I am not actually sure how much of that was my fault, as the weather was shockingly rough and we were rowing in an old wooden tub of a boat that had a damaged and pliable skeleton and no splash guards. Well, whatever the reason, the water just poured in and once that started the flexible old boat just sank.

I stopped coxing after that, but not because of the sinking. Something else was happening, something that would alter my world and shock my family.

I was worried I was pregnant.

We were approaching fourth-year exams and this was nothing short of a disaster. It was a dark time of fear and anxiety and fervent hoping beyond reasonable hope that my fears were unfounded. The stress we were under was to test David and me to the limit of our relationship.

But there was no way of denying the truth. I was pregnant.

No amount of pleading and bargaining with God could alter this fact. We had got ourselves into an unspeakable mess.

It was a highly stressful and anxious time for David and me as we grappled with the truth and tried to come up with a solution without having the means or skills to really find one. We are a Catholic family and how I was going to tell my parents remained an impossibly difficult and terrifying thought. David's parents lived far away in Maseru, Lesotho, and had no idea we were even a little bit serious.

Once again, I found myself unable to deal effectively with my predicament. I withdrew and simply avoided the problem, pushing through my exams and refusing to speak to my parents or David's parents. Stupid, yes, but it showed how I struggled with the hard things.

I grew up in a big family. My father, Louis Albert, known as Bertie, is Mauritian and grew up in Curepipe. He was the third-youngest of 11 children. When they were growing up, the prospects in Mauritius were limited and one by one they left, spreading themselves around the world. My father was no exception and left Mauritius in 1953. He went to Rhodesia, now Zimbabwe, to study commerce through correspondence at the University of South Africa (UNISA).

Five years later, degree in hand, he left Rhodesia for South Africa to work and do his articles in Cape Town. There he met my mother, Doreen Blackman. My mother had recently lost her father to lung cancer and lived with her mother Mary and four siblings in suburban Cape Town.

My parents were married five months later in September 1958 and over the next eight years had five children. They moved to Johannesburg in 1960 with two children in tow and their next three children were born there. I was the third child, and my parents elected to have me born at home. It was the only way my father could actually witness the birth of one of his children. I had an elder brother and sister, Stephen and Monique, and a younger brother and sister, Marc and Claudine. We were all given French names but we did not speak French at home. My father spoke excellent English, which became the language we grew up with. We had a happy childhood. We lived in two homes during my childhood years, both of which were filled with wonderful large gardens, a life-sized doll's house, swimming pool, tennis court, and numerous games and activities. We rode our bikes freely around the neighbourhood and played in the veld that abutted one of our homes.

My father was disciplined and worked hard, making his way to the top in the diamond industry to become the financial director of De Beers. My mother did not work outside the home and was always there for us. She was a selfless woman, devoting herself to care for the five of us, and my father, who was climbing the corporate ladder. As most mothers do, she worried about us excessively. We were the centre of her life. We were lucky to have a grandmother, whom we called Danna, who lived in the Cape. She was a formidable woman in her own right, intelligent, a woman who could fight for what she believed in. She became a skilled artist, and her work is spread through all our family homes. We spent glorious, long holidays in the beautiful Cape fishing village of Hermanus in her seaside home, Pisces, and her home, Silverglade, in Constantia, Cape Town, soaking up the sun, the beach and the very best of family life. We were all reasonably bright and hardworking, and managed school relatively easily.

I fitted the stereotypical mould of the middle child to perfection. I was always the one who kept the peace and avoided conflict. I wanted attention but had no idea how to cope with it when it came along. Most of all I craved approval, and became a perfectionist. I sought permission for everything; I wanted people to like me, which often superseded my ability to show my true self. I feared being left out of anything. This insecurity has been an enduring weakness throughout my life. My self-confidence and belief in myself have never reached their full potential.

'A woman today must have a career,' my mother would tell her daughters. This may have grown from her own experience of not having a career. She wanted us to have opportunities and be independent. Perhaps she wanted us to have other central focuses in our lives.

David was the elder of two brothers. A few months before he was born, his parents immigrated from England and settled in Vereeniging, an industrial town south of Johannesburg. David's mother Dorothy, or Curl as she was affectionately known, taught biology at General Smuts High School where David and his younger brother Roger went on to matriculate. His father John was a mechanical engineer and had come out to South Africa looking for new opportunities and greater prospects. David and Roger had a carefree childhood; they played furiously and explored their world, on bikes, on foot, camping in the mountains and at the sea. They were both bright and did well at school. David became deputy head boy, displaying the natural leadership that manifested throughout his life.

But all that seemed very long ago and somewhat irrelevant to me at the moment. I had bigger issues to deal with. How was I going to tell my family I was pregnant? I knew I was going to shock them and upset them terribly, and I avoided it for as long as possible. I knew they would be hurt and angry. I felt I had let them down. Deep inside me I carried a little secret, a tiny little cellular life steadily dividing and growing, and I simply had no idea how to tell everyone. What should have been joyous had become an anguished time. I knew without a shadow of a doubt that I wanted my little baby. It was agony not to be openly excited about being pregnant, and to have virtually no idea how it would all work out. I started making vague plans with my best friend, Nici Verriest, who was living in Namibia at the time. I thought I would go and stay with her, quietly disappear from my life in South Africa, have my baby and face the consequences later. It was impractical and illogical but I was getting desperate and David seemed equally helpless.

Nici was a huge support to me at a time when I had few people to turn to. My younger sister Claudine sensed my stress and figured out what was happening. We were very close and she supported me emotionally where she could, but she was too young to know how to deal with the situation. I approached the Faculty of Medicine to tell them my predicament and am indebted to Mrs Phyllis Hyde, then the secretary of the faculty, who showed inordinate kindness to me during this difficult time. I was granted leave of absence from the faculty, to return the following year. Miraculously, David and I managed to pass our fourth-year exams, an extraordinary achievement, considering the stress we were both under.

We were still avoiding telling our parents.

I was not planning to go away with my family over December as I knew I would be unable to deal with being so close to everyone. My mother had other ideas and insisted I come down to Knysna, as they had recently bought a holiday house there and they wanted me to see it and for the family to be together. I avoided the subject of the holiday for as long as possible, being uncharacteristically vague and uninterested. Under pressure from my family to come to Knysna, I told my mother I could not come without David and she agreed. Perhaps she realised at that stage that things had become a lot more serious between David and me. I drove down with David and my brother Marc. I sat quietly in the back, hardly talking, depressed and insecure. I was afraid. I had no idea how the next few weeks would unfold.

Eventually, however, it was my parents who finally confronted David and me. They noticed I was pregnant; my mother had seen I was depressed and withdrawn and had looked hard for a reason.

It was a traumatic time and not a way I would have chosen for my baby to start his early foetal life, but what could we do? We were in it. Deep in it. We were in a world of anger towards us, we were responsible for our situation and we paid the price by having to face the world. Unlike today, when there is less negativity, shame, guilt and anger surrounding pregnancy outside of marriage, at that stage it felt to many as if the end of the world had come.

After the initial shock and fury had erupted, simmered and then calmed, my parents were able to be objective and consider the options. They opened a door for us by suggesting we consider getting married. This was something we had not contemplated as we were students and had no source of income. It had been one of those unthinkable thoughts. It was only after they made it possible that we allowed ourselves the option of considering it. Suddenly it all fell into place and seemed so easy, so obvious. For David and me it felt completely right; we simply flowed into that decision, as if it were the most natural course of action.

It was a decision that many frowned upon, criticised and doubted. One of the priests we spoke to flatly refused to marry us as he felt the marriage would not last more than a couple of years. We were adamant, however, that this was the right way forward and, despite the censure and general lack of confidence in us, we believed we had the commitment and resolve to make our marriage work. There is no doubt that we questioned ourselves on a far deeper level than we might have done had circumstances been different. We spent hours focusing on the future and how we would manage. The priest who married us, Father Ignatius Fidgeon, helped us considerably during this time. He was a shining light as he guided and led us in his uniquely gentle and non-judgemental manner. I was profoundly grateful for his kindness and unremitting support at a time that had been so painful and confusing for us.

After making the decision to get married, everything calmed down. David and I felt immense relief as the burden of our secret evaporated. We were happy and excited, finally owning the fact that I was pregnant proudly and openly. Our families recovered and rallied around us like soldiers, reinforcing their support and belief that we could do this.

We were married on 29 January 1987, in a small ceremony at the iconic St Charles Borromeo Catholic Church in Victory Park, Johannesburg. With

Father Fidgeon leading us, we bravely and firmly said yes to each other, committing our lives and futures irrevocably. The ceremony was followed by an equally small reception at my parents' home in Northcliff. A few close friends and family attended the wedding. I was very emotional. The tension had been enormous and I cried throughout the entire ceremony, no longer able to hold back the pressures I had borne for five months. At the same time, it was one of my happiest days and I knew intuitively that things would be fine. We would be fine. The two of us were young, naïve and unprepared but not lacking in courage, determination and sheer hard work. We had energy and were committed to each other. But more importantly, we were in love and wanted to be together, and were excited for the future.

After a two-day honeymoon in the Magaliesberg during which I got really sick with a viral flu-like infection, we moved into a two-bedroomed flat in Yeoville and started our married life together. We were both 24 and in the latter part of our medical degrees. We had very little money except for the financial help from our parents. Life was extraordinarily tough, but we were tough, and although things looked daunting and had changed dramatically for us, it was also exciting and we were extremely happy.

I had a year's leave of absence from the university. David was in his fifth year and went to the hospitals and campus every day. While he was away I attacked the flat, scrubbing, cleaning, painting and generally refreshing our new home. When he returned I had all sorts of jobs lined up for him, shelving, repairing, hanging curtains – the list was endless. We made a good team and over the years it has remained like that, with me planning and organising and him doing the manual part of the job.

After we were married David did not row. It was a sort of unspoken natural progression that, between studying, being married and having a baby, rowing would fall away. I did not really think too much about it as life had become a lot more complicated and the possibility of rowing seemed unrealistic. David took on his roles as husband, soon-to-be father and doctor with the energy and generosity that is so characteristic of him.

The doctor I saw had his rooms in Hillbrow and I used to walk in to see him for my check-ups. On 5 May 1987, David walked with me to see him. I was heavily pregnant and considerably uncomfortable. The doctor felt I was very close to having my baby. We walked home and by the time we got home I was in agony. This was not what I expected, the well-described, conventional early labour, the slow build-up of contractions. This was something far from gentle or slow. This was as if I had been hit with a bat in the stomach and I was now doubled over with intense, constant pain, pain that made me very afraid. David drove me to the hospital and the doctor confirmed I was in active and advanced labour. I was in a sea of pain, and felt overwhelmed and frankly terrified. With almost no time to gather myself and adjust to labour, a mere three hours later I delivered the most beautiful, healthy 4.1 kg baby boy, Matthew Joseph Brittain.

I can honestly say that having my baby made me the happiest I had ever been in my life, and each time I had a child it made me more perfectly happy than I thought possible. Having children and being a mother was completely normal and natural for me. David felt the same way; we seemed to slide into the role of parents remarkably easily. Being parents seemed fundamentally right for us.

Matthew was gorgeous. I could not believe we had produced such a beautiful baby. To me he was flawless and perfect. David and I were ecstatic. We coped well with the considerable adjustments to having a baby and somehow he just fitted into our lives, adding another dimension to our already full and complicated days.

My leave of absence gave me the chance to spend seven months with Matthew and support David, who was finishing his fifth year. I went back the following year to continue my degree as I still had to finish my fifth and sixth years. This would be followed by my internship.

Those were hard years for us. For senior medical students, the work was predominantly clinical. Students were allocated to units and wards where they spent time working with patients and learning how to manage illnesses, injuries and surgical interventions. We worked mainly at the Johannesburg, Hillbrow, Coronation and Baragwanath hospitals as students. These were the largest teaching hospitals available to us and the standard of medical education was very high.

Baragwanath Hospital, as it was then known, is a large teaching hospital affiliated to Wits and situated on the outskirts of Soweto. At that time, the government had declared a State of Emergency in a desperate attempt to control the political uprisings in the designated 'black' areas. The state of unrest and political turmoil were at their highest and Soweto was a seething, volatile place. The nationalist government's apartheid policies were under massive pressure and the awful regime was thankfully crumbling. But they were not going out without a fight; tragically, this dreadful mentality cost the lives of thousands of people. The Armed Struggle was gaining momentum. As medical students we were exposed to highly traumatic cases such as gunshots, multiple stabbings, rubber-bullet injuries, beatings, teargas injuries and victims of horrific necklace burnings, as well as car accidents, burns and domestic violence. It was a gruesome time and there were times when I had to push myself to continue. I had to complete the clinical years and learn as much as I could.

David graduated in 1988 and began his internship at the Johannesburg General Hospital, as it was called at the time, in 1989. We moved from Yeoville to the doctors' flats allocated to that hospital. It made things easier for him as he was within walking distance of the hospital. I was a final-year medical student and finding the year pressurised and stressful, with a packed academic timetable and trying to manage a home and baby. One of the professors in whose unit I was working picked on me one day during a ward round and I burst into tears. He was immediately remorseful. When he found out about my situation, having a small child and finishing my degree, he tried to help me by getting some support for me in the form of counselling. I did not go for the counselling but I was touched by and appreciative of his kindness.

We pushed on through the tough times. David was working long hours with night calls and weekend duties. I was completing my final year. Life was challenging and in no way simple for us. At that time, our parents were our rocks. They were enormously supportive of us and helped us in whatever way they could. They were devoted to Matthew. When he was born he had all four grandparents as well as five great-grandparents still living. They adored him. Just as his announcement had caused shock and almost split the family, his birth had had the entirely opposite effect, drawing our families together with bonds I did not think were possible. It was a special time for our family, bringing healing and joy. I think having a child can do that.

My mother and father were living in Johannesburg and David's parents lived in Ladybrand in the Free State, so we naturally saw my parents a lot more. They supported us where they could, helped us financially, looked after Matthew and generally tried to shoulder a little of the burden for us. My mother drove to our flat every day to fetch Matthew for the afternoons so I could finish my studies.

During this time, my mother and I had the closest and best relationship we had ever had. It was a gift to me; despite the difficulties we went through, that time will always be special to me. Growing up, I was always a little afraid of my mother. She was busy, with five of us and running a home. My father worked long hours and she always seemed stretched. Later, when I went to university, I wanted independence but my mother felt I would not cope. She was against my moving out. Looking back now, I understand the difficulties and conflicts. They were inevitable, normal. As a mother myself, I can grasp her reasoning. At that time, however, I did not see it that reasonably and it caused some resentment.

I was scheduled to start my internship on 1 January 1990 at Baragwanath Hospital and that day was looming heavily in front of me. I knew the workload would be high. I would need all the support I could muster.

Sadly, however, tragedy was not far away.

I graduated in November 1989. It marked the end of an era. The nineties would begin with David completing his internship and me starting mine. I needed a break after the stress of my final-year exams, and flew down to

Knysna with Matthew to spend two wonderful weeks with my mother at her holiday home on Leisure Isle. My father joined us towards the end of that time. Soon the time came for Matthew and me to get home to David. On 17 December 1989, my parents said goodbye to Matthew and me at the airport in George, where we boarded a plane to fly home to Johannesburg. I was very emotional at the airport and said a tearful goodbye to my parents. Despite feeling enormously happy and relieved to have completed my degree, I was nothing short of terrified of my impending internship and the responsibility I would be expected to bear during that year.

My parents were driving on to Hermanus to stay with my grandmother for a few days. Danna had played a constant role in my life. My parents were planning on visiting her and, later, attending a party to celebrate my uncle's 25th wedding anniversary in Cape Town. I remember turning at the door of the aeroplane to wave goodbye to them but they had already left as they still had a long journey ahead of them and it was getting late. To this day I can still feel that sharp pang of disappointment and hurt that they had already left and were not there to wave us goodbye. Matthew and I flew home to David, who met us at the airport, delighted to see us both again.

Much later that night, at 11 o'clock, the telephone rang, waking us up with a jolt. David answered. I sat up in bed, alert, and David's voice immediately changed to an urgent plea, 'Bertie, what's wrong, what has happened?'

At that moment I knew without a shadow of a doubt that something unspeakable and terrible had happened and instantly I knew what it was. I heard my father speak to David, who then passed the phone to me. My father sounded terrible. 'I am so sorry to tell you, Danielle, but your mother has died. There has been a terrible car accident. She is no more, she has gone.'

In a set of horrific circumstances, my mother, my rock, had been killed in a tragic car accident near Swellendam in the Cape. It had happened three hours after they had said goodbye to Matthew and me at the airport.

I felt at that moment that someone had taken a white-hot metal rod and driven it straight through my heart, ramming a hole so big I thought I would die. An agony so fierce and intense that it paralysed me shot through my body like an electrical shock.

It was the worst time of my life.

My mother had just turned 54. It was three days after her birthday.

I was hit by a grief so hard, swift and complete that it split me into pieces. It was the most intense pain and suffering I had ever been through and nothing, not a single thing in my life, could have ever prepared me for it. The world as I knew it shattered, fracturing into shards. I felt an indescribable sense of abandonment and loneliness, and had no way of knowing whether I could manage for even one day without my mother.

How was I going to manage without her, with my internship pending and my little boy to look after? Never before that day had it even entered my head that my mother could die. I always thought I would die before she died. It seemed the most unnatural thing to happen. I had no idea how I would carry on and live the rest of my life without her. As a child, I had this childish, reassuring thought that by the time I grew up they would have worked out how we could all live forever.

I found the reality that she would not know my life from this moment on, that I would walk the rest of my journey without her, indescribably painful. I could not bear it.

My brothers Stephen and Marc, my sisters Claudine and Monique, my father Bertie, David, and little Matthew, we were a broken family, huddling together to try to stop ourselves from splintering.

I wanted to crawl into a deep, black hole and never come out. I was profoundly and inexorably wounded. I did not think I could heal. And I raged. At God, at the universe, at the world. I raged that every other person out there was carrying on with their lives as if nothing had happened, while I was feeling that I was dying of grief. I felt alone in this. I had been one person before my mother died, and was a completely different person afterwards.

Through an overwhelming, thick mist of pain, I managed to push through. Getting up each day, feeding and caring for Matthew, making plans for him, delaying the start of my internship by one week, were matters that had to be attended to; despite being paralysed by grief, I had to do them. I have always had a strong sense of commitment and the inner life force is inexplicably strong within me. Somehow, being in that black hole brought its own bleak comfort and healing as the blackness took in its own energy and generated some form of substance and matter, galvanising me to keep moving.

I had to begin my internship. The week of compassionate leave was almost over. Many times, a voice deep within me spoke: *Leave it now. You cannot do this without her, without her help and support. You have been through so much. Don't do it*. It was the voice I wanted to hear. My self-doubt and inferiority raged on in battle: how would I manage the year? Was I good enough? But I was way past the point of no return. That path was irrevocably set. Bravely, shakily, weak and vulnerable, I faced my fears, and the unthinkable, and started my internship.

There are times in grief when unexpected lights help one through the darkness. During those first few months of my internship, working in Obstetrics and Gynaecology at Baragwanath Hospital, I will always be deeply indebted to my friend and colleague Andreas (AJ) Karas, who helped as much as he could to ease my workload as I struggled with unremitting grief. It seemed impossible.

But, like many impossible things, it was possible. I did it. Once again in my life I began to realise that, although there are many, many things I lack, I am fundamentally a survivor and I do not lack courage. I learnt that, despite being shattered by grief, it is still possible to keep functioning and moving forward. I learnt too that, despite overwhelming doubt and fear in my ability, I *can* bear it. Despite the paralysing anxiety, I can pitch up, face it and take it on.

David tried to shoulder as much of my pain and grief as he could. Witnessing my suffering on top of his own sadness about the loss of my mother was hard on him. David always tried to fix things that were broken; he was gifted at this. But he could not fix my grief. I had to endure it and learn to manage it. He was a lifeboat for me in the raging sea of despair and Matthew was my lighthouse. There was still joy. Matthew was two and a half years old when my mother was killed and, despite his smallness, he seemed to grasp the concept that his 'Ganny' was not coming back. At that early age he too learnt about loss, hardship and survival, about how to keep going because that is what he saw his parents do. He absorbed it all.

We kept going. It was the only way. Day by day. Week by week. We fought to survive.

Despite unspeakable pain and deep wounds, it was possible to survive.

There is neither a beginning nor an end to that continuous movement of life, to those staggering and momentous events that knock us down and build us up. They move through us, changing and moulding us, altering our shape and form. Like giant protoplasms we move and shift, engulfing the experiences and becoming the change.

These are the narratives of our lives, the stories and events that turn us into who we are and shape us, for better or worse.

4

‡‡‡‡

EARLY DAYS

Johannesburg, 1987

Heart, cover your tracks
The blood that you spill, will wash what you lack
Soul, sew up your wounds
Test out your engine, give it some room

Mind, pick up your pace
Capture the thoughts you always chase
Soul, open your wings
Lift this cage higher than any dream

[...]

Heart, flesh out your webs
The past that was tangled, will unwrap and shed
Soul, sing out your songs
Clear out your throat, belt it out strong.
— A BOY AND HIS KITE, 'COVER YOUR TRACKS'

Our three-strong family continued bravely, hurt and lost but slowly realising we would survive. I felt as though we had unravelled but we could still get up and go on. The wound was deep but it did not stop me moving on. I missed my mother terribly, yet I could still breathe. I had not been turned to stone.

Life kept moving.

It was always going to keep moving.

Matthew was strong-willed from the beginning, a bright, intelligent little boy who grasped concepts quickly and challenged us constantly. He wanted things his way and truly believed that most things, if he thought about them and put his mind to them, were possible. He was feisty and determined, and when he wanted to do something he did everything he could to make it work.

He pushed the boundaries, always wanting more. He mastered numbers as well as language and reading easily. He had a vivid imagination and he tried everything. He sat on the ergo machine at the age of two. He was determined to ride a bicycle and would not rest when, at the age of three, he saw another little boy on a bike and wanted nothing more than to ride. He did not give up until he was riding a two-wheeler proficiently. He tried to build a rocket that would fly to the moon, and had plans and drawings of what the rocket would look like. He had other plans to dig a tunnel under our house, he had boxes that became cars and boats, he built rafts and go-karts, and in his imagination we owned horses. In Matthew's own mind he became the game, the character, the concept.

I was now well into my internship at Baragwanath Hospital in Soweto. I had managed to get through the first month and was starting to relax into the work; my anxieties and fears were better controlled. During my second month of internship I made an important discovery. I was doing Obstetrics at the time and was assisting a young registrar to perform a Caesarean-section operation in theatre. I suddenly found myself on the floor, having fainted. The obstetric registrar casually asked me, 'Are you sure you're not pregnant?'

A light went on.

I was pregnant.

David and I had spoken about having another baby but we wanted to

67

wait until after I had completed my internship. Matthew was getting older. He was already almost three. Both David and I knew he needed a sibling, a more permanent friend and partner. Well, the permanent playmate was on his way. Once again, we had got the timing all wrong and this time it would interrupt my internship, a brutally tough year for anyone, never mind a young mom with another child on the way.

Medical internship is a year during which you are expected to work like a machine. It is fraught with an insurmountable fatigue, beyond what one has ever experienced. Working a 90-hour week on average, I would drive home from a long shift with the windows down, music blaring, eating and drinking whatever I could lay my hands on, trying to stay awake at the wheel. It was the norm to work shifts of 30 hours or more when on intake. It was a ridiculously tough year. I was generally overstressed and exhausted. You were the first to be called to see patients, so you had to be confident and skilled enough to make assessments. When my unit was on call I worked in the medical or the surgical intake wards. At Baragwanath Hospital, the surgical intake ward was known as the Surgical Pit. Any patient who had suffered trauma or could require surgery was shunted to the Surgical Pit. It was a terrifying place where seriously injured trauma patients were rushed through to the resuscitation room where we tried to save their lives.

I found the year intensely dehumanising. I was constantly exhausted and found myself suffering from a profound disconnection from patients. There were always crowds of people waiting to be seen and it felt like an impossible feat to ever get on top of things. The risk of contracting HIV/Aids was high and the medical staff had become paranoid, donning aprons, gloves, masks, glasses, any form of protection to avoid the risk of being infected with contaminated body fluids.

There was also a lot of violence in Soweto because of the State of Emergency. It was not a safe place. I used to take a shortcut home through Diepkloof, one of Soweto's suburbs. One day, a German medical student working in an exchange programme at the hospital was shot and killed at one of the traffic lights on that same route. His death was a terrible shock for everyone and brought home to us the extreme violence we were living with on a daily basis. I stopped using the shortcut.

I also very quickly learnt another truth in medicine, a truth probably mirrored in many professions: the work was never done. It was impossible to get to the end of the day and feel that you had accomplished everything. There was always more work to be done: more patients, more tests, more reading, just more of everything. There was no limit to the depth of the work.

This has never eased. Throughout my medical career, I have felt that the demands are unceasing.

The pressures of the year took their toll. During the year I developed viral meningitis and another intern, with whom I worked closely, later developed tuberculosis in his knee. We were constantly under pressure and the fatigue was immense. It was tough being pregnant in this environment. As my pregnancy advanced, David would come and help me by doing some of my night-call duty. He was always so generous and kind about helping me, besides being one of the most capable people I know.

I missed my mother, her calm way of coping, her pleasure in helping, her wonderful presence in Matthew's life. I missed her concern. Who would worry about me the way she had? And I missed the joy she would have had in my pregnancy.

We were learning to be a tough family that could handle what came at us. Despite the difficulties and the poor timing, we were overjoyed and excited to be having another child. It was some respite for our sad, bereft family.

As a result of being pregnant I had to delay the completion of my internship and shift my attention to the birth of my baby. On the morning of 9 November 1990 I visited my doctor, who felt the time had come to intervene. I was induced that morning as I was post-dates and my baby was getting bigger by the day. Labour for me never eased itself in – it simply arrived like a brutal tidal wave of pain that to this day remains the most intense physical pain I have ever endured. Fortunately for me, the shocking intensity was short-lived and three hours after the start of the induction, I delivered another baby boy.

Lawrence Andrew was born at a massive, healthy 4.2 kg. To me he was beautiful, but what mother does not think her baby is gorgeous? In my eyes he was as perfect and flawless as Matthew had been. I was overwhelmed by love for my new baby. I always felt that if I had not seen my babies after their birth and had to pick mine out in a room full of babies later, I would have chosen the right one. They just had that look about them, that they were ours, as if we had developed our own unique brand of baby.

Shortly after Lawrence's birth, David faced the unwelcome prospect of national service. At that time, South Africa conscripted all white males into its army for two years of military service. In 1989, this was reduced to one year. Every year since starting university, David had applied for and been granted deferment, which was the case for most medical students. But he completed his internship in 1989 and was working as a medical officer at Baragwanath. He wanted to begin specialising but the army refused to grant him further deferment. He was conscripted in early January 1991 and spent three months doing basic training. We did not see him during that time.

I was depressed without him and struggled to manage Matthew and a six-week-old baby on my own. Looking back, I realise that I more than likely had a degree of post-partum depression, which was inevitable in some ways as it was not long after losing my mother and I was lonely and physically exhausted. It was tough on David too. He worried about the three of us at home and was anxious to get on with his specialising. My family, especially Claudine and her boyfriend at the time, helped me considerably through this period.

After completing his basic training, David's circumstances improved and he was posted to Witwatersrand Command in Braamfontein, Johannesburg. We were able to lead a normal life again, with him coming home every night after work. He managed the military medical services for the entire Witwatersrand area and was very successful in this work.

After much deliberation, he made a decision to join the permanent force for two years as it was better paid and we were struggling financially. He was good at his work; when the two years were up, they offered him a chance to stay with the army and climb the ranks to commandant. He worked extra casualty sessions at night at Germiston Hospital as well as at a large local general practice to supplement our income. David is one of the most phenomenally capable people I know and has always seemed able to shoulder an enormous amount of pressure, difficulty and hardship. He seems to absorb difficulties, finding space for any problem. He turned down the offer of a career in the military in favour of specialising through the University of the Witwatersrand.

I had been fortunate to have my parents pay my university fees but David had taken out a large student loan. Over seven years he had amassed a debt and we had to slowly pay this back. There was no money for extras. We did everything ourselves to save money. There were no dinners out or luxuries. That came so much later. As our family grew, the boys witnessed this aspect of our family life, the financial struggle and being aware that we had to be careful. My father had the foresight and generosity to create a family trust for the purpose of paying for his grandchildren's education. This was and remains an unparalleled support for us and I owe my parents much gratitude for this and acknowledge the enormous difference it has made in our lives.

Matthew was at a small nursery school in the mornings and he was encountering a problem with his teacher. He was running into a war with her and neither of them was prepared to back down. The teacher insisted that he ate his peas and Matthew hated peas and flatly refused to comply. Eventually, I had to step in. He was three years old and could take on an adult – he was that strong-willed, determined and uncompromising.

I had to split my internship over two years, leaving it a month before Lawrence was born and returning eight months later to complete it. Without the full year of medical internship, it is not possible to register or practise as a doctor. I had no choice. So it was back to Baragwanath

Hospital to complete the year. It was during this time that I had the first of a few sequelae of the radiation therapy with which I had been treated back in 1978. I developed thyroid nodules and had to have half my thyroid surgically removed to ensure there was no malignancy. Fortunately, all went well and I sailed through that operation, proceeding almost as if nothing had happened.

Lawrence was a relatively easy baby after Matthew. The two grew up as good friends, with Matthew clearly Lawrence's keeper, always scheming and pushing and getting Lawrence to do what he wanted him to do. Lawrence was a willing comrade, unless it was something he did not want to do. At that point, nothing could convince him to do it. He simply refused. He was easy-going until he reached that point, and he then became as strong-willed and determined as his brother. He was sure of himself from an early age. With his blond, wispy hair and earnest blue eyes, he was adorable, good-natured and easy to be with. He was funny and had the most infectious laugh I had ever heard.

That early brotherly bond was cemented in their play and we put a lot of effort into this aspect of their lives. Thankfully, it was the era just before hard-core computer games and the boys benefitted from playing outdoors. We believed in them playing as much as possible to help their physical and imaginative development, and encouraged it in every conceivable way. We lived on some amazing properties as we moved around Johannesburg to accommodate our growing family. One of our favourite homes was an enormous farm-style property on an acre of land in Ferndale. We named that home Longacre. I was devastated to leave it when we later moved to Linden to be closer to the boys' school.

Wherever we lived, we created something special for the boys, encouraging them to play. Our gardens were always filled with treehouses, secret gardens, soccer fields, jungle gyms, trampolines, rope ladders, climbing walls. We had spectacular birthday parties for the boys, with massive bonfires and fun things for the children to do. We had playrooms and bookshelves stocked to the ceiling. In many ways we were the perfect team.

I had the ideas and David put them into action. He was resourceful and extremely good with his hands. He could fix anything if he put his mind to it. We used to call him Sylvester McMonkey McBean, the Fix-it-Up Chappie from the book *The Sneetches and Other Stories* by the genius Dr Seuss.

In 1992 South Africa was going through the long-awaited changes so desperately needed in a country ravaged by the effects of apartheid. Nelson Mandela had been released from prison in February 1990, a glorious and momentous day in the history of this country. The democratisation of South Africa had begun. The country geared up for its first democratic election and change swept through the land as the appalling bastions of apartheid were finally dismantled.

Suddenly, the Olympic dream became a reality again for many South Africans. The country set about putting a team together for the 1992 Barcelona Olympics. Rowing was part of this team. South Africa sent a heavyweight men's eight to Barcelona, which included some of David's old rowing mates and colleagues from his Wits University days. The crew included Robin McCall, Andrew Lonmon-Davis and Ivan Pentz. Paolo Cavalieri, one of the stalwarts of South African rowing, was one of the team managers. They raced to eighth place at the Olympics. It was a momentous and special time in the history of South African sport, and for rowing it marked the beginning of an exciting new era.

I should have anticipated what happened next. I should have known. But I had no idea.

One day, unexpectedly, David said, 'I want to go back to rowing. I want to try to make the next Olympic Games.'

I stared at him in a daze. 'What? Are you serious?'

'I want to row at the Atlanta Olympics in 1996. They have brought a new division into the Olympic rowing competition and created lightweight events. There will be a lightweight coxless four and a lightweight double scull. I think I can do it. I think I have a chance to make it. I'll need to lose some weight. I've been speaking to Gareth Costa. He wants to go and he feels we could have a chance together in the lightweight double.'

We had been married for five years, we had two small children, both of us were working as doctors and we had moved five times since getting married. Our lives were full and busy and I had no idea how rowing would fit into this schedule.

David was 28 years old. He had not rowed for five years.

Gareth Costa was a slightly younger athlete rowing for the Wemmer Pan Rowing Club in Johannesburg. David had never rowed with him but knew him quite well. He was a talented rower and had won many local championship events, including the famous Buffalo River Silver Sculls. He too was working and had a young family. He had never taken a break from rowing and had kept going after he finished school. Gareth was young, driven and athletic; they would make an impressive duo.

I would be dishonest if I did not admit that my heart sank. Hard, and far. I knew what this meant – I knew the level of training he would be expected to complete and the amount of time it would take. I was not wildly excited about the prospect. But I also knew it was something David had always wanted to do and I could not deny him the chance. He had given up any chance of international rowing at university and a few years later, when we got married and his life changed, he gave up local rowing. Emotionally it clearly had left a void, a place within him that remained incomplete and unfulfilled. I could not say no. He deserved to try. I wanted him to give it his best attempt.

It was the start of four long years of David training hard – really hard. To say it was not an easy time would be a complete understatement. I wanted to support him but there simply was not enough time in the day in which to fit everything. It was a difficult time for all of us; we all wanted a piece of David and there just was not enough time for him to divide himself up fairly. I was working as a medical officer at Baragwanath Hospital, we had two small, energetic and boisterous children, and David was specialising in haematological pathology at the Johannesburg General Hospital. He worked in a department of high-achieving cum laude graduates, who had neither the understanding nor the will to understand his rowing aspirations. They made life somewhat difficult for him and he was constantly trying to prove he was doing his share of the work. In addition, he was trying to make the lightweight division of rowing, and had to lose enough weight to make the 70 kg cut-off.

Could it have been any harder? I asked myself.

As a family we had to dig into our reserves and find the energy to both support and allow David the chance to make it to Atlanta. I had to be generous; to be perfectly honest, it was not the easiest thing I have done and it did not come that naturally. But I put my head down, focused on the goal and tried to support him as best I could. The two little brothers were exposed to their father's training and dieting at this time when their little minds and bodies were like sponges, absorbing everything happening around them. This process influenced Matthew in particular, an astute, bright child who internalised the extreme discipline and level of hard work this took. He was five years old when David started training again. Lawrence was still very much a toddler at one and a half, and was quite happy to be following his brother and Daddy around.

Where possible we went with David, watching him train and race at Roodeplaat Dam, north of Pretoria. We became friends with Gareth and his wife Leanne. They had two little girls and went on to have a third daughter. We were in it together, bound by common difficulties and a common purpose. It was a joke between us that Gareth had the girls and we the boys. 'It's because I am doing all the work,' he used to tease David.

During this period, I discovered I was pregnant again. I was working with professors Ken Huddle and Roy Shires in Endocrinology and Professor Mohammed Tikly in Rheumatology. I loved the work and had I been able to specialise at that stage of my career I would more than likely have chosen rheumatology. I was delighted to be pregnant again, both David and I loved the thought of another baby. Somewhere deep within me I cherished the idea of having a daughter, a little girl who would balance our family. I also knew that a boy would be very special, familiar to me and another friend for Lawrence and Matthew. I knew our lives were busy but neither David nor I had ever taken the easy path. I continued to work for as long as possible into the pregnancy. How did I manage? I expanded my outlook, absorbing what needed to be done and then getting on with it, head down.

Our third gorgeous little boy, James Michael, was born one beautiful Spring Day, 1 September 1993, at a time when South Africa was in the middle of exciting political changes.

The morning I was going into hospital, we had a domestic crisis. A pet bunny from next door found himself in our garden. Our dog, Numpie, thought heaven had arrived and proceeded to chase said bunny around the garden. David rushed out after Numpie, with Matthew and Lawrence in tow. David managed to dive on the bunny and save his life, returning him triumphantly to the neighbours. Exactly five hours later, after an induction and another rapid delivery, James Michael emerged into our world.

We had effectively made our lives a thousand times more difficult by having a third baby at a time when we were already stretched, but we loved having the children. Having babies made me the happiest I have ever been; these were the best times. James was the smallest of the three, weighing 3.8 kg at birth. He was another adorable baby boy and his two brothers crowded around him, fascinated. Matthew was six and Lawrence three, so they could be involved in his care and were intrigued with his growth and development.

Three little brothers. When James was born, David and I were instantly outnumbered.

James was a good-natured, easy baby, and simply got on with being part of a growing family. He had to fit in as our lives were busy and there was not a lot of leisure time in our family. He had a lovely nature and we considered ourselves blessed to have three healthy, energetic little boys. He had a quietness and an intelligence about him, and a clever, witty sense of humour. One of my fondest memories of James as a toddler was the time he decided to become a lion. He had been watching the movie *The Lion King* and was passionate about the story, as were all the boys. They could recite the dialogue almost word for word. For a few months James thought he was a lion, moving like one and growling and roaring. He had become Simba and Mufasa. To this day, he will look at a wildebeest and mutter about them being Mufasa's murderers.

David and I always joked that we were made to have children. Immediately after James was born, David whispered to me in the delivery room, 'We have to have another baby after this.' It was a little secret for me, something I would look forward to. I never wanted them to grow into the next stage. I loved them the way they were. Each time they entered the next phase, though, I loved them even more. Each stage brought its own charms and difficulties but we grew and adapted to these inevitable changes in our children.

But the reality was in the moment.

David had committed to the process of training his body to be faster and stronger. He threw everything he could into the programme. Wynand (Wig) Dreyer, one of the coaches of Wits University Boat Club, undertook to coach David and Gareth in the double scull and did so in 1992 and 1993. The entire Viking Rowing Club, for which both Gareth and David rowed, came out in full support of them and offered a boat and some financial assistance for their tours to the World Cup Regattas in Lucerne. From 1994, they joined the national lightweight squad, falling under coach Paul Jackson, the same coach who later coached Matthew to the London Olympics. Being part of the lightweight squad meant they now had a chance to make the selection for the top boat, the lightweight four. This gave further impetus to their training and motivation as they pushed on, hoping to make it into the four.

Gareth and David worked hard at their training as well as managing their careers and young families. Their perseverance and dedication were extraordinary. David would wake up early every morning, at about 4.30, to meet some of the squad at a regular meeting place on Grayston Drive, Sandton, and drive out to Roodeplaat Dam to train. He would return to the Johannesburg Hospital at about 9 am and put in a full day's work in his department. He would leave work early, at 3 pm, to travel back to the dam to train or to go to gym with the group. This caused some dissatisfaction among his colleagues, who felt that he was not doing his quota of work. He devised a system that split the work up evenly, and which showed that he was doing his share of the work but in less time. He also attended tutorials and lectures, as he was specialising in Haematology. This effectively meant he was studying on the job. He often fell asleep in tutorials. This may not sound too serious, but if there are only two of you in the tutorial it is a little awkward. His professor, Barry Mendelow, was very understanding and generous towards David. In his way, Professor Mendelow played a vital role in David's life, one of those people who becomes a turning point in one's journey.

The harsh and bitter truth, however, was that David did not make it to the Atlanta Olympics. He simply was not fast enough. It was brutal: one day he was part of it, and the next day he was not. In April 1996, Paul Jackson took David aside and said, 'Look, David, on nearly all the assessments you are a couple of seconds behind the others. This is a consistent finding. For this reason, you are not in the lightweight four selected for Atlanta. We have decided to take you as the spare man.' He was direct, but not unkind. There is no way of softening a decision like that.

'I did not make the selection. I was not fast enough. They want to take me as a spare man to Atlanta, but I am too old for that. They must take someone younger who will continue to row later for them. I am done now. I tried, but did not make it. I have other options and a career and a family to consider,' David explained to me later, trying to make sense of the decisions.

Gareth, on the other hand, did make the selection. Paul Jackson continued as the coach of that crew, which comprised Gareth, Mark Rowand, Roger Tobler and Mike Hasselbach. They took a young athlete, Shaun Tagney, as the spare man. The lightweight four raced in Atlanta in a new event in the Olympic line-up, making the B final and coming ninth overall.

I was devastated for David, his dream, all the work, for myself and the hope I had invested. It was a painful time for us. The disappointment cut deep as the fanfare surrounding South Africa going to Atlanta was considerable. South Africa celebrated being fully back in the Olympic fold and put together a team that showed promise. They even painted a South African Airways jet in the South African colours for the purpose of transporting the Olympians. I felt bruised for David; he was hurt, but he accepted it and ultimately understood the decision. It was a hard lesson, learning to be proud of something from which you have been dropped. That lesson requires maturity.

It was the first Olympics in which South Africa was able to shine. Penny Heyns won two gold medals and Marianne Kriel a bronze medal in swimming. Josia Thugwane won gold in the men's marathon and Hezekiel Sepeng won silver in the 800 m athletics.

The real disappointment for David was that at his age his Olympic chances were over. There were no second chances. His dream to row at the highest level died that day. I felt that too many things had stood against him having a real chance of making it: his age, his circumstances and, most likely, the five years of rowing he missed after we got married. It was too long a break from rowing to come back and really have a chance. He simply had too much to cope with in the rest of his life, trying to hold down a heavy work schedule, study and manage the demands of a young family.

He decided to stop rowing. It was a brave, final decision made one day and then carried out the next. He just stopped. He has never gone back to competitive rowing. He was 32 at the time. To this day, he does not enjoy rowing with scratch crews. To David, a crew needs time to settle and grow together. He still loves rowing and occasionally rows in a scull for his own enjoyment, but almost never rows with a crew.

From that time on, David devoted his time and energy to preparing for his final Haematology exams. Within four months of not making the team for Atlanta, he had qualified as a specialist in Haematological Pathology. He went on to study further and completed another two years of clinical work, specialising in haematological diseases and qualifying as a clinical haematologist in 1998. He had effectively been studying for 18 years.

What helped us both was the knowledge that David had given everything he could to the process of trying to make the Olympics. What helped even more was the knowledge that there was a life after rowing – there were other ways in which one could give of one's best.

The growing young brothers witnessed David's profound hurt. They saw my distress too as I had invested much in the process. They also saw the inner resolve and strength to get up from being smashed down, change the direction of a life path, and keep going. They saw that it was not the end if a door slammed shut. This was a valuable lesson for the boys. They saw that the inner void could be filled more by trying than by succeeding. I believe that the loss sowed within Matthew the seeds of a deeply rooted and unquenchable hunger to succeed and subsequently each brother subconsciously embodied that drive and hunger to win. David's Olympic dream was over, but that same fervent dream was seeded quietly in the boys and they carried it silently, deep within themselves, for many years until they faced their own opportunities to succeed.

At an early, impressionable age, the boys had been exposed to the Olympic dream, the spirit of excellence. Matthew would later speak of not only his father's Olympic dream but also of Josia Thugwane's win as a major inspiration to him. What followed was a deep and quiet belief and conviction that he too could one day race at the Olympics.

True to David's whispered words three years before, we had our fourth and last child, a beautiful son. Charles Albert was born at an impressive 4.4 kg on 2 January 1997. I was staggered by the sheer size of this baby boy I had produced. I am not a big person, and to deliver these enormous babies – well, frankly, I impressed myself. Baby Charles was the only one of the boys to carry family names. He was named after his great-grandfather Charles on David's side, as well as my father Albert.

To be honest, there was a time in the pregnancy when I hoped for a girl, but I knew before the birth that another little boy was on his way into our lives. I wept briefly and selfishly for a private moment when I heard there would be no little girl. After that there were no more tears.

I would be the mother of boys.

I think I was destined to have only boys because I had suffered a horrible miscarriage eighteen months before Charles was born and that had been a tiny baby boy too. I was 35 years old when I had Charles. There was an age gap of ten years between Matthew and Charles so, despite our poor record of family planning, we had spaced the boys well, which made having four children a whole lot more manageable.

The three brothers were fascinated by baby Charles and spent hours helping me and running errands for me when I was busy with him. James saw Charles as finally being the playmate he needed as the elder two were much busier at school and he was often excluded from their activities. James had just started pre-primary school and Lawrence and Matthew were well on their way through primary school. James was ready for his own permanent friend. Charles just seemed to fit into the general chaos of our family, the busyness and energy. He completed the brotherhood and brought a sort of balance into the other three boys' lives.

I was overjoyed with my four little boys. I felt special, in an elite group of Mothers With Four Boys. I liked that. I was immensely proud of them. They were exuberant, boisterous children, full of boundless energy so characteristic of boys and the very young. I loved the energy they brought to our lives, but there were plenty of times I found it draining and utterly incomprehensible, times when I wondered how on earth I had landed myself in this situation.

It was not always easy to work and have a family. I struggled but I knew it was the way I wanted it to be. We were hard workers with a strong work ethic. We had made the decision early on that I would not specialise as I wanted to spend more time with the boys. I worked part-time as much as possible as I wanted the boys to see me as a working mother, that it was possible for women to have careers, and that life could be pushed to the limit. Memories of my mother and her belief that modern women have rights to careers had left their powerful mark. I wanted the best of both worlds.

David turned down a number of work opportunities earlier on his career that would have set us up comfortably much sooner. But he chose his specialisation instead, managing diseases of the blood and lymphatic system. Once he qualified he moved into private practice and worked hard to get the work flowing smoothly. Having his own practice sounded good, but in reality it meant that everything fell on his shoulders and he was ill-prepared for some of the difficulties of managing a practice. He learnt the hard way and had to learn fast.

Throughout the years, David has worked with science, pushing to know more and do more. He has always been fuelled by a deep hunger for understanding the biology and science behind the illness. He has the unique gift of being scientifically driven, but compassionate and interested in the human spirit.

I continued to work at Baragwanath Hospital for many years in the Department of Medicine doing Rheumatology and Endocrinology. Baragwanath still has a special place in my heart.

In 1996 I left Baragwanath Hospital to take up a position at the Witwatersrand Hospice, known as HospiceWits, a year before Charles was born. For a long time, I had felt the pull in that direction of work. Losing my mother and having had my own experience of illness at a young age had set me up internally to manage the highly distinctive and unique work involved in the relatively unknown field of palliative care. I loved the work. It was enormously fulfilling, and highly rewarding. People would say, 'I do not know how you do that work. I would find it too difficult as I am too sensitive. You must be able to cut yourself off.' They were wrong, though. It was precisely because I was sensitive and empathic that I could do such work.

Most people have no idea what palliation means. For me, the work encompasses caring for people who have limited time left to live. They have a seriously advanced illness that is no longer responsive to curative treatment. They are dying. Medical care bent on curing the patient is unable to fulfil its role and becomes palliative. The work ensures as much quality of life for the patient as possible while preparing both the patients and their families for the inevitable end. It was the time in my career where I fully grasped the understanding of ethical principles, and the concept of doing good rather than harm and weighing up the benefits against the risks of any decision.

I sometimes think I gave my best during those years at Hospice. The work enabled me to accompany many as they walked extraordinary roads towards the end of their lives. I was lucky to work with an incredible team of doctors, nurses and administrative staff, many of whom remain good friends to this day. I went on to specialise in Palliative Medicine, completing a master's degree through the University of Cape Town in 2006.

My younger sister Claudine and her husband Julian were our closest friends during those early years. We spent much time with them. Their eldest daughter Beth was six months younger than Charles. They went on to have four children, three girls and a boy. They had the girls and I had the boys. Their son Oliver became almost like another son to me and as he grew up he became Charles's younger brother. Charles jumped at the chance to boss Oliver around just as he had suffered at the hands of three older brothers. It was a joke between us that when all our children were together it looked as if we had eight children as the ages fitted that mould perfectly. Their children felt like my children in so many ways. We had a lot of fun together, supporting one another in those early years as we negotiated our way through the multitude of difficulties in parenthood and family life.

Young children breathe in the rhythm of the family in which they grow up. Every family has a distinctive pulse. The way in which a family moves and copes with daily life and momentous events sets the tone of that family. Our family rhythm gained momentum as each life event moulded and changed us. As a family, we tended to make choices that were not necessarily the easiest. These were decisions that pushed us just a little harder, a little further past the boundaries that limit potential. They set us up for the risk of disappointment, but also the joy of success. We immersed ourselves in whatever we did. We persevered and worked hard. The boys internalised this rhythm and learnt, in their own individual and personal ways, how to move to it.

My father's family, the Lincolns, have a powerful motto they hold close: Strength in Adversity, or, in Latin, *constans contraria spernit*. I felt this motto resonated deeply within my own family.

We are strong despite the hardship. We bear the unbearable, we beat to the rhythm of strength and courage.

5

BROTHERHOOD

Johannesburg, 1997

He felt as if he were swimming out to sea, and the tide was sweeping him farther and farther out [...] he was terrified that if he could not save his brother, he would drown, too.

– JONATHAN WEINER, *HIS BROTHER'S KEEPER*

Our family was active and busy right from the beginning and we have never stopped being on the go. We pushed hard and expected a lot from ourselves.

David continued to train, albeit at a more conventional level, doing things like running, cycling and gym. He seems to be one of those unfathomable people who remain naturally fit and athletic no matter how little training they do.

We took the boys walking and hiking from early on. I am indebted to David's parents and their close friends, the Bennetts, who often took them camping and hiking in the Magaliesberg and engendered a love of the outdoors in the boys. To this day they have secret places in, and fond memories of, the Magaliesberg.

We spent a lot of time in our garden, always planning and doing things. We constantly had projects on the go. The boys were part of these projects and worked alongside us, helping in their own unique ways. David and I once dug up a tree – a privet, a horrible invader – only to find a day later that the boys had dug their own hole, planted the invader and were trying to resuscitate it.

As with all parents, we excelled in some ways and fell far short in others.

Over the years we never found the best way to discipline the boys. We tried negotiating with them, making them apologise, sending them to their rooms. I did a fair amount of shouting and screaming at them, and smacks did happen, but that stressed me more than anything so we agreed to stop those. We fined them, but then often forgot to take the money. We tried to be strict with food and junk food: 'No pudding until you have eaten your dinner.' David and I did not always agree on disciplinary issues. I feel we could have been better at presenting a more united front when it came to discipline.

We tried to encourage the boys to stand up for themselves, face difficulty, and not turn and run away. We learnt not to jump in too quickly when things were going wrong, but rather to encourage them to figure out how to solve the problem themselves. I once made the mistake of marching in to see the Grade 4 teacher, telling her that Matthew was being bullied by another child. She listened carefully and then said calmly, 'Matthew gives as good as he gets.'

I never did that again.

As doctors, we treated their childhood illnesses and ailments when necessary. They were healthy children, with few illnesses. We were lucky with respect to the common ear, nose and throat infections that plague so many children. The boys never had ear infections, grommets or tonsillectomies. They had the occasional bout of tonsillitis and that was the sickest they got. They would spike temperatures of almost 40 degrees; we would have a look at their throats and diagnose the tonsillitis. Within 12 hours of starting antibiotics they would be back to normal. Lawrence was delirious once from a fever and saw soldiers marching towards him through his curtains. Matthew had a couple of more dramatic infections, viral encephalitis and tick bite fever. On one occasion when he was sick he told us, 'I want to see a proper doctor.' I think he thought we were a bit casual, and he wanted the real thing. On another occasion, we surgically removed a plantar wart from Lawrence's foot on our kitchen table. I have to say the plantar wart never regrew. Matthew and Lawrence both sustained broken arms in their younger years and James needed stitches on his forehead. We used proper doctors for those injuries.

We were hopeless with tooth-mouse duties. We often forget and had the awful job of explaining to the boys that our tooth mouse was a very busy mouse with a lot on its plate and had probably just forgotten to take the tooth and leave money behind. We were a whole lot better with the Easter Bunny and Father Christmas duties and had quite a bit of fun with those.

We had fabulous family holidays in Knysna. In 1986 my parents had bought a house named Helford, situated on Leisure Isle. From that moment it became our personal piece of paradise. We went there every year and often more than once a year. That home enabled us to have glorious holidays, crammed with activities perfectly suited to energetic and sporty children. The days were filled with walking, beach days, swimming, sailing, boat trips up the river, water-skiing, cycling and canoeing. We bought the boys a large canoe in which they could all fit comfortably and under Matthew's leadership they would canoe their way up and down all the rivers in and around the Knysna area. Knysna was the closest to heaven the boys knew.

We used to pack the car with bikes of all shapes and sizes: plastic motorbikes, tricycles, and varying sizes of two-wheeler bikes. As they got older, ergometers, which are indoor rowing machines, became part of the baggage; we eventually took three with us, as well as a few rowing boats on a few occasions. We have taken a single scull a few times and even went as far as taking a double scull one year and a pair another year. As the boys got older, the ergometers took over the patio with their distinctive whirring sound, getting louder and louder as the number of them increased.

Our road trips were part of our holidays and we made up general knowledge quizzes for the boys, asking them questions and scoring them. Travelling through the Karoo was, and still is, one of my favourite journeys.

When I gaze at the huge, open sky stretched out over the dry vastness I always have the feeling that the sky holds everything together, stopping us from falling into a thousand directions and pieces. The sky knows and contains everything, both the hardships we endure and the joys we experience.

As parents we brought different qualities to the intricate process of bringing up four little boys and turning them into solid men. We gave them the best we could, like any other parents. I was definitely more sensitive and quiet; I worried a lot, becoming anxious and stressed about the boys, the future, the world.

I got overwhelmed easily and was overly self-conscious. I was diligent and committed to everything I took on. If I said I would do it, I would do it, no matter what. I struggled to delegate tasks and tended to do everything myself, at times working myself to wreckage. Conflict stressed me and I was forever trying to soothe the fights between the boys, attempting to find ways of stopping them from attacking one another. I was a perfectionist in my younger years and nearly drove myself and my family crazy with this. Over time I have thankfully dampened that trait and learnt that some things just do not matter that much. I did not lack courage and inner strength. When I studied for my master's in Palliative Medicine the boys were astounded by how hard I worked for it. They certainly did not inherit my ability to study for long periods – or, rather, they inherited David's ability to grasp concepts quickly and retain knowledge easily.

As a father David was a good role model, hardworking, honest and intelligent. He was generous in so many ways and wanted to solve problems. He could be relied on to help and get things done. He had enormous reserves of energy and nothing was too big a job for him. He was more laid back than I was and soothed some of the stress and anxiety for me. He dealt with situations head-on, and was unafraid of conflict. In this we were poles apart. What I at times felt was him being tactless was perhaps my being too cautious or timid. There were times when I felt he pushed but could have held back – and, equally, when I could have pushed harder but instead held back.

Matthew was a leader, a clear thinker, honest and challenging, always pushing for more. He was mentally strong and sniffed out weakness in others. He was outspoken about mediocrity and abhorred the modern way of thinking that gave everyone recognition no matter how bad they were. He felt it made no sense to not have winners and a merit-based system. He felt people should not be protected and the lessons learnt from coming second were valuable. He was tough, but also sensitive. As a young child he sobbed his way through movies like *Bambi* and *The Lion King*. We had to leave the drive-in one year when he sobbed so loudly after Bambi's mother was killed that we could not control him and were disturbing the cars next to us. He cried after he caught a small squid in Knysna one year, weeping out of guilt and remorse for the poor thing. He had the ability to cut you down sharply and reduce you to tears, but was also sensitive enough to be the first to notice if something had upset you.

Matthew had a wicked sense of humour: in high school he once made up a fictitious name when they were being taught by a student and kept this up for a long time until the librarian caught him out. He once signed James's homework diary and wrote a message in the diary to James's teacher, telling her that James was clearly not working hard enough and that she should feel free to beat him as often as she wanted to. James told me later that she saw the funny side of this and roared with laughter.

He was a risk taker. As he grew up this got him into trouble at times but also grew a spirit of recognising uncertainty and being more daring than most people. He knew when to hold back but he also had a feel for when to attack, an ability not to hesitate but to trust himself.

Lawrence always saw the best in people. It would take a lot for him to speak out against someone. He usually found an excusable reason for someone else's behaviour. He was a calm child who got on well with his brothers and friends. He made good, lasting friendships at school. In primary school he was passionate about Warhammer and played the game endlessly.

I found it inexplicably difficult to get cross with Lawrence. He had a way of looking so shocked and wounded that you felt simply awful for having shouted at him. The brothers did not hesitate to point out that Lawrence got off far too easily and if I was cross with Lawrence I aimed it at them.

As Lawrence grew up, his ability to absorb situations with relative calmness began to prove a great strength. He had a considered outlook on life situations that set him up to grow his inner self-confidence, but without arrogance or superiority. He was always looking for ways to improve. He learnt to hear hard truths and absorb them without reacting in a negative way.

James had a kind nature and was the most helpful of all the brothers. He was artistic and would draw for ages. He read prolifically. He was constantly being caught reading in class as he considered his book far more interesting than the topic being taught. He was hauled out to the principal's office on a few occasions, once when he folded an important school notice into the most amazing paper sailboat and was caught by his teacher. The principal saw the funny side of this; besides, the boat was actually a work of art. James annoyed my father in Mauritius when we travelled there on holiday by reading virtually the whole time and missing out on all the sights and history of the country. He was bright and witty and had self-confidence, which, considering he had two ruthless elder brothers, was a blessing.

He loved the trampoline and would bounce away for a few hours every day, talking to himself and creating his world. He loved rugby and was the only one to continue playing rugby at school up until matric, where he played in the second team. He had a good understanding of the game and an intelligence when it came to playing it. All three of the others gave up rugby in Grade 10 as they elected to row for longer periods through the winter.

Charles was a happy, smiling baby until the age of one. After that he earned the name 'the delicious monster', coined so appropriately by his granny, David's mother. I travelled to a conference in Australia for ten days when Charles was eighteen months old, leaving David in charge.

His parents moved in to help him. This was not good for Charles and he suffered severe separation anxiety for a long time after that. I was not in favour of leaving the boys but at that time I thought it would be fine and felt guilty that it had not worked out.

As a toddler he was best of friends with my sister Claudine's children, his cousins Beth, her brother Oliver and the two youngest, Emma and Abigail. Charles was the only one of my children lucky enough to have grown up with cousins. Of my siblings, I was the first to have children. Oliver and Charles once set about building a tunnel between our two houses. Their perseverance was considerable. They started the mighty tunnel project in Claudine's garden but unfortunately it failed dismally when Oliver's father Julian fell into the hole one night. It could have been serious; thank goodness that was not the case. But it was the end of the digging operation.

Charles has a dry sense of humour and tends to be the more anxious of all the boys, probably taking after me to a greater extent than the others. He was good at sport at junior school; he had the best ball skills of all the boys when it came to soccer and cricket, and he was a skilled swimmer and a proficient cyclist from an early age. His benchmark was three older brothers and parents who were busy and working, establishing careers and managing the family. In many ways he did not grow up with the full effect of all his brothers as Matthew left home to go to university when Charles was eight.

The bond between the boys was fundamentally solid and close, and they would stand together for most things. They were a brotherhood, a tribe, moving together like a pack. That bond remains strong to this day. At times, of course, they would fight terribly, almost as if they hated one another. When they lost their tempers, they nearly killed one another. There were times when I felt I was losing it, incapable of containing the energy and physicality they brought into our lives. There were times when I felt I could run away.

But it was all normal. It was what happens in families.

They were quite capable of giving each other a good bashing and their play could be rough. They were into playing with sticks; a stick of any size and shape would do. They would make them into swords and bows and arrows, jousting sticks, weapons of any sort. They once took their sticks into my garden and systematically and brutally hit every flower and bud off every plant in the garden. I am not sure what they were thinking, but later they told me they were soldiers. I came home to find my garden decimated. When I phoned David to tell him how awful they were, he consoled me, and said 'Just make them clean it all up. Please don't kill them, Danielle.'

We had a no-gun policy and refused to buy the boys toy guns as they grew up. They begged and pestered us for guns but we were adamant. Somehow we both felt there was enough gun violence in the world without adding to it. Of course, they got around it by making their own guns which took the form of large potato guns, shooting potatoes astonishingly far.

When Charles was nine years old, they were playing with one of their innumerable bows, shooting arrows, when James – mistakenly, caught up in the moment of the game – shot an arrow at Charles, hitting him in the eye. Until that point, apart from the odd wound needing stitches and two broken arms, I had got off lightly from an injury point of view considering I had four boys.

That luck ended that day.

This was serious, really serious. The injury caused severe blunt trauma to the entire anatomical structure of his eye. It was a grim time because the injury progressed to full retinal detachment and Charles needed surgery to save the eye. He went into surgery on 14 September 2006. We paced the waiting room, anxious for this to be over. He came out of the anaesthetic raving uncontrollably, in distress. We took him home as soon as we could, back to familiar surroundings where we could contain his distress.

His eye was saved, but he lost more than half his vision. We were devastated for Charles, knowing that he would go through life from this point less than perfect and would bear the brunt of a terrible accident. It was a hard lesson for all the boys. The ease and speed with which things can go fearfully wrong hit them hard.

Charles had learnt to face up to hardship and real disability early in his young life. At the age of nine, he had to come to terms with permanent and residual damage. There was nothing we could do but push on and keep moving forwards.

I was shocked by the way many people handled James at the time: 'So this is the brother who did the damage.' It was unnecessary. Neither David nor I blamed him. Yes, he had caused it. It was a terrible mistake, but it was an accident. His intention had not been to hurt his brother. A person's intention was always important to me.

The boys mischievously pretended to many people after that: 'Charles had an eye injury and has a glass eye.' I could see people staring at Charles's eyes, trying to work out which was the glass eye. Funny, yes, but tragic, as it very nearly ended up that way. Charles carries the injury quietly, and has never allowed it to hold him back in any way.

I was outnumbered in the family. My femaleness got lost somewhere in that potent mix of masculine energy and testosterone. I think a daughter in the family would have tempered the boys, made them perhaps less intense, more careful. In many ways I hid my girliness too much, not showing them how a girl would react to a situation. Our family was unbalanced. The four brothers were physically active, energetic, busy children. As they grew up, the rough and tumble, the hard-core physicality of the boys and David, the often crude conversations in what could be frankly termed toilet talk, were all a challenge to me. I had grown up with two brothers, so I had some idea of the male psyche, but never to this extent.

There were some specific issues that came with the territory of having four children, in particular four boys.

By far the biggest was the issue of food.

They could eat. A lot.

It never ended, really, feeding the growing machines. They wolfed down everything I made. I shopped and cooked, and cooked and shopped. At one stage, around the time when David was training for Atlanta, Matthew told me, 'Mommy, if there was an Olympics for cooking, you would win the gold medal.' If I made it, they ate it. They loved their food and packed as much of it away as possible.

On the other hand, David's lightweight training days had rubbed off hard on Matthew. He was fastidious about what he ate as an older child, giving up junk food for a long time as he prepared his body for competition. He even became vegetarian for a year after he caught the squid, which proved a challenge for me.

There was a natural rivalry that existed between them. Simply stated, there was constant competition between them.

They each wanted to be the best, the fastest, the strongest, the tallest, the favourite. There was a long-standing bet as to who would be the biggest. In the beginning David used to win everything, taking quite childish pleasure in being able to beat them. He never 'let' them beat him to make them feel better. In this, he taught them a valuable lesson. They had to be good enough to beat him. It was a grim day of facing reality for him when Matthew beat him for the first time on the bike in one of their so-called hotspots. And then Lawrence beat him. Then James. Then Charles. The wheel of life turned when the boys became stronger and faster than their father.

Contrary to their firm but very incorrect belief, we had no favourites. They were all our favourite children, because they were all different, each having something special, as well as something considerably less favourable. We loved them equally and completely, 'To infinity and back,' I would tell them, based on the delightful children's book by Sam McBratney, *Guess How Much I Love You.*

Then there was the issue of privacy. Or should I say, lack of privacy.

Having four children meant they were everywhere and it was hard to find a moment alone or a space that did not have some evidence of them in it. Rooms in our homes were constantly changing as their needs changed and they were either sharing a room or having their own space, depending on their ages and who was closest to whom.

Then there were pets.

We had a range of pets through the years, from bantam roosters and

94

hens and hamsters to rats, cats and dogs. The pet rats were quite a challenge. Matthew named the rats Reepicheep after the leader of the talking
mice in the book *Prince Caspian* by CS Lewis and Mathilde after one of
Roald Dahl's characters. We thought we had two females until one morning we found some minute little pink things snuffling around Mathilde in
the sawdust at the bottom of the cage. Overnight, we had quite suddenly
and unexpectedly become the proud owners of five tiny baby rats. When
they were a little bigger Matthew took them to school to give to his friends.
His friends loved them and he succeeded in giving them all away. The next
day, however, they all came back except one. None of the other mothers
was going to tolerate rats. We decided that the friend and his mother who
had kept the baby rat were hard-core people. They went up considerably
in our estimation. One morning we went to wake the boys and Mathilde
had tried to get out of the cage and got stuck. Her mate, her partner, had
devoured her! We were appalled, quickly removing the remains before the
boys woke to the murder scene. I drew the line at that point and it was the
end of our days with rats.

We loved cats and had four over the years. We had various dogs. Roxy
was an Alsatian we adopted from neighbours, Numpie a black Labrador
cross who was very skittish and highly strung, and later came two huge
Alsatians we raised from puppies, Tank and Cassie. All our dogs, when
given half a chance, would bound out the gate at full speed and run away
into the suburbs. The boys chased long and hard after them as we struggled
with their boundless energy. We never quite got the discipline of the dogs
under control.

There was mess, constant evidence through the house that we had
four children. My ordered mind struggled with this, and it took years to
finally relax slightly about the chaos. I am indebted to have had wonderful
domestic help in my house; Ivy Moyo has been my lifeline for what seems
like forever.

Then, of course, there was laundry.

The laundry started off with nappies, thousands of nappies over a period of 12 years. I did not use disposable nappies; to this day I feel they are a terrible environmental burden. As the boys grew, so did the volume of laundry. It started reasonably and I should imagine fairly normally, as in any family. I had already had some experience of sports kit from David, but as the boys grew and rowing became their lives and training became a daily event, I was ill-prepared for the amount of sweat-drenched training kit resulting in never-ending volumes of laundry.

It was never easy but I would not have changed it for anything in the world. Being the only female among five males, all with strong personalities, was also special and I felt that being the woman and the mother put me at the centre of the family. When I was around, things seemed to flow so much better. I was able to absorb more of the difficulties, taking things easily in my stride. One of the most heartbreaking things I saw during my time at Hospice was a young mother dying and leaving her children behind. Who would ever love those children the way their mother had loved them? Those moments left me with the deepest sense of sorrow and loss, without doubt reliving the loss of my mother and the feeling of being abandoned.

Because both David and I worked and possibly because we had the same profession, somehow the responsibility of being in charge of the family seemed to be evenly spread between us. David and I always did things together and shared responsibilities. One day Matthew asked me, 'Are you the boss of the family, Mommy? Or is Daddy the boss? I don't know who the boss is.'

If I were to choose one thing, one activity I enjoyed most with the boys, it would be reading. I loved reading and was fascinated by how brilliantly writers could put words together. I never read a book without a pencil, and would underline everything that resonated with me. I passed this on to the boys and enjoyed reading to them. We read stories together on the couch almost every night and, with the exception of the times I fell asleep in exhaustion reading to them, we got through volumes of books. We had a huge library that we'd collected over the years, entire series of books, and the boys read these over and over. I encouraged them to read and they were all good readers, especially Matthew and James. James used to devour books and at one stage held the record for reading the most books in his primary school.

We loved movies and watched them with the boys as much as possible. The boys would watch the same movies over and over again, and could virtually recite the entire dialogue of some favourites. I think it would be accurate to describe our family as intense and passionate. When we like something, we immerse ourselves in it completely and become totally involved. When the magnificent movie series of *The Lord of the Rings* came out, we saw each new movie in the trilogy on the very first night it came out and probably saw them at least 20 times after that. We could quote the full text. We bought the extended version of the movies. We had read the series to the boys and loved the film version. We were passionate about *Star Wars* and *Harry Potter*, never understanding how someone could not embrace the stories. I considered JK Rowling a genius. I had adopted a more open approach to action science-fiction movies like *Star Wars* after my brother Marc pointed out when the boys were small, 'Danielle, you are the mother of boys and you do not know who Darth Vader is.' I rectified that situation as soon as I could and became as passionate about *Star Wars* as they were.

As they grew up, schooling became central in their lives. All four of our boys went to De La Salle Holy Cross College in Linden, Johannesburg, for their primary-school years. Sport played an important part of these years. They played soccer and cricket, were good swimmers and decent tennis players, and enjoyed running, especially cross-country.

Lawrence was good at swimming but average at soccer and cricket. He reached a point when he needed swimming training as opposed to lessons. He refused to go for training. He simply did not want to swim. I tried to pressurise him but I realised there was no point if I was going to have to force him to get up and train every day. When Lawrence says no he means no, and he will not budge. Like many of us, he can be stubborn

97

and extremely self-confident. With the exception of Charles, they were all average at soccer and cricket.

Academically, they were solid. Matthew was the strongest. At the annual school teacher-parent meetings I got tired of hearing the same from the teachers: 'They can do better. They are lazy and not working hard enough.' They were not the proverbial teacher's pets – far from it. I used to find this awkward as I am fundamentally a rule keeper, a peacemaker. I toed the line. I used to say to Claudine, 'If only one of them, just one of them, could be a goody-goody it would make me feel better.'

We could have pushed them to achieve more. Later, Matthew would say, 'You should have pushed us harder. You should have been stricter with us.' David and I have always believed there is a fine line dividing achievement through being pushed outwardly from achievement through taking responsibility for yourself inwardly. I am sure there is a strong case for both. Strangely, Matthew only spoke of it regarding academics – when it came to sport, specifically rowing, that sentiment was never expressed.

As they got older they started cycling. My brother Marc was instrumental in encouraging them to cycle. During one Knysna holiday, when Lawrence was eight, Marc woke him up to join the 'elite' older group of riders comprising himself, my father on many occasions, and David and Matthew. He bounded out of bed, 'Aah, thanks for waking me up!' He was so excited to be included in the early-morning family cycle and being considered good enough to be asked to ride with them. As they entered their middle-childhood years they continued to cycle, and they loved it. When James and Charles got older, they too joined the pack. They would cycle all over Johannesburg in the early mornings. They had their routes, riding up Northcliff Hill being one of them. They were all about 12 when they rode the 94.7 Cycle Challenge for the first time.

The boys had cheap bicycles for a long time, and we handed everything down the line. We did not believe in buying the best for them – they needed to prove what they wanted. I guess we did not believe in making it too easy; they first needed to show resolve and intent. We were careful with money and worked hard for what we had; we both wanted the boys to embody this principle. At times my father would pass his bikes down to the boys. It was only later, much later, when Matthew took cycling more seriously after rowing, that the boys started riding better bikes.

We trekked down to Knysna for the annual Oyster Festival held in July, and they all rode the cycling races, some of them doing two of the races back to back. Matthew and Lawrence were good cyclists and at one stage I wondered whether they would take it further. When he was 15, Matthew rode the Knysna 80-kilometre road race and the next day the 80-kilometre mountain bike race. He was always determined. Later, when they were actively training for rowing, Matthew and Lawrence cycled the 94.7 race twice, back to back. We used to watch the Tour de France avidly and were passionate Lance Armstrong supporters. Lance's battle with testicular cancer and his triumph over this adversity touched me deeply. I had huge posters of him in my office at Hospice. It was a devastating day for us when it eventually transpired that he had been doping.

But it was not cycling coursing through our boys' blood like the very oxygen they breathed. It was rowing and the love of racing that would become their future.

One by one the boys left De La Salle at the end of their primary-school days, choosing high schools that offered rowing. These were defining moments in each of their lives and choosing rowing was a turning point for each of them. They would each discover themselves as they learnt to master the technical complexity of the rowing stroke as well as the challenge of rowing in a crew.

Matthew was the first and had told us from a very early age that he wanted to row at school. Watching David had sown that seed.

We tried to find senior schools that suited our boys. I am not sure if we made the right decisions in this regard. Each of the boys have since both loved and criticised their chosen schools for being too much of one thing and not enough of another.

We chose to send Matthew to Crawford College in Benmore, Sandton.

Academically the school was strong and suited his intense personality. He began rowing in Grade 7 and had the fortune of being coached by heavyweight South African champion Ramon di Clemente. There is no doubt that Ramon's passion, drive and discipline rubbed off on Matthew. He was in Form 4 when Ramon and Donovan Cech raced the heavyweight men's pair at the 2004 Olympics. Matthew went to school later that day so he could watch the race at home. Don and Ramon came third, winning the bronze medal. It was South Africa's first Olympic rowing medal and a huge achievement for them, their coach Christian Felkel, and South African rowing in general. This result fired Matthew up even more and fed his resolve to excel in rowing.

Lawrence was equally adamant he was going to row. We sent him to Parktown Boys' High School in Johannesburg between 2001 and 2005, a large boys' government school, the school my brothers had attended. He was determined to follow in his brother's footsteps and take up rowing. I wanted Lawrence to go to an all-boys school where he would be able to develop in his own space and time. Kevin Stippel was the master in charge of rowing and was supportive and absolute in his belief that Lawrence could one day be very good. Lawrence had good friends who played a big role in his life, and except for a few years when, to my horror, he became frankly disturbingly gothic, dyeing his hair black and donning black clothes, his high-school years were relatively uneventful.

We encountered further grief and loss during these years. When David was 15, his mother Dorothy, or Curl, had been diagnosed with breast cancer. She had been treated with surgery and chemotherapy, and had overcome the disease. For 25 years she remained cancer-free and very well. She lived to see all her grandchildren born and played a vital role in their lives. It was a painful day for us in 2001, when she relapsed and developed secondary cancer spread, an inconceivable number of years after the primary diagnosis. From that moment the disease moved rampantly through her. John and Curl came to Knysna for the December holidays in 2001. We had a wonderful holiday but the painful realisation was that Curl did not have long to live. She was excruciatingly thin and barely ate. She crammed as much as she could into those short weeks, spending time with family and friends, walks on the beach and picnics. I think she knew the end was close.

In the last month of her life, David and I drove to and from Ladybrand in the Free State, where they lived, every weekend to see her and support John, David's father. All my palliative training seemed to come down to this one momentous and final purpose. The drive to Ladybrand took us through the breathtakingly beautiful eastern Free State, with fields and fields of yellow sunflowers bravely facing the sun. The extraordinary light reflecting off the sandstone mountains will always bring tears to my eyes as the sadness and beauty remain interwoven and evoke strong memories of Curl. I used to think to myself that I was bringing her the sun and the light when I arrived with bunches of sunflowers.

It was a heartbreaking day for us when she died at home in Ladybrand on 26 February 2002. The boys were particularly close to her and were old enough to understand and feel the pain of her loss. Sadly, Charles was only four years old so he has little recollection of her. Her charming name for him in those early years, 'the delicious monster', still reminds me achingly of her.

She had been a close mother figure to me when I married David, became a mother myself and lost my own mother. She always told me, 'I am so glad David married you, Danielle, and that you are the mother of four of my grandchildren.' Once again I was confronted with grief and the reality of loss, of continuing my journey without her, more alone than before.

Nine years later, in September 2011, David's father John was diagnosed with pancreatic cancer and died within six months of the diagnosis. We lost one of the strongholds of our family structure. John was one of the least judgemental people I ever knew, hardworking and dependable, and his loss was considerable. He worked as an engineer right up until his death and remains one of the most intelligent people I have ever known. The loss of his mentorship for David and the boys was enormous. The boys were left with one surviving grandparent, my father Bertie.

James followed Lawrence to Parktown Boys' High School, equally determined to row at school. He was sharp and insightful, and this, coupled with a witty sense of humour and relaxed manner, gave him an edge, a resilience, and a kind and generous nature. Of all the boys, James was always the one I asked to do the difficult things, like check on the dogs at three o'clock in the morning if they were barking when David was away, or check on strange noises. When driving to Botswana in 2014 to watch Charles rowing in the Africa Youth Games, David and I realised, with that awful sinking feeling, just before the border, that we had left our passports behind in Pretoria. It was James we called and asked to drive to Brits and meet us with our passports, knowing he would come to our aid kindly and without question.

Many people criticised our decision to send the boys to Parktown, a government school, feeling that their children could only be sent to private schools. It was an attitude I struggled with, and still do. Both Lawrence and James benefitted greatly from what the school offered. They remain intensely loyal to their school and made lasting friendships there. We were involved parents, and were part of the rowing club management. My father was also involved, donating two rowing boats to the school, one of which was an eight. The boat was named *Redgrave*, after Sir Stephen Redgrave, one of the most famous oarsmen in the world. The other boat was a four named *Resolute*, in keeping with the Lincoln motto, strength in adversity.

Sadly, Parktown has since struggled in rowing and slipped further and further back in performance. But performance in schools seems to follow a cyclical nature of highs and lows – as things always change, there is promise that their performance will improve. Recently, they sent athletes to the Junior World Championships once again: in 2019, Cameron Taberer and Callan Barrell were the first to be sent since Lawrence and coxswain Nick Holt were sent in 2008.

Right through junior school, Charles had been dragged to regattas to watch his brothers row. As a young boy, he was bored. In fact, he detested rowing, telling me he never wanted to row at all. We were happy with this decision and suggested he continue with cricket and rugby, and take swimming more seriously. I should probably not have been surprised, however, when Charles told me during his final primary-school year that he had changed his mind and now wanted to row when he got to high school.

We were in the process of moving to Pretoria at that stage so we made the relatively easy decision to send Charles to St Alban's College, which was the only school in Pretoria to offer rowing. He fell under Coach Tiago Loureiro at St Alban's and had the fortune to learn from one of the best technical coaches in South Africa.

In his third year at St Alban's, as part of the school's requirement and tradition, Charles completed The Journey, a much-feared and anticipated 21-day hike. The Form 3 boys were divided into groups, given daily maps and food, and basically left to fend for themselves, hiking from St Alban's to somewhere close to Nelspruit. They covered a distance of around 450 kilometres in total. They did their own map-reading and cooking. They were given lodgings at the end of each day's hiking and there were teachers hovering in case of emergency, but for the most part they were left to make it on their own. In an emotional ceremony of farewell, our family watched our youngest son and brother go off to make a transition into manhood. It was a deeply moving and heartfelt moment saying goodbye to him, and then later welcoming him back. All his brothers came to the school to welcome him home, a sign of the respect they felt for his having completed The Journey. He returned weighing a massive 7 kg less than when he had left. The brotherly bond felt strong to me on those days. I think the boys were secretly envious of Charles – they had not had this opportunity at their schools.

I was spared some of the more challenging and hard-core experimentation that can complicate and cloud teenage years, but certainly faced others. There was the highly anticipated and expected buffing up of their builds and muscles, the acne, the thickening of their skins and the deepening of their voices. The sweaty kit intensified, and the appetites became more ferocious than ever. Lawrence was the most experimental of all the boys.

His gothic years were a challenge, taking all my tolerance and patience to not make too much fuss but to remain calm, turn a blind eye and hope that he would outgrow the phase.

He and his friends were caught with a bottle of vodka when they were 15 and that caused much stress among the moms. We were more tolerant because we knew it was not really a problem, and was actually quite normal. Alcohol was not much of an issue among the boys; their training prevented it. That is not to say they did not want it. They just could not drink vast amounts of it, and I was grateful for that. Smoking was forbidden. I had always told them that I would not tolerate smoking at all and Matthew told his brothers that if he ever caught them smoking he would cut their arms off. Drugs, well, I do not think it even entered their heads to experiment with drugs. They were into sport and that's where they put their energy and passion.

The active busyness of our family channelled itself into rowing and we literally became a rowing family. It was rowing talk that began to dominate our family conversations as we rapidly became immersed in it. David had a wealth of experience and a deep-seated and passionate feel for the boat. He understood the hydromechanics of rowing: what made boat speed. He loved the pleasure of feeling the boat moving with a rower as the blade sliced into the water and pulled through the resistance. He had a good eye for seeing the faults in a boat and knowing how an athlete should work to move one. Interestingly, he never imposed his views on the boys, unless they asked for his advice. It was a sort of unspoken agreement to hold back and let them discover their own way.

I am sure there are many who believe we pushed the boys into rowing but nothing could be further from the truth. It was always them. Somewhere, somehow, the sport had entered their souls at a very early age. It was what they wanted, and still is what they want. We stood by as the support, the framework they could rely on to hold it all together. I was a realistic parent, not one to make out that they were better than they were. If I thought it would go badly I would tell them. At times I was criticised

104

and misunderstood for this, and there were some who felt I did not believe in the boys. David never wanted the boys pushed at all, and had a fundamental belief that if the desire to row and win did not come from within them it would not last.

The difficulty was that, as the intensity of the rowing increased, so came the highs and lows, the outstanding victories but also many more devastating losses. It was hard knowing what to say to them without sounding glib and superficial. Matthew once told us, 'You can say two things, and two things only. Good luck and well done. Nothing else.'

There were many solid male role models and mentors for the boys during their childhoods, their teenage years and along their school journeys: my father Bertie, David's father John, my brothers Marc and Stephen, my brothers-in-law Julian and Steve, and the boys' school rowing masters and coaches Ramon di Clemente, Kevin Stippel, Tiago Loureiro and Ernie Steenkamp. There were also key women who mothered the boys and loved them dearly: David's mother Dorothy, my sisters Claudine and Monique, and my sisters-in-law Diane and Judy. Many years later, both of my brothers and their families emigrated. Those were sad days for me, losing part of my family, but especially sad for my boys, who lost out on the ongoing input my family would have had in their lives. There were many others on the boys' individual journeys who played significant roles in those vital earlier years. Cousins, friends, parents of friends, teachers, school principals, extended family – the list is endless.

As the boys grew up into their later teenage and university years I faced a new and exciting chapter in their lives.

Girlfriends.

Suddenly, matric dances were coming and going, girls were coming to visit the boys and have Sunday lunches with us, and if we went out as a family we had girls joining us. It was a welcome time for me. At last there were females, and I had some other way of teaching the boys about girls and their way of thinking that was not just my way of thinking. Finally, there was a smidgen of balance in their lives. I loved their girlfriends and formed my own relationships with them. I was sad when inevitable break-ups happened, and would feel, *But what about us – me and her?*

As time went by some of those girlfriends stayed, becoming partners, forming lasting, deep relationships with my sons. I always felt that any girl taking on one of the boys would need to be strong and independent. Alicia, Nicky and Stacey are all on this path, walking their own journeys with my boys, and I am proud of them. More than anything I am grateful for the love they give my sons. It gives me greater joy that my sons love them back.

The boys themselves became role models for one another. Matthew was a solid role model for his brothers and still is today, remaining as hard on himself as he is on others. Lawrence has the ability to see the best in a situation and shoulder difficulties that come his way. He is outwardly easy-going but his inner core is pure granite. James has an innate kindness and generosity, but is able to stand his ground with no difficulty and has developed a resolute self-confidence and belief in himself that has over-ridden the middle-child complex. Charles is a mixture of everything. He embodies aspects of all of us and in some ways has had it the toughest; it has not been easy forging himself from such a strong line of personalities and contrasts. He is strong and resilient and the only person he is harder on than others is himself.

The bond between the brothers has always been strong and deep. They were and remain, without a doubt, a brotherhood. As I witnessed this bond developing, I realised its value and wanted them to stick up for each other. 'If I am cross with one of your brothers, you must not get cross with them too. You must take their side. They need you then,' I used to say to them. Some of my greatest moments of joy and satisfaction are the moments when I witness their brotherhood. I see it as something unparalleled in its strength and value. They should treasure and maintain it forever.

It was within the boundaries of our family that the boys really developed to be the best they could be. Our family, like many other families, was messy and imperfect, but always a safe place where they belonged completely. Being part of a family was the ultimate gift we gave our children. Their brotherhood was an extension of that gift and became, in return, a gift to us.

6

卷卷卷卷

REACHING FURTHER, PUSHING HARDER

Johannesburg, 2000

March on. Do not tarry. To go forward is to move towards perfection.
March on, and fear not the thorns or the sharp stones on life's path.
— KAHLIL GIBRAN

Rowing had begun to dominate the boys lives – and ours. It never felt burdensome, though. As a family, we flowed easily into the rhythm of the training, the racing, the energy and preparation needed for the boys to succeed. In a way they made it easy because they wanted to succeed. The drive to do it and do it well came entirely from them.

They all began rowing at under-14 level, which in South Africa equates to Grade 7. With the exception of James, they all rowed full-time at school from Grade 10, stopping all other sport. James continued to play rugby in winter during the rowing off-season.

We followed them from one regatta to the next, usually to Roodeplaat Dam, north of Pretoria, but also to East London for the Buffalo River Regatta and Port Alfred where the annual Schools and University Boat Races were held. When they started the international circuit, we followed them to regattas all over Europe. We gave them as much as we could, as much as they would take from us.

Matthew only raced sculls at school, both the single and the double scull. Crawford College had a very small rowing team and was unable to put bigger crews together. He was a natural lightweight, and came up against some bulky heavyweights when he raced the single sculls. He repeatedly faced a promising, hefty young athlete from King Edward VII School in Johannesburg. That athlete was Shaun Keeling, who would later row with Lawrence in the Rio Olympics. Throughout Matthew's school rowing career, he raced against Shaun in the single sculls and always came second to him.

Matthew hated coming second. He wanted to win. Coming second was, well, second. It did nothing short of firing him up, powering his drive and spirit more than anything else. He internalised the losses and drove himself harder, striving to beat Shaun. At the annual Gauteng Schools Championships in 2005, his final year at school, he came second to Shaun but both of them broke the course record that year. In his final South African Schools Championships, he came second in the sculls to Shaun but won the double sculls with his school rowing partner, Michael Meerkotter.

In the South African rowing system, junior athletes are given the opportunity to row at the Junior World Championships in their last two years of senior school. Trials are held immediately after South African Schools Championships and continue for about six weeks. It is an intense time for the junior athletes if they want to make it into the junior squad. The competition is stiff and parents often have expectations of their children, making it a tense and pressurised period.

Matthew was determined to make the team selection for Junior World Championships in 2004 when he was in Grade 11, but after a long and drawn-out selection process he did not make it. He was bitterly disappointed as he firmly believed he would be selected. I too believed he would be selected and felt an uncomfortable weight of despondency settle over me when he was not. It was not my first taste of the bitterness of selection, reminding me of David's loss back in 1996. It was certainly not my last.

Matthew's future rowing partner, James Thompson, rowed in a coxed four that year for Junior World Championships and claimed the bronze medal in that event. Matthew had only one answer to disappointment, and that was to work even harder. He made the selection the following year, in 2005, at last being able to represent South Africa at the Junior World Championships in Brandenburg, Germany. He rowed in a double scull with Dominic Kester, a brawny young man from Bishop Bavin School in Johannesburg. Shaun Keeling rowed in the single scull at that regatta and came 14th overall. Matt and Dom rowed to a win in the D final, which meant they came 19th overall. Matthew was devastated by this result – he thought they were a lot faster and was shocked by the speed of the rest of the world. It was a brutal realisation that the international regatta scene was fast and professional. Being fast in South Africa did not mean being fast against international crews. It was Matthew's first taste of the hard reality of international racing.

I had an inkling that they might not do well. David had gone to watch them training at Roodeplaat Dam one Sunday morning and came back concerned. 'Danielle, there are some technical problems in the boat; their timing is an issue,' he told me. David had experience and good insight, so I knew he was speaking sense.

I travelled to Brandenburg with my father and my brother Marc. My sister Claudine, who was living in England at the time, flew over to join us. Brandenburg is just north of Berlin and we spent some time exploring the historical city. The history is chilling. Throughout the city are remnants of the Berlin Wall and memorials to the atrocities of World War II. Berlin has rebuilt itself into a beautiful city but at the same time acknowledges the horrifying past, without hiding or changing anything. I wanted to see it all, to face it, a small sign of respect for the suffering of millions of people.

On his return home, Matthew passionately opened up to me. 'I don't want to lose like that again. It was awful. I am going to work harder and train better. I know exactly who I am going to team up with now and I'm going to start as soon as possible.' He was bouncing around the room, explaining his plan. The very next day, when everyone else was taking a break from rowing, he was on the water, training again with a new partner

– Marco Biaggio, a young lightweight rower from St Alban's College. Unlike everyone else, who stopped rowing until after the matric exams, Matthew continued training right through matric, rowing when he could. He was unique in his drive and the will to do better. He was equally unique in finding solutions to his problems.

He finished school that year and had already set his path clearly ahead: he made the decision to go to the University of Pretoria. He had the foresight and knowledge to realise that elite rowing in South Africa would gravitate to Pretoria and he knew that this was what he wanted.

He knew something else of importance: he had identified a key person in his journey ahead, a person who would slowly build South African rowing into an elite entity, forming a centralised squad system. Matthew knew that this person was a young, upcoming coach, Roger Barrow.

I did not know it then but Roger would play a major role in all of my boys' lives in the future. He had started the School Rowing Academy programme at the High Performance Centre in Pretoria in 2005, which was affiliated with the University of Pretoria. The programme was designed to identify potential rowing athletes, offer them a place in the school and train them to become elite athletes. Roger had previously set up rowing clubs in Johannesburg at St Andrew's School for Girls and St John's College, as well as at the University of Johannesburg, then called the Rand Afrikaans University (RAU). He had begun to work his way up the coaching ladder by taking junior crews to World Championships and assisting coaches of senior crews at Senior World Championships. Matthew knew Roger and had spent time talking to him, so he had a good idea that Roger would be a key person in developing rowing in South Africa. Roger went on to become the official national coach in 2009, a position he still holds today.

When he entered the University of Pretoria in 2006, Matthew continued to train with Marco Biaggio. At the annual selection regatta held in May 2006, Matthew raced in a pairs matrix with a variety of partners to identify the fastest athletes. Unfortunately, Marco was dropped. Matthew was now teamed with James Thompson to row together in a pair. James had a similar vision and passion to come to Pretoria.

They were both selected to row in a lightweight coxless four with Pete Lambert and Grant Celliers, and were coached by David's old rowing partner, Gareth Costa. It was strange to see the wheel turning, and Gareth now coaching Matthew. The four rowed at the Under-23 World Championships held in Hazewinkel, Belgium, in 2006, in a mind-numbing, blistering heatwave that hit Europe that summer. I travelled to Belgium with David to watch the rowing. We stayed in Brussels, a city more geared for deadly cold than blistering heat. It was a challenging trip. I struggled with the heat and the travelling difficulties we encountered between Brussels and Hazewinkel.

In terms of the rowing, both the crew and the coach had high expectations, even though it was their first experience of international rowing at under-23 level and the entire process of weighing in and making weight.

The racing was nothing short of a disaster.

They came stone last.

The reason? It is never just one thing that causes a boat to do badly. It is usually a few things that simply do not line up on the day. But in this case, it was predominantly related to poor weight management and overt dehydration in some of the crew members.

The result reduced Matthew to despair. Losses like that were bitter and humiliating. But he was never one to despair for long. He became more resolved, more focused, and vowed to me, 'I never want to row again with people who are not at weight during the season.' He was building up intelligence about rowing, savviness and confidence.

By the start of the new rowing year, which is usually in September or October, James Thompson and Matthew had masterminded a plan. They neither belonged to nor were part of the School Rowing Academy system and a unified South African squad did not exist at that stage, so they had to fend for themselves and sort things out alone. They organised themselves, arranged for their parents to buy a boat, and approached Roger Barrow to coach them. He was busy with the Academy but agreed to let them tag along.

He would help them where possible, stipulating, 'You need to be all in or nothing.' Neither one of them were half-hearted in their plans.

The 2007 season saw Matthew and James pairing up in their new boat, a beautiful lightweight pair they named *Maximus* after the main character played by Russell Crowe in the epic movie *Gladiator*. When possible, Roger coached them. They were a powerful combination. James was lean and well-built, a good combination for a lightweight rower. Matthew, tall and lean, was a natural lightweight. They blossomed under Roger. I used to joke with Matthew, who was forever quoting Roger this and Roger that, 'Matthew, if Roger told you to jump in a fire because it would make you faster, you and James would do it.'

They were fast, disciplined and hardworking. Matthew was clinical, hard and steely in his preparation, despising any sign of weakness. According to Andrew Grant, one of the subsequent national coaches, 'Matthew was one of the most competitive people I have ever met.' He was an exceptional trainee and trained harder than many people.

Matthew and James were selected for the Under-23 World Championships to be held in Strathclyde, Scotland, in 2007. I met Roger for the first time at the annual awards ceremony that year, held before they left. He told me, 'They are fast, they will do well.'

In an agonisingly close finish with the young Italian pair of Andrea Caianiello and Armando Dell'Aquila, they won the silver medal, losing to Italy by 0.3 of a second. Both Italy and South Africa broke the world record that day. Strangely, it was the second time in his career that Matthew had broken a record but come second. It was a great result; they had made their mark and stepped up into the realm of medal-winning performances. It does not matter how much an athlete loves rowing and training, they love winning a lot more. It will always be about winning. And medals. The only thing dampening the South Africans' day was not beating the Italians and winning gold.

It was my first experience of my sons making an A final and winning a medal on an international stage. But it was not the first time I had watched my boys race and the stress was the same: almost unbearable. I buried my face in my South African flag, unable to watch.

At that time, in 2007, winning medals at World Championships was a big deal for South African rowing. Our country tends to have an inferiority complex, often not believing we are good enough, that other countries are so much better than we are, and have so much more than we have. We were not, however, completely unused to winning medals. The senior men's pair of Ramon Di Clemente and Donovan Cech had tallied up two silver medals and one bronze medal at World Championships between 2001 and 2005, and had won the bronze medal at the 2004 Athens Olympics. South Africa had won a silver and a bronze medal at the Junior World Championships in 2000 and 2004 from junior coxed fours and a bronze medal at the Under-23 World Championships in 2006 from a lightweight men's pair.

That evening, David and I celebrated their result with my father, Bertie, who had travelled to Scotland with us, and James's parents Gigi and Gus Thompson. We were delighted for the boys; their success was showing how capable they could be.

Their performance gave James and Matt the opportunity to race at the Senior World Championships to be held later that year (2007) in Munich. At that time it was the custom in South African rowing that, if a crew medalled at Under-23 World Championships, they would be sent to Senior World Championships to compete in the same event. The 2007 World Championships was a big event. It was the all-important Olympic Qualification Regatta for the 2008 Games to be held in Beijing the following year, so the pressure was enormous. South Africa sent a men's lightweight four and a men's heavyweight pair to Munich to try to qualify for the Olympics.

The international rowing hierarchy has a very clear and organised structure and is governed by FISA, the international rowing body. Aspiring young athletes have the opportunity to first-row at Junior international level. The cut-off for this is 19. After that, athletes move up to under-23 level, where the cut-off becomes 23 years. At this stage they race people of similar age and the standard is relatively constant. These are important steps in the journey of an elite rowing athlete as they allow young athletes the chance to develop appropriately before moving into a senior level. Once in senior-level rowing, the narrow field falls away, opening up into a much wider spectrum. There is a vast difference in standards at senior level as young inexperienced athletes pit themselves against older, tougher, more experienced and physically better-conditioned athletes. There is no age limit in senior rowing and there are many examples of elite rowers continuing to race at this level until the age of 40.

The squad at that time was a less unified team than it is today. The heavyweight men's pair was coached by Christian Felkel, the lightweight men's four by Steve Hasselbach and Roger was coaching the lightweight women, who later qualified through the Africa Championships for the Beijing Olympics. All three crews worked hard independently, and although the goal was the same they did not work as a centralised, cohesive unit. Much effort and energy went into these crews up to Athens and Beijing, with success in the form of a bronze medal for the heavyweight pair in Athens and two crews qualifying for Beijing.

Matthew and James were to race in the lightweight men's pair, which was not an Olympic event. They were hoping to medal and Roger believed they had a chance. His belief was valid: the Italian pair who had beaten them at under-23 level went on to win the gold medal in the event.

The heavyweight men's pair with Ramon di Clemente and Don Cech qualified comfortably for the Olympics. The senior lightweight four, which included Sizwe Ndlovu, Rod Macdonald, Bruce Turvey and Warren Wellbeloved, did not have the same outcome. Unfortunately, half of them were sick, and Sizwe and Bruce had to be flown home as they were too ill to row. In a last-minute, desperate attempt to qualify the lightweight four, which was a priority boat, a decision was made to put Matthew and James into this boat, replacing the sick athletes who were now back in South Africa. Their coach Roger, now superfluous, was also sent back to South

Africa and the young pair had to fit into a different system. With very little time to practise, settle in and develop a feel for the boat, Matthew and James had to race a highly pressurised event to try to qualify the lightweight four for Beijing. Some mistakes were made and, in deciding how to place the athletes, James and Matthew were split up, with Matthew stroking and James in the bow. A strong pair was now weakened within a boat that had lost two of its crew members.

It was asking a lot.

Too much.

The lightweight four did not qualify. They came 21st overall and needed to come 11th. They were way off.

It was too much too soon; Matthew and James had been thrown into a raging current and expected to swim against it. They could not do it.

Yet.

Afterwards, Matthew told me, 'I cannot believe how fast that event was. I have never been in such a fast start.'

A year later, in 2008, James Thompson and Matthew once again rowed in the lightweight pair at the Under-23 World Championships in Brandenburg, Germany, and repeated the same result, coming second to the same Italian crew and claiming the silver medal. The Italian pair were simply too good.

Following the Beijing Olympics, the South African national rowing squad system collapsed. It was unsustainable. The Academy collapsed, the various divisions of the national team collapsed, coaches were lost. Many factors caused this. Predominantly, though, major funding issues cracked the system wide open. Christian Felkel left South Africa and joined British Rowing. Lightweight coach Steve Hasselbach retired from coaching and the lightweight squad disbanded. Sizwe Ndlovu, grieving the recent deaths of his parents and the loss of his Olympic dream, took a break. Warren Wellbeloved emigrated to Australia and Rod Macdonald stopped rowing. Lightweight rowers Bruce Turvey and Tony Paladin both started working but maintained a rowing presence, hoping they would get another chance

116

some time in the future.

Roger Barrow emerged, stepping into the gaping hole and becoming the national coach with the unenviable task of drawing all the fragments together. He took over the reins of the flailing system, taking the next four years to solidify the programme and centralise South African rowing into a squad. It was clear that a more professional approach was needed to advance the sport. The concept of professional athletes began to filter through; it became one of Roger's major tasks to fund the growing squad and engender the concept of full-time athletes.

The system needed support. One of biggest bastions of strength came from a key person whose association and deep commitment to rowing had spanned nearly 50 years. Paolo Cavalieri first started rowing for his school, King Edward VII School, in the early 70s. He was chosen to represent South Africa as a junior sculler in 1976, but sanctions were mounting against South Africa and he was prevented from taking part. He studied at the University of the Witwatersrand, where he became an integral part of the University Boat Club. Later, after completing his degree, he went to France, searching for work opportunities. Ironically, it was rowing that gave him the passport to fitting into the country. He arrived with very little. He could not speak French, knew no one, and had no work experience at all. But he knew rowing. He joined a rowing club, and that was what drew him into the country and the culture.

On his return to South Africa five years later, he took on a more administrative role in rowing. In this time, South Africa had been readmitted to international sport and he managed the rowing team sent to the Barcelona Olympics in 1992.

Paolo took a break from rowing after Barcelona, although it remained a passion. In 2001 he bumped into Ramon di Clemente, who was rowing for South Africa in the heavyweight men's pair, and learnt that Ramon and Don were training part-time, living in cities 450 kilometres apart, with virtually no financial assistance at all. Paolo realised he was needed in South African rowing. He stepped in, offering financial support in the form of sponsorship and employment, which continued for the next seven years. In this way, he started the process of developing a system that would support full-time athletes.

In 2009 Paolo became head of the International Commission, a subcommittee of Rowing South Africa (RowSA), a position he held until the end of 2020. The role of the International Commission was to select, prepare and support athletes and crews for international racing. It was around this time that he both met and started working with Roger, who had taken over as the national coach. Roger had the vision of creating a system of full-time athletes. Paolo understood and was able to support this vision. Roger and Paolo worked closely together from that time, and that relationship has developed over the years into a powerful working combination.

Paolo's work and involvement in rowing continued. After the London Olympics, South African rowing once again fell into crisis, with no money or prospect of funding. In 2013, with a community of former international South African rowers, Paolo established a trust. Team Powerhouse Trust came to rowing's support, enlisting sponsorship from the rowing community, former rowers, unrelated benefactors and commercial sponsorship. The main sponsorship came from successful South African businessmen and ex-rowers, with support from some large companies. Without the trust and the financial support from these people and organisations, rowing would undoubtedly have fallen apart. In particular, Paolo has played a pivotal role in South African rowing.

During this time, South African rowing was not the only system coming under pressure to grow and change. Tuks was under pressure to create a rowing club. Other South African universities had long-standing rowing clubs and Pretoria lagged behind. Tuks had a rowing club but did not operate independently; it was affiliated with Roodeplaat Rowing Club and formed part of that club. It was an effective partnership, enabling interested students to row. Matthew and James joined the Roodeplaat/Tuks club in 2006, together with a few athletes who formed part of the Rowing Academy that was growing under Roger's leadership.

From this time, Matthew and James were instrumental in building the Tuks Rowing Club. From a mediocre club, it started to develop into a more competitive outfit. Initially, Matthew and James kept the peace and fell in with the existing protocol. But it was clear that they wanted something better and, within a year, with enormous support from the Director of Sport at the university, Professor Kobus van der Walt, they had engineered a breakaway from Roodeplaat Club, and Tuks Rowing Club (TuksRowing) became independent.

The club had its own space, bought its own boats and equipment, and set up an independent management structure. Matthew and James were strong leaders and set the tone and precedent for the club. They had the same philosophy and vision and led from the front, creating a culture of winning within the club, rather than one of just participating. They wanted a culture that emphasised the importance of training. They both knew that solid training set the stage for the possibility of winning.

From 2007, TuksRowing went from being average to being highly competitive. Matthew and James knew that the club needed the best possible athletes who understood the ethos of training and had the hunger to put a winning crew on the start line. The club started to attract more school-leaving rowing athletes and it actively recruited potential athletes. The culture rapidly became entrenched. In the annual University Boat Race, Tuks came second to Rhodes in 2008 and won for the first time in 2009. They have gone on to win every year since then. At the annual University Sports Awards function, TuksRowing has won Student Sports Club of the year six times, a testimony to its success. The standards set by TuksRowing are high but its superiority is based on hard training.

While all this was happening in Matthew's world and he was growing his dream of rowing at elite level, his younger brother Lawrence was equally determined to take up rowing and follow in Matthew's footsteps. Matthew was in Grade 11 when Lawrence started high school in 2004. Lawrence stopped swimming and began rowing. He never looked back. He loved it from the first day he rowed at under-14 level when he joined the biannual

Parktown Boys' school rowing camp at Roodeplaat Dam. I took him to the camp and saying goodbye to him left me with a deep aching feeling as I realised he was growing up. This ache would become more and more familiar to me over the years as slowly and inevitably the boys became independent. With the immense pride and happiness of seeing my boys grow up, there has always been a longing for the time when they needed me more than anything on earth.

Lawrence thrived. He was doing something he loved, and following that path came easily to him. He did well at rowing and was an asset to the team. He won the Most Promising Young Athlete award in Grade 9. His crew won the under-15 boys' octuple in Grade 9, breaking the record and holding that record for the next year. He stroked the Parktown Boys' First Eight from Grade 11. One of the fathers of a crewmate commented to me one day, 'Lawrence is the stroke of the First Eight and yet you would not know it. He is very humble and unassuming.' In a large boys' school like Parktown, being in the First Eight was akin to making the First XV in rugby, but on a much smaller scale. It was extremely important to the boys; the pride they felt from being in that boat was enormous.

In his matric year, Lawrence wanted to try the single scull event as it was such a prestigious one at South African Schools Championships. From under-16 he had been in the sweep side of rowing – the opposite of sculling, when each rower holds one oar and the boat is balanced by an even number of rowers – and this year was no exception. He was racing South African Schools Championships in the senior eight, four and pair, and had not touched a scull for two years. He went on to win it, a somewhat unexpected and unprecedented win from a relatively unknown athlete who rocked up on the day and beat everyone. Matthew said, 'I cannot believe he just won a race I spent five years trying to win. And he did not even train for it.' Racing to second place was a tall, skinny young athlete, John Smith. This race marked the start of a long rowing relationship between John and the Brittain brothers.

Lawrence was selected to row for South Africa at the Junior World

Championships in his matric year after missing out on selection the year before due to a knee injury. He was paired with Dane De Reuck, who came from one of the top competitive rowing schools, St Benedict's College. The competition was to be held in Linz, Austria.

I travelled to Linz with David, Charles and James, and my father Bertie. The Junior World Championships followed the Under-23 Championships in which Matthew had just rowed, so we first travelled to Berlin to watch the event in Brandenburg, and then flew to Vienna. Travelling to Linz from Vienna entailed a two-hour drive. It was pouring with rain, and dark, making it an unpleasant one. We were relieved to arrive safely in Linz and check into our hotel. Matthew joined us a day later to watch his brother row. A powerful and indelible memory was our visit to Mauthausen, the most chilling concentration camp memorial I have ever seen. Walking through the buildings and the grounds, down to the quarry where the prisoners laboured, brought to mind horrifying images of the trauma that people had faced. We left there emotional and sombre, coldly reminded of just how inhumane man can be to man.

After the regatta we enjoyed a week's holiday in Austria. But before the holiday came racing. I was becoming more familiar with the routine and stresses of international racing.

Lawrence and Dane won the C final, rowing to thirteenth place in the Junior World Championships in 2008. Lawrence did not like that position; he wanted something better and had already witnessed Matthew winning two silver medals at Under-23 World Championships. He was clear about what he wanted.

He wanted to win.

In his mind, Matthew's silver medals made it possible for him to dream about winning.

So many promising young athletes stop rowing after school. It is a trend that has continued through the years and, despite some talented rowers achieving top results at school level, most of them do not continue beyond that. Rowing is one of the toughest sports to train for and excel in, and many school-leavers have had enough of the hard training it requires. They tend to complete matric and then fulfil other aspirations, or go on to study at university. Their parents often want them to think about a career. Rowing at elite level is usually not seen as a career in the same way a football or rugby player is seen as having a career. The reason for this is probably a financial one. There is virtually no money in rowing and making ends meet is difficult. I think of rowing as a full-time career, but a very poorly paid one.

Many school athletes perform because of pressure outside themselves, from the school or the coach or their parents. Their true desire does not come from within. I have noticed in life that whenever I had to convince someone to do something they were not entirely sure they wanted, things tended not to work out for the best. It is the same with rowing. Young people must *want* to row. It cannot be coaxed or pushed or driven from anywhere except the inner drive. It is simply too hard for that. It takes courage and determination, and a massive amount of support from family and friends. To become a successful elite athlete takes years of training and conditioning.

Many parents have mistakenly thought their children will do better academically without the time pressures of rowing. I strongly refute this. In my opinion, it makes no difference to their results. If the child does better without rowing it is because they did not want to row. If they want to row, everything falls into place. And this is not just about rowing. When I have wanted to do something in life, it has always worked on some level. I made it happen.

Matthew blazed the trail for Lawrence, so in many ways Lawrence had it a bit easier. After matric, he followed Matthew to the University of Pretoria where he asked Roger if he could train with the squad.

Roger eyed him. 'You can, but you need to do two things if you are going to stay – you need to lose weight, as you are too fat, and you need to be here, coming to the sessions and doing the training.'

It was Lawrence's first experience of the brutal honesty so prevalent in elite sport. Many may criticise such honesty but for an athlete to make it to a winning position they have to be able to handle it – in fact, they have to search for it, demand it.

In the following year, 2009, Lawrence was teamed with big, brawny Murray Chandler, a heavyweight rower in the Tuks Sports Academy who had come from Selborne College in the Eastern Cape. They rowed the heavyweight men's pair together and were coached by a young, enthusiastic coach, Grant Dodds. Lawrence developed rapidly in this combination and learnt much from Murray, who was bigger, stronger and more experienced. They won the B final at Lawrence's first Under-23 World Championships in Prague. They faced the British in that race, and beat them. Mohamed Sbihi was in that pair, the biggest heavyweight rower I have ever seen. He went on to row for Great Britain in the senior four and the eight, medalling every year from then, including a bronze medal in the eight in London in 2012 and the gold medal in the British four in Rio in 2016.

At the same under-23 regatta in Prague, Matthew rowed in the lightweight pair with a new partner, the young John Smith who had matriculated from St Alban's and, under Matthew's persuasion, presented himself to the University of Pretoria. John came to Pretoria with the sole intention of rowing for South Africa.

Prior to that point, Matthew had been having a hard time. James Thompson was no longer eligible for under-23 competitions. Lightweight rowing had disbanded after the Beijing Olympics, so there was uncertainty surrounding their future. James and Matthew joined a few potential lightweights who were hoping that lightweight rowing would reform in the squad, and that they would be given a chance to compete for places in the senior group. Together with Sizwe Ndlovu, who had come back to rowing after a break, Tony Paladin, Polly Polasek and Brett Paconek, Matthew and James fought for a place in lightweight rowing. At the lightweight men's trials held in March 2009 at a rowing camp in the farming town of Bethlehem in the Free State, the athletes raced against one another in a relentless selection process in which James and Polly emerged on top. They were selected into a lightweight double and went on to row to 12th position at the World Championships later that year.

Matthew was under pressure and felt he might be losing ground in the fight to the top, that his rowing was not improving enough. He was demoralised. He was still in the under-23 age group but there seemed to be no one with whom he could row.

But in rowing, as in life, things never stay the same. They change constantly.

At that time John Smith had come to Tuks to train but was nursing an injury to his foot. He was not selected for the March camp to Bethlehem and therefore not included in the trials. No one really took him seriously. He was training alone and waiting to be noticed. He raced South African Championships in the single scull, and although he was beaten, he was up with the pack for a large portion of the race. 'That race put me on the map. I was beaten but at last I got noticed,' John says.

Matthew noticed him. He called him later and said, 'Come, let's make a pair, let's do this.' They got together, found themselves a boat and started training.

John had not rowed in a sweep boat before, nor did he know much about lightweight rowing. He had to make the adjustment. Matthew took charge and helped him, teaching him about lightweight rowing. 'Matthew was a beast. He understood rowing so well. He knew how to train and how training helped you to be the best. It was such an advantage for me,' John told me.

They were coached by a new upcoming coach, Dustyn Butler. He had recently left his position of coach at St John's College to join the squad. They had a good season of training and were selected as the under-23 pair to race at the World Championships in Račice, near Prague.

They came into the Under-23 World Championships feeling strong and ready for battle.

Once again, our family travelled to Europe to watch the racing. I am grateful we were in a position to watch the boys race and see parts of Europe I had never seen. My father loved these trips, and it meant a lot to him to watch his grandsons rowing. My sister Claudine joined us from England for the week. Prague was a spectacular city to explore in between the racing.

But it was the racing that captivated us. Matt and John started out in the competition looking precise and fast, impressing everyone by winning their heat. They were the fastest crew in the heats. They looked good enough to win the gold medal and beat the same Italian pair that had beaten Matt and James for two years. They were relieved to have such a good heat and the win ensured that they went straight into the A final. Looking back, however, it would probably have been better to row another race before the final, allowing them to settle and consolidate their racing.

The final did not work out the way they thought it would, the way I thought it would.

They came a disappointing fourth. Caianiello and Dell'Aquila, the same Italians who had beaten South Africa into second for the past two years, won again. This time, however, South Africa was beaten by the French and the Dutch as well, two crews who had never beaten Matthew in this event.

What makes one thing happen, when you expect another? What decides it? What makes it go the other way when the outcome hovers on an edge?

In rowing, as in many sports, so many aspects need to line up perfectly at the exact moment of racing to enable the crew to deliver a sublime race and win a gold medal. Matt and John had a bad race in the final. But the real problem had started well before the final. It started after the heat. They won easily and as a result were lulled into thinking they had already won the final. They made the mistake of thinking they had the win before they had actually raced, a mistake that cost them a medal. They learnt a painful lesson. They should have medalled; they were fast enough to have won the gold. Matthew says, 'We thought we had it. We did not have the pressure and purpose needed to go out and win that race. It was soul destroying.'

Later, he reflected, 'There is nothing more dangerous than over-confidence.'

John and Matthew were shattered. It was a horrible disappointment for them, as if they had smashed into an unexpected brick wall. For those of us watching in the stands, it was an equally crushing blow. I hated seeing them broken, having to face their loss, the chance that had come their way but slipped quickly out of reach. But they were learning that, to follow an international rowing career, you need to bear the painful losses and still move forward. They had to face the suffering, the adversity, and get back up and fight. High-performance sport requires huge amounts of tenacity and perseverance. When things were tough for the boys, David and I would say, 'It is a long, hard process.' We have never stopped saying that.

While Matthew's journey continued, Lawrence was disgruntled and tired of not making the A final. He loved training, but more than anything he loved racing. He was a born racer and seemed to have the right temperament for the stress associated with racing. He was always excited to race and seemed to embrace it. He wanted to step up and progress to A-final level. He may appear less intense and serious than Matthew, but this is not the case. When it comes to racing, he has a unique fearlessness and a deep hunger to win.

His moment came the following year, 2010, at the Under-23 World Championships held in Brest, Belarus. Lawrence and John Smith had come into the season without rowing partners as their partners from 2009, Murray Chandler and Matthew, had moved up to senior level. As they were the only under-23 male athletes, they were lumped together. They were an unlikely combination as John was lightweight and Lawrence heavyweight. They got into a boat and started rowing together. They made it work. They had no coach; they trained themselves. They gave themselves their own pre-race pep talk before the South African Senior Championships and the subsequent Selection Regatta.

They had something.

After the Selection Regatta, they were selected as the under-23 men's heavyweight pair and were allocated to coach Andrew Grant, or AJ as he is more familiarly known. Lawrence was strong and brought power into the boat, and John had to fight to keep up with him, which helped develop his strength. John had the capacity and ability to make these changes, as well as the belief that he could overcome any difficulty. They sensed they were fast. They raced the South African junior men's four during training pieces and beat them, which gave them a lot of confidence. At the same time, they were in the relatively safe position of having no expectations on them; they were unknown, a new combination, and they were simply enjoying rowing together.

South Africa came into the under-23 regatta as the unknown entity and had a less than favourable start to the tour. During a long layover in Dubai on their trip over, John suddenly asked Lawrence, 'How important is your passport?'

Lawrence stared at him and said, 'It is probably the most important thing in your luggage.'

John whistled. 'Ohhh boy, I think I've left my passport on the plane.'

The plane had left with John's passport, and John was now stranded at Dubai airport. Airline officials located it, but the plane had flown on to Germany and was only returning in three days. AJ decided to stay with John and the two of them camped out in the rest lounge for three days, eating the food provided and sleeping on airport loungers. AJ found a small gym in the airport for John to do some cycling on an exercise bike and some explosive gym and weights. To keep themselves motivated, AJ and John watched video clips of the Canadian eight training, coached at that time by the legendary Mike Spracklen. These clips kept John's motivation up as he held the Canadian eight in high regard.

AJ had made the decision to send Lawrence ahead to Belarus with the under-23 South African women's team, comprising Kirsten McCann, Kate Christowitz and Claire-Louise Bode and their coach Ben Tipney. Lawrence trained alone on the ergometers at the regatta venue until John's passport returned to Dubai and AJ and John finally arrived in Brest. They arrived on Wednesday evening and racing was due to start on Friday. While AJ and John were stranded in Dubai, Lawrence and Ben had been working on rigging the boat. On Thursday morning, AJ had a brief look at the boat and sent Lawrence and John off on their first row, the day before racing started.

The pair were excited and relieved to finally be rowing. They barely noticed the setup in the boat and their spirits were high. They rowed and felt happy with the boat and relaxed at the hotel until the afternoon row.

At the next session, AJ said, 'We have to ensure the boat is perfectly set up for you so check it out properly to see that you are happy.' During their afternoon session, John said, 'It feels horrific. There is something wrong in the boat.' They stopped every 100 metres, rowing to the bank for AJ to reset various components. The entire session went on like this.

AJ became irritated with them. 'You were so sure it was all fine this morning. Go back to the hotel and leave me here with the boat. I will get it right.' He did not want them around him while he worked on the boat as he was afraid it would affect their confidence going forward. He spent the next few hours on his own, fiddling with the boat, checking and rechecking, sending messages back home to Roger to check the rigging of their boat at home. Roger actually drove out to Roodeplaat Dam to do this, to make sure that no one had made a mistake.

Often in life it comes down to going the extra mile.

Coaches spend a vast amount of time ensuring the boat is correctly set up. The process of setting the boat up is known as rigging. The position of the shoes and footboard, the height and angle of the rigger all need to be carefully measured to ensure the boat is rigged for optimal biomechanical efficiency and synergy. When travelling to competitions, this becomes even more important as athletes want the new boat to feel exactly like the boat they are used to rowing at home. Many other factors influence the way a boat is rigged, such as the size of the athlete and the type of boat and blade used. Coaches usually measure every distance and angle of each part of the boat before the team travels. Mistakes of the smallest millimetre or degree can make a difference to boat speed. The athlete might feel uncomfortable in the boat and be unable to apply force and connect with the boat correctly. Just as a cricketer or a golfer has the perfect sweet spot to strike the perfect shot, the boat also has the perfect mechanical setup for perfect connection.

AJ spent the late afternoon and evening painstakingly checking the rigging and making minute adjustments.

The competition started the next day. The pair was to race the heat and at that stage they had been for only two rows in a boat that did not feel perfect. None of the other crews in their event were particularly concerned about these two unknown South Africans who had arrived late and seemed incapable of rowing more than 100 metres without stopping.

The pair pushed off for an early-morning row before the race. They knew immediately that the boat was perfect. They could relax. They practised a few starts. The boat surged ahead. AJ had worked miracles and got it right. They were happy and they were fast.

John said to Lawrence, 'If we come out of the blocks like this, no one will touch us.'

He was correct. They were the fastest crew out the start of the heat. This almost surprised them. The German crew rowed through them at 1 000 metres and were up on them when Lawrence glanced across and saw how hard the German crew was working – much harder than John and he were. This was another surprise; he suddenly realised they could win.

With 500 metres to go he called out, 'I want to win.'

John replied, 'Okay.'

It was all they needed. They surged ahead to win the heat.

They faced a strong Canadian pair in their semi-final. The pair included a big heavyweight oarsman, Colin McCabe, who had been taken out of the same Canadian eight of which John was in awe and whose racing videos he had watched in Dubai.

Lawrence asked AJ the night before, 'Do we save ourselves for the final?'

AJ replied, 'No. Go for it. We have come here to race and win. Go and win.'

They won their semi-final, beating the feared Canadian pair. This was a crucial win for them. It gave them confidence and set them up for the final.

They were safely into the A final and were the fastest crew on paper. Now, their nerves started to build. The anxiety needed to be managed and AJ was a key person here. They were worried they were going to lose.

'Show me the medal you are so afraid of losing. You have won nothing yet. Canada has not won. No one has. You need to go out and win this race. Then we can talk about being afraid to lose. You have nothing to lose. You cannot be scared of losing something you don't yet have. Be excited about the challenge of going to claim the win rather than afraid you might not meet your new expectation', AJ said.

This was an important message and calmed them down, putting the race into perspective for them.

On the day of the final, AJ received a message from Ramon di Clemente stating simply, 'Believe.' Ramon had enormous stature in the team and was, in many ways, the idol of the younger rowers. To hear this from him was inspiring and motivating.

David and I had travelled to Belarus to watch the racing. The trip had been one of the more difficult, with transport and accommodation challenges. Once again I felt that mixed emotion of fear and excitement as racing approached. We sat on the stands with the rest of the South African supporters. Kate Christowitz, who had rowed in the women's pair earlier and come fourth overall, turned to me and said, 'They are going to win. Lawrence won the C final in Juniors, the B final last year and he is going to win the A final today.'

The Canadian supporters in front of us asked us which events we were supporting. When I said the South African heavyweight pair, the woman almost laughed at me, saying, 'I'm afraid they don't stand much of a chance against the Canadians. These two come out of the Canadian eight.'

I kept calm and simply answered, 'Well, let's see what happens.'

What happened was a win, but not by the Canadians. It was a solid victory, an impressive result from an impressive crew.

The Canadians could not hold Lawrence and John off, and could not respond to their call to win. At the 1 000-metre mark the South African pair were in the lead, one length up on Canada. John thought, *This is going to be a huge race for second place.* He knew they were not going to give their lead away. They were two fearless warriors fighting in battle and would not easily relinquish the win.

They crossed the finish line 1.5 seconds ahead of the Canadians.

About standing on the podium later while receiving their gold medals and singing the South African anthem, Lawrence reflected, 'It is one of the greatest feelings in the world being on the podium and knowing that you are the best in the world at something.' It was a feat that shot South African rowing onto a new level: the first gold medal achieved at a World Championship.

I spoke to the boys back home after the race and Matthew said, 'This is massive, Mom. This will do so much for rowing in South Africa.'

At the same regatta, Kirsten McCann raced to third place in the light-weight women's scull, winning the bronze medal and the first medal for South African women's rowing at World Championship level. She had represented South Africa at the Beijing Olympics in 2008 and was disappointed with her 14th place. She stopped rowing for a year after Beijing due to academic pressures and returned to training later in 2009. The medal at Belarus fuelled her hunger to race; she knew she could do better. She completed her academics after Belarus and returned to full-time training with the squad in Pretoria in 2012, training solidly and consistently from then until the Rio Olympics in 2016.

Things continued to go well for Lawrence. In 2011 he won the silver medal at the Under-23 World Championships in Amsterdam with a new partner, David Hunt. David was close in age to Lawrence and had rowed for St John's College in Johannesburg. He was a tall, lanky athlete who had decided to study engineering at the University of Pretoria but was also keen to continue rowing. He was trying to fit it all into his packed life. Lawrence and David were fast and showed promise. They were coached by AJ, who was rapidly building his reputation as an international coach.

They had not trained that much together as Lawrence had been selected for the senior men's heavyweight pair with Ramon di Clemente, and David was in the senior men's heavyweight four, and both were training for the Olympic Qualification Regatta in Bled. Their focus was on the qualification regatta and the enormous task of rowing for Olympic qualification.

The under-23 regatta was almost of secondary importance; training in the senior boats took preference, and Lawrence and David literally got into the under-23 pair two weeks before the event. They lost out on a gold medal to the high-quality British pair of Constantine Louloudis and George Nash, and claimed the silver medal. The following year, at the London Olympics, Louloudis went on to stroke the British eight, winning bronze, and Nash won bronze in the men's pair event. Both Louloudis and Nash won gold in the men's four at the Rio Olympics.

AJ went on to coach the under-23 division for another two years, winning a further silver and gold medal from the combination of David Hunt and the young Vincent Breet who had come through St Benedict's College as an extremely promising athlete. AJ progressed rapidly and became a senior national coach shortly after the London Olympics, joining Roger Barrow in his continued quest to build South African rowing.

Following the Beijing Olympics in 2008, Ramon and Shaun Keeling continued to row together into 2009, showing promise by coming second in one of the World Cups. Unfortunately, things began to deteriorate between them. They came sixth later that year at the World Championships in Munich. Their conflict resulted in a breakdown. This, coupled with some health issues, saw Shaun not rowing in that combination again. He had come to a turning point, a key moment in his rowing journey. He almost stopped rowing; it was a difficult period for the young athlete as he negotiated his way through that time.

Ramon continued and raced with a new partner, Pete Lambert, at the World Championships at Lake Karapiro in 2010. They placed seventh overall. The following year it was Lawrence who was selected for the senior pair with Ramon. In the meantime, Shaun had decided to continue rowing, and felt that he had more purpose. Shaun and Pete made up a heavyweight men's four with David Hunt and a powerful young man from Cape Town, Josef (Joe) Muller, to row on Lake Bled in an attempt to qualify a men's four for the London Olympics the following year.

Following their silver medal win at under-23 level in Amsterdam in 2011,

Lawrence returned to South Africa to train further in the senior men's heavyweight pair with Ramon, and David Hunt returned to the senior heavyweight four.

Ramon had represented South Africa on the international stage for a staggering 18 years and raced at three Olympics. Together with Donovan Cech, they raced to sixth place at the Sydney Olympics in 2000 and won a bronze medal at the Athens Olympics in 2004. In between the Olympics, Ramon and Don had won two silver medals and one bronze medal at World Championships and numerous medals at World Cup events. When Don left rowing at the end of 2007, Ramon raced with Shaun to a fifth position at the Beijing Olympics in 2008. Ramon was undoubtedly one of the pioneer athletes of South African rowing. Together with Donovan Cech they put rowing on the map of South African sport.

Ramon was hoping to make it into another Olympics. Lawrence was equally hungry to race for a position in the Olympics. There was a massive 16-year age gap between Lawrence and Ramon. Ramon was already racing at Junior World Championships when Lawrence was only a year old.

But life has a way of being unpredictable and twisting itself around when things get comfortable. The harsh reality is that no one gets everything. Everyone has talents, but conversely everyone lacks other qualities and traits. Talent comes at a cost. There is a levelling process, a balance far beyond our understanding and expectation.

Disappointment was in store for both Ramon and Lawrence.

The qualifying regatta for the 2012 Olympics in 2011 was held on Lake Bled, one of the most exquisite pieces of rowing water I had ever seen. South Africa took five boats to the regatta, with four of the boats in Olympic-class events. The Olympics only allows certain boat classes to qualify. Other events are classified as non-Olympic events and can only be raced at the annual World Championships. A men's lightweight four, a men's and women's heavyweight pair, and a men's heavyweight four were the boats hoping to qualify for the Olympics. South Africa sent a men's lightweight pair comprising Sizwe Ndlovu, who had returned following an injury that required wrist surgery, and was now back in lightweight contention, together with youngster Steve Mattushek. The boat was unfortunately scratched at the regatta due to an injury with which Steve had been struggling.

The men's lightweight four and the women's pair, comprising Lee-Ann Persse and Naydene Smith, both went on to qualify their respective boats for London.

The heavyweight men did not do as well. The four did not manage the qualification, coming 13th overall. They were two places short of a qualification spot, needing to come in the top 11 to qualify for London. Shaun said, 'From the beginning it was touch and go whether the four would make it.'

This was a bitter and wretched defeat for the South African men's pair, and for heavyweight rowing in South Africa. The despair David and I witnessed in Lawrence and Ramon, and in their coach Roger Barrow, was agonising for us as Lawrence's parents and as South African supporters. Of the four boats sent to Bled to qualify, only two had managed. I had never been to such an intense regatta before and the stress weathered by the athletes and coaches was harrowing to see.

Matthew explains it to me. 'A normal race is all about winning and doing your best. The pressure comes from trying to win. It becomes clear during a normal race whether it is possible to win. People crack under the pressure and fall behind; they might even stop going all out when they see they are far behind. In an Olympic qualifier the pressure is totally different. No one cracks, no one breaks under pressure, no one wants to be the crews who do not make it. Everyone fights to the line. The race becomes about not losing. The thought process is completely different.'

As the mother of two athletes at Lake Bled, I was torn. On the one hand I was gutted for Lawrence and felt helpless, wishing more than anything that I could take some of his deep-seated distress and wretched disappointment from him, but on the other hand I was overjoyed and delighted for Matthew and also about the achievement of the lightweight four. Such was the extent of the emotion. Poles apart: great joy and crushing despair in the unparalleled world of high-level sport.

Ramon had a powerful effect on Lawrence. His knowledge and experience were immense and he taught Lawrence an enormous amount. Without a doubt, Lawrence benefitted massively from rowing with one of South Africa's greatest stars. Being older, Ramon had a set way of rowing and the technical dynamics of the pair struggled. He had a way of rowing that had been effective with Don. He wanted to replicate that way with Shaun and later Lawrence. Every rowing pair is different and the athletes need to adapt to different rowing partners. Ramon struggled to adopt Roger's new vision. The triangle between Ramon, Lawrence and coach Roger was never balanced. The triangle should have the coach at the apex with the athletes in equal positions at the bottom. Ramon was trying to mentor Lawrence during their training sessions. Also, unbeknown to everyone, Lawrence may well have started on his own secret path to illness at that stage. There were many possibilities and reasons on which to reflect, which may have contributed to the disappointing result.

In a way, what happened between Shaun, Ramon and Lawrence comes down to the complexities of managing an older athlete in the squad system. This is a universal problem in sport, in business, in any field of life. How does the team manage an older individual who has a vast amount of experience and so much to offer but at the same time a more entrenched and rigid approach? How does a team incorporate a younger, less experienced person into a highly functioning system so that both still give of their best and conflict is minimised? The dynamics are intricate and need careful management. It would take a highly experienced coach to manage it and at that stage Roger was young and had walked a long road with Ramon, who was more like a friend to him. This was a dangerous situation and made life awkward for all involved.

Ramon was the idol of all the younger athletes. They looked up to him and held him in high esteem. They had enormous respect for him and his word was highly regarded. This made it even more difficult for the younger athletes as it was an honour to row with him and they wanted to listen to him.

Roger learnt from that time. To this day, he is careful with his approach to athletes, recognising the need to keep a professional distance – a feat that will always be challenging because they spend a lot of time together. He always says, 'If I get too close, if they become my friends, I cannot say the hard stuff or tell them when they are not pulling hard enough.'

Later that year, Ramon made the inordinately painful and difficult decision to retire from rowing. Losing an experienced senior athlete of that calibre was a massive blow to South African rowing. Together with Donovan Cech, they remain the two athletes who grew South African rowing into a significant entity in the international arena and highlighted the sport within South Africa and South African sport's governing body, SASCOC.

Matthew says about Ramon and Don: 'They were a crew that people looked up to; they gave so much hope to young rowers in South Africa, because they had done so well. They made it possible to believe that rowing could do well, that hard work could be rewarded. I knew Ramon better than Don and he was my hero. I learnt so much just from watching him. He trained professionally and I learnt that no obstacle was too much for him. Don was a phenomenal athlete, he rowed technically well and could really turn on the power when it was needed.'

Ramon has good insight into growing the sport of rowing in South Africa. 'It is important to have a culture of information retention as well as sharing in order to shorten the time an athlete with potential can take to reach the top and then stay successful at that level. The secret to achieving medals is to retain data and keep key people in the system for longer. If people with the knowledge leave, it extends the time before athletes can achieve Olympic medals, if at all.'

Following Ramon's retirement, Lawrence and Shaun were selected to train in the men's pair in the early part of 2012. They were training for the famous annual Henley Royal Regatta in England and a last chance to qualify for the London Olympics at the Late Qualification Regatta in Lucerne in June 2012. They had rowed well together in the season building up to that regatta and left for Lucerne feeling that they were in with a chance. There was a lot of expectation and excitement surrounding this crew and qualifying for the London Olympics.

It was not to be.

They were under pressure from two experienced and fast crews from Poland and France, and failed to qualify, coming fourth overall when they needed to come first or second. The French pair won and Poland came second. Shaun later said, 'We should have beaten the Polish.'

Lawrence agreed: 'We did not own the race enough and go out and claim it for ourselves. We allowed the French and Polish to grab it. We needed to be more aggressive. We did not have enough belief.'

The French crew went on to claim the silver medal in the men's pair at the London Olympics, showing the calibre of crew the South Africans had faced. Lawrence and Shaun's hopes for rowing at the London Olympics were decimated. It was once again a massive blow to them, to Roger Barrow, and to heavyweight rowing in South Africa.

Representing South Africa at the London Olympics was thus left to the lightweight men's four and the women's heavyweight pair, both qualifying through Bled in September 2011.

Once again David and I witnessed a race from the grandstand in Lucerne, hoping and praying fervently for success but realising during the race that Lawrence and Shaun's Olympic dream was disintegrating before us. It was heart-wrenching to witness Lawrence suffer another defeat of that magnitude. Athletes in this state retreat into a private space in an attempt to gather themselves and make sense of the loss. They are wounded and need time to recover.

It reinforced for me how tough the road was, how long, hard and humiliating it was, filled with indescribable losses. To put it in perspective, the losses far outweigh the victories on this particular path.

Shaun and Lawrence took a break and were forced to watch the Olympics from a distance. For Shaun it marked the end of a difficult and rocky part of his journey. For Lawrence, he felt he had not yet given his best. He felt he could win. Their disappointment fuelled their resolve and served to deepen the well of tenacity and perseverance. The gold medal claimed by the lightweight four gave them hope and encouragement to return, determined to persevere.

After the London Olympics, Matthew returned to rowing after a short break, ready to start again. There was an ergometer trial early in the season and, in his inimitable and determined style, he put his body on the line, pulled hard and hurt his back again. He was advised by the neurosurgeon to take a year off to allow his back to settle and recover. He agreed to this. He engaged in a series of biomechanical exercises to strengthen his back and improve his core muscle strength. However, some injuries do not settle. The damage to his back was irreparable, and the degeneration to his lower lumbar spine could not be reversed.

When a year of physical recovery and relentless introspection was over, he made the painful but carefully considered decision to stop rowing.

From that moment at the beginning of 2013, Matthew never rowed at international level again.

It was a grim day for South African rowing. They lost a skilful athlete with a brutal work ethic who would be missed throughout the squad. Lightweight rowing paid for the loss. In 2013 the lightweight four raced at the World Championships in Korea with John, James, Sizwe and newcomer Mike Voerman. They came sixth. A year later, the selectors decided against a four and selected John and James into the lightweight double.

South Africa never selected a lightweight four again, and after 2016, FISA disbanded the lightweight four event at Olympic level.

Matthew decided there were other things he wanted to do. He had plans to marry his partner, Alicia Enslin, and they tied themselves to each other in a beautiful ceremony and reception in Pretoria on 14 December 2013, a special day for me as it was my mother's birthday. He had plans to work, travel, cycle and study further. He never fully trusted his back to withstand the extreme level of training he knew he would have to subject it to for a further four years to achieve a similar result. And it would have to be a similar result. Anything less than winning would not be good enough for him. He cycled seriously for two years on the mountain bike circuit. He was skilled on the bike and pushed hard. In a conversation I had much later at the Rio Olympics in 2016 with James Read, one of the elite South African mountain bikers, he said, 'We were a bit worried when Matthew came onto the circuit.'

Sadly, however, that too fell away from Matthew when he injured himself in a cycling accident with his younger brother Charles, both of them landing up in Casualty one Sunday afternoon. The cycle had started out as a training ride for the brothers but ended when Charles misjudged a speed hump and fell hard. Matthew was close behind him and crashed into him. Charles ruptured his acromio-clavicular joint, where the collarbone and scapula meet, and Matthew fractured the head of the radius and disrupted the scapho-lunate ligament, a ligament in the wrist.

Matthew was furious about the accident. Until that point he had a clean record from a falling point of view. The fact that Charles had been injured softened the anger and Charles was grudgingly forgiven. Matthew had been preparing for two serious mountain bike rides and was in the best physical condition he had been since stopping rowing. He was hoping to do well in the races. The injuries tore his hopes apart and took a number of months to heal fully.

He never cycled again at that level. High-level sport had finally ended for Matthew. He was 27 years old. From that moment, his life journey took him in a very different direction.

Four months later, Matthew and Alicia left for London to pursue work opportunities.

A few years later, Matthew told me, 'There is life after rowing. I missed it when I left but I love the direction my life has taken from then.' Success in rowing often heralds success in life.

A chapter closed and I felt the sense of pride mixed with the deep ache that has become more familiar to me as my boys grew up and forged their own paths in life.

But rowing in our family was not over, not by a long shot.

Lawrence had dreams to fulfil, and James and Charles had begun their rowing journeys in their school years. Both followed the trail their brothers had pioneered. Despite it being a well-trodden path, it has been neither easy nor very comfortable for them. They have had to make their own footprints, despite the big ones left by Matthew and Lawrence. Most people incorrectly assume that James and Charles were under immense family pressure to row and perform. The truth is that neither of them began rowing nor feel they have continued to row because of the achievements of their brothers or pressure from me or David. If they have felt pressurised, it is a result of their own aspirations and inner drive.

James came through Parktown Boys' Rowing Club and had a more difficult path through the years. His age group did well in the early years, but as they moved up to their more senior years they never really achieved the result they so desperately wanted. The group were extraordinarily close as friends and many of them remain close to this day. James went to Tuks in 2012 and rowed for the university that year. He knew that if he wanted to take rowing further and try to make it into the squad, he would need to train a lot harder and work his way up. 'I never felt I was exceptional at rowing during school. I knew I would need to work my way up from the bottom if I chose to pursue rowing,' he explained to me.

He was not sure he wanted to take that path. School rowing had been fraught with many disappointments but he loved it and wanted to row for the Tuks club, so he pursued this path, rowing for the Tuks Boat Race crew with Lawrence in 2012. Tuks won Boat Race that year, James's first big victory in rowing. Earlier that year he had watched the 2012 Olympics and witnessed Matthew's gold medal. Those two events fuelled the inner drive to take rowing more seriously and he started training with the squad at the start of the new cycle in 2013. He was selected to row at the World University Games in Russia in 2013 in a lightweight four. They came eighth overall in that event. A year later he was selected to represent South Africa in the Under-23 World Championships in the lightweight single scull in

Varese, Italy, and came 18th. In 2015 he rowed in Korea as part of World University Games and raced the single scull again, coming eighth. In 2016 he came sixth in the A final at the Student Championships in Poland, his best result yet. He continued to row for Tuks throughout this period and rowed for the Boat Race First Eight four times, winning each time.

It continued to be an uphill path but James persevered, trying to make it into the senior squad to deliver the performance he hunted for. He was not ready to give up yet. He continued to scull as a lightweight sculler. He is the lightest of the four boys and struggled to get his weight up. He is the only lightweight I have ever known who never even stepped on a scale before the official weigh-in. James has always understood what was needed to be faster. He knows how to look at a situation and pick out the flaws. He can look at himself honestly and critically. The scull is not an easy boat in which to train; it demands extreme mental toughness as there is no one else to shoulder the burden. The sculler is alone and fights alone, battling the inner voices without respite, with little support. It is a cruel truth in sport that the weaker athlete gets less from the coaches and support staff, so weakness begets weakness and the cycle of not improving sufficiently continues. Despite all these challenges, James continued to train with spirit and determination.

Charles sculled at school, as is the tradition at St Alban's. The school does no sweep rowing during the season until the end of each year, when a senior crew is selected for the annual Boat Race on the Kowie River. In his first year at school Charles initially found the pain of rowing unbearable. It was only after he started winning that he began to understand the meaning of the pain and begin the process of learning to accept it. Charles initially found it tough to follow Lawrence and Matthew's path as the pressure on him was great. He had to withdraw a little and allow his own ability to grow alone; it was uncomfortable growing in the shadow of others. His coach during his school years, Tiago Loureiro, allowed Charles to develop at his own pace in the first few years without pressure. He had insight, knowing that Charles's fire would soon burn strongly.

Charles came second in the prestigious single and double sculls at South African Schools Championships in both of his senior years, losing to Daniel Watkins and Nicholas Oberholzer respectively. He won the quadruple sculls in both years. He was selected to race at the Junior World Championships in Hamburg in 2014, in the quadruple sculls, with Nicholas Oberholzer, Nicholas Farrel and Christopher Mittendorf. It was the first of some losses and Charles was devastated to come 23rd overall. He was being considered for the junior men's double the following year, but due to the cycling accident with Matthew just prior to selection he was unable to participate further. Charles required surgery for his disrupted acromio-clavicular joint; his chances of racing overseas that year were wrecked. He had to concentrate on rehabilitating his shoulder as he was not yet ready to stop rowing.

Charles has the passion and drive for racing, as well as a core of steely hardness. He is disarmingly tough. He rows well and is technically skilled. He is ready to spread his wings and soar as high as he can. He wants to taste it all – and even though he understands the nature of the process, he is impatient and easily gets frustrated with himself and others when he feels things are not good enough. He is as hard on himself as he is on others and his expectations are high. After matriculating from St Alban's he continued to row through Tuks, joining the squad and training full time.

He was selected to row in the men's coxed pair with heavyweight Leo Davis at the Senior World Championships in 2016 in Rotterdam. They suffered a disappointing 13th overall. Charles was ill with a viral upper respiratory infection before the race, requiring medical treatment. It was physically tough to race in this condition and Charles had to hunt for his inner strength to overcome the fatigue and lethargy. A year later, he raced in a coxless four at the Under-23 World Championships in Plovdiv, Bulgaria, with Garth Holden, Tim Miller and Mzwandile Sotsaka. Their result was a further disappointment for Charles: the crew came 12th over-all. I think many saw his frustration as unremitting negativity rather than a deep hunger to improve. For Charles there is winning and then nothing.

'Winning is what keeps me rowing.'

Inevitably, questions arose in people's minds. Why were the losses so enormous? Why did the pain feel so visceral, so brutal, as if a vital part had been hacked away? When I explained the particular race and event and the loss to people, many would respond, 'But they did so well. It is such an achievement to row at that level. They should be proud of what they have done. It is good enough.' They are both completely correct and profoundly mistaken in this conclusion. If the goal is to participate and get to that level, then it is good enough. But if the goal is to win and be outstanding, to want to be that good and attain that level of perfection, then it is not. This is about pushing harder and further, moving out of a comfort zone and into an extreme level of excellence. This is about striving relentlessly to achieve beyond the forgettable, beyond mediocrity. About being outstanding and moving beyond the limits we impose on ourselves.

As a parent, I have become hardened to the disappointments. I understand and almost expect them now. I have seen such heartbreak along the journey that I have had to build my own resilience and ruggedness. I learnt that, just as the athlete has to bear the losses, as parents so do we. Witnessing our children's pain nearly tore me apart on many occasions.

As their parents, I feel we have offered unceasing support of our time and finances, without expectations of glory. I recognise that to row at this level, to even contemplate and believe in the possibility of a medal-winning performance, takes years of staggeringly hard work and commitment. It is a job that requires extraordinary dedication and large reserves of energy and skill. There are so many who ask about the boys' rowing and then say, 'But what else do they do?' They cannot comprehend that this is a job like any other job, a career like any career, just shorter, with a more defined lifespan. Few understand how much work is involved, how much physical output is required. It may not pay that much, and in a financially driven world that is incomprehensible to most people.

I am grateful to those who see it as a professional sport and recognise the boys' efforts as professional sportsmen. My father has always understood this concept and that unmitigated understanding has been of great support to all of us, but especially to me. I do not see it as a sacrifice, but rather a choice they make to be the best in the world. We will give forever to them – these are our children, our legacy, our joy.

Would I have chosen rowing as a career for them? It is not my role to choose a career for my children. I can only provide the support, the means, the values for them to make their own decisions. I can say that seeing your children focused, passionate and working hard is one of the greatest rewards for a parent, irrespective of the career they choose.

I feel that David and I could have given our boys no greater gift than to support them in their courageous and extraordinary quests. Few can push that hard, past the edge of pain into the realm of excellence. They deserve every bit of our support, and my advice to people in a similar position is to support their children in every way possible.

As parents, we have a duty not to place our own limits on our children. We need to allow their dreams.

I have seen those dreams become reality.

7

🚣🚣🚣🚣

WOLF PACK

Pretoria, 2009

Now this is the law of the jungle, as old and as true as the sky,
And the wolf that shall keep it may prosper,
but the wolf that shall break it must die.
As the creeper that girdles the tree trunk,
the law runneth forward and back;
For the strength of the pack is the wolf,
and the strength of the wolf is the pack.
— RUDYARD KIPLING, *THE JUNGLE BOOK*

I have seen enough rowing to grasp that it was never meant to be simple. If it was straightforward, many more people would be doing it. Any job that consists primarily of pushing the body far beyond what is comfortable will be demanding and difficult.

I remain intrigued how poorly known and understood rowing is within the broader community. It is often confused with canoeing and the concept of the boat moving forwards despite the rowers facing backwards is somewhat bewildering. There are many boat classes in which to race, but the most important to grasp is the basic division of rowing boats into sculling and sweep rowing. Sculling refers to the athlete holding two oars, one in each hand, and moving them both symmetrically and equally through the water. Sculling boats have one, two or four rowers in each boat. In

145

sweep rowing, each athlete holds one oar with both hands on one side of the boat. With a partner holding an oar on the opposite side, they move the boat forwards by rowing in pairs, each oarsman balancing the boat with his or her body. A sweep boat always has a minimum of two rowers, but can have four or eight.

Over the years I have developed a profound respect for the degree of complexity involved in rowing a boat. It requires a complex, hydro-dynamic, mechanical action using the body, arms and legs. Generally, it is not well understood that rowing relies on the legs to drive the boat more than the arms. The rower moves on a slide that runs up and down the boat and uses the power in the legs to drive the oar through the water. The arms and the body coordinate the last bit of the drive to send the boat on as far and as fast as possible.

The oar, or blade, has a handle on one end and a spoon on the other. It passes through a gate in an outrigger and this point is the fulcrum by which the boat is levered along the water past the spoon. The whole body is applied to this mechanism, but the bulk of the force or drive comes from the rower's legs. The objective is to move the boat as fast as possible. The body's movement in the boat needs to be controlled; if it is too rushed, the weight will kill the momentum of the boat.

The more aspects of the rowing stroke the athletes master, the more effi-cient they become. Training and practice perfect the rowing stroke. No one is born skilled in rowing; technical talent needs to be found. A talented athlete brings an inborn natural feel for the movement of the boat and is naturally athletic, but perfecting the stroke takes discipline and hard work.

In the sporting world, rowing is unremittingly tough, requiring years of physical and mental hard work. Both aspects need to be conditioned and trained. I think of rowing as a machine made up of cogs; everything is linked. Each movement requires the preceding cog to be moving perfectly. It is a system dependent on each link for its strength and synchronic-ity. Rowing training is an intricate and vital combination of endurance, speed and strength on a base of technical skill. The training builds aerobic capacity as well as anaerobic tolerance. A rowing athlete has to be able to tolerate the pain of anaerobic work and sustained intensity.

There is no doubt in my mind that training consistently is the key and first step towards winning. Training with purpose and application is the second step. The race is never won on the day; it is won at each and every session in the weeks and months and years before, each session completed with intent and focus. Session after session, day after day, week after week. It means pitching up at every session and making that session matter. It is not enough to just complete the training. The athlete needs to be looking for more, searching for ways of doing it better. There is no space for complacency and satisfaction. This is no secret – but knowing it is one thing, and putting it into practice is on a completely different level. When I spoke to Matthew about training, he had great insight: 'Training is often done when no one is watching. Then it must count and matter even more. The pressure to succeed must be internal pressure. It cannot come from outside or you will not succeed.'

Aspiring young rowing athletes cannot schedule training or decide when it will be convenient to train up to an elite level. Missing a year or two to study or work or do other things may cost a potential athlete too much in terms of training and technical skill. A rowing athlete needs to be able to weather the shock and humiliation of losing, then regroup and attack again and again with determination. In rowing, the losses far outweigh the wins; there is little glory. Most athletes need to be prepared to put in anything from four to twelve years before they see the results of which they dream.

When I first met David, he was training hard for the Wits University Boat Club. He set the tone for training. Matthew was next, and quickly grasped the importance of training. Whenever any of his brothers felt that things were a bit unfair and they were being outdone in some way, he would say, 'Make yourself fast, work on yourself, that way you will never be left out of a boat selection.' He grasped the invaluable lesson that success meant taking responsibility for yourself and the outcome.

Matthew emphasised the quality of training and understood the power it could bring to performance. He wanted to train at elite level for one reason only, and that was to win. To win gold. 'You have one chance; there are no second chances,' he says.

Roger Barrow understood the importance of training. He spoke of the squad being on a high-speed train moving forwards. Staying on that train and getting to the front of it needed continuous hard work. Matthew was on that train. Lawrence followed him. Later, James and Charles followed. In all the years of rowing training, I never once heard the boys complain about training. It was part of them, what they did day after day, week after week. In short, they were trainable and open to the difference the training would make.

Roger made decisions based on how much of a difference they would make to the speed of the boat. He would ask, 'Will it make the bow ball go faster?' The bow ball is the rubber ball that sits at the end of the boat, protecting the boat from hard knocks. It is used to measure the start and finish of the race; the bow balls line up on the start and the first bow ball to cross the finish line wins.

In the process of training the body to adapt to greater loads and higher speeds, the mind is also trained. Professor Tim Noakes conceptualised and proposed the 'central governor' theory. According to this theory, it is the brain that has ultimate control over how much muscle is recruited for use during exercise, which in turn determines how hard the heart needs to work to supply those muscles with an adequate blood supply. The concept of 'muscle recruitment' and how much muscle is used depends ultimately on survival, on how much danger the brain perceives the body to be facing. The brain wants to protect the body when it perceives suffering and danger. The fitter and more conditioned the body, the more muscle can be used and the better the performance without the risk of serious damage. Training the mind to know how much more it can tolerate and how much further it can push the body becomes a key to performance. The rowing team worked with a bright sports scientist, James (Jimmy) Clark. His thoughts on this theory resounded meaningfully for me: 'There is always more muscle that can be recruited. You never recruit every muscle fibre.'

Witnessing my sons' rowing journeys, I learnt that training to become a world-class rowing athlete is a process that cannot be rushed. There is no short cut, magic wand or silver bullet. It takes time to grow and develop into that person. There is no place for impatience and looking too far ahead, beyond the reality of the present. In a world where everything is on fast forward and the desire and expectation is for instant gratification, rowing training is the antithesis. It takes strength of character to commit to this process of delaying gratification and facing the pain of repetitive training – and often, repetitive losses.

Successful athletes are trainable. They can absorb the demands made on them by the coaches and make the changes successfully. They are able to improve. In this way they respond to the training and this sets them up to succeed.

On an emotional level, training is like a roller-coaster ride. Emotions change repeatedly and swiftly depending on the measure of progress. If the boat is not progressing and increments in speed are absent, emotions flag and the work begins to feel impossibly hard. Just as quickly, the mood of the athlete will soar in response to small victories and improvements. If the sessions are not going well, it is important to keep at it and complete the work during such hard times. Being demoralised brings perspective but negativity is dangerous and needs to be contained and prevented. Individuals bring varying amounts of optimism and negativity into the boat depending on their personalities. These must be managed to bring out the best, the right balance.

It is not always possible to enjoy training – it is often quite the opposite – but achievements along the way help build courage and inner strength to keep going. Winning helps. Winning always helps. Rowers have to believe they can be good enough to win, and that it is possible to achieve the speed that supports winning. The concept of self-belief is powerful but also fragile. It is easier to believe in yourself when all is going well. It is much, much harder when things are waning. Matthew says, 'It can break you to

149

know how many times you have to fail before you get it right.'

Despite the intensity of the journey, there needs to be joy, what coach Paul Jackson refers to as *joie de vivre*. The athletes who have *joie de vivre* do not allow the potent world of sport to knock them down for too long. It is the love of rowing, a passion to build momentum and feel the joy born from the boat cutting through the water, that brings the athlete back time and again. In his book *Encore Provence*, Peter Mayle refers to the 'essential ingredient, *joie de vivre* – the ability to take pleasure from the simple fact of being alive'.

Relaxation is essential for recovery. Under-relaxing will result in burn-out as quickly as, if not even more quickly than, overtraining. Rowing athletes train two or three times a day. They spend a fair amount of time recovering to be able to do repetitive sessions. Without proper recovery, the body starts to tire. Adequate recovery is part of the job of being a rowing athlete. Training and recovery become the athlete's world.

Training well mentally and physically are key elements in the process of rowing, but I think there are a few, subtler, aspects that an athlete needs. Paul Jackson speaks of boatmanship and the importance that skill, instinct and finesse can bring to a boat. They need a savviness to pull it all together. These aspects form the language of rowing. Some are subtle and some not so subtle, but the margins to win are small and fundamentally everything needs to be geared towards boat speed.

The squad thinks of itself as, and compares itself to, a wolf pack. A wolf pack is deadly and ferocious when hunting; the pack instils fear in its enemies. As a pack they are ordered and structured with a strong, sophisticated hierarchy. They have complex dynamics and the pack mentality maintains stability and engenders extreme loyalty and devotion to the group. Pack members respect their position and follow the alpha leadership in almost all things. The wolf pack relies on powerful instinct and intuition, as well as a high intelligence. A wolf pack travels and hunts as a group and will defend its territory to the death. Their quest is to live together and be stronger than the fear.

Just as a wolf pack moves and lives, so does the rowing squad. They train as a pack, they travel and race together. There is a sense of purpose and adventure and there is pride in the pack. There is a definite hierarchy in the squad, with the overall alpha leader being the head coach, Roger Barrow. Older athletes mentor younger athletes, demanding and expecting a certain level of behaviour. No athlete wants to be the omega wolf, shunned by the pack because of weakness.

It is easier to train together because the pack supports each person. The squad has a set, prescribed programme that is ordered and structured, so self-motivation is less important. The programmes are set weekly and allow athletes to train without the burden of deciding what to do. It is more difficult to find motivation to train alone than to train in a squad. The squad has a complex momentum of its own and feeds itself, each person feeding off the drive of the squad, in this way maintaining a high level of competition. South African rowing is good because the athletes train hard. Like the wolf pack, they aim to be stronger than the fear.

But athletes don't just train. They don't just practice. The main aim of training is to build up to the pinnacle of racing. Rowing athletes know about racing. They race all the time. They race high-intensity pieces during their training week. They race ergometer trials. They race at local regattas. They race at highly pressurised selection regattas, hoping to make crews for the international season. They race at international level, in World Cups and World Championships. No matter how often they race, it never gets easier. They just keep pushing harder.

Training and racing is what they do.

Rowing training happens in a highly competitive environment. Each week athletes race against each other a number of times, pushing themselves to beat their colleagues and, in some cases, their friends. The group races week after week, pitting themselves against one another. It is merciless, but it is this competitiveness that engenders speed. Out of the competitive environment comes teamwork forged from the struggle. Teams and crews are formed and changed and reformed and tested. Rowing is the ultimate team sport as the boat needs everyone working in perfect unison. At the same time it recognises the individual roles of each athlete. Individual motivation and belief feeds the team.

As the improvements start happening, the athlete gains confidence. An elite rower will be looking for a 98 per cent performance, based on times measured against the world's best rowers in a similar boat class and age category. It is not good enough to be the fastest in the school or the club or the university or the country. It is not enough just to be fast. An elite athlete must strive to be faster. To be the best in the world, you have to open yourself and fight against the best in the world. Being a talented rower is not enough. It is a helpful starting point but hard work counts for far more.

There are few other jobs or work systems that publish the performance of their employees on a weekly basis. In rowing, performance is published after each racing session, sometimes three or four times a week. There is nowhere to hide. Those invested know the condition of each squad member as strengths and weaknesses are exposed every week. It is virtually impossible for athletes to fool themselves into believing they are better than they are because the numbers do not lie. Hard as the truth may be, it is the truth. It can be humbling, even humiliating.

Before athletes can race, they need to be selected. They are selected for crews and boats, camps and tours. The weekly times and prognostics prepare them for selection. Despite this, selection will always cause conflict. The selection process is often painful, and is fraught with crushing disappointment for those who do not make it. It is largely based on numbers; who is the fastest on paper? Athletes often make the mistake of judging their overall standing on a few good performances, when consistent speed counts for far more. At times, there is little to differentiate between athletes in terms of their numbers. At that point, it will come down to coaches and selectors making decisions about who they feel will make the biggest difference in a boat. Who rows better and moves the boat faster? Who will fight harder? Who is the most compatible person in a crew? The selection process is as objective as possible, but there is a narrow window of

152

subjectivity that belongs to the coaches and their understanding of what is needed. The better the coach understands the boat and the crew, the stronger the decisions they make.

I have often wondered what keeps an athlete going. Without doubt, it is the dream, the hope that keeps them hunting. Most athletes want to hear they are fast. A balanced athlete needs to be prepared to be hard on themselves, confronting themselves and being critical, but at the same time acknowledging the small victories along the way.

Since 2009, the South African squad system has been sustained by the head coach Roger Barrow. As the leader he is unremittingly proactive, a few steps ahead of everyone else. He is driven by finding solutions to problems. Over the years, a number of assistant coaches have helped him. Andrew Grant, AJ, became the longest-serving assistant coach; others have come and gone depending on the need at the time. Dustyn Butler, Paul (Jacko) Jackson, Tiago Loureiro, Marco Galeone, Grant Dodds and Mpumi Geza, as well as a myriad of school coaches, have all played roles in the development of the South African squad system, from junior through to senior level. But it is under the hard work and sustained leadership of Roger that the squad mentality has matured. He brought an enormous energy and vision to the programme and he is key to the development of the system.

The key players from Beijing to London and then Rio were coaches Roger, AJ, Jacko and Dustyn. In a wolf pack, however, there can only be one alpha leader.

AJ backed Roger as the leader and settled into his coaching of the under-23 group, followed by the men's heavyweight four for qualification at Bled and later, after London, the senior women's squad, whom he coached to the Rio Olympics.

Jacko worked well with Roger as the head coach and leader. After the lightweight four gold medal, he went on to coach the lightweights in Korea 2013 but the crew disbanded after that. He later became involved with the men's heavyweight four and coached them to Rio 2016.

Dustyn was a talented coach who was instrumental in coaching the successful men's lightweight four. According to the athletes in the light-weight four, 'Dustyn was the unsung hero. His technical ability and prowess were outrageous. He had a superb rowing eye and was completely dedicated to the task.' But, as with many highly charged work environ-ments, a split came after the London Olympics and Dustyn left the squad. South Africa had lost a good coach.

Coaching rowing is an intricate process. The coach has to be able to explain the complexities of skilled rowing, and design exercises to improve its technical component. Coaches also have to engage and draw the athlete to points of focus. Watching the athlete and the crew closely, the coach is in a position to know every stroke taken, to see the mistakes and to make changes. The process incorporates improving the physical shape of the athlete. The stronger and fitter the athlete, the better able they are able to absorb the technical, training and physiological demands of the sport. The coach needs to prescribe work to bring out the best in an athlete. Fatigue needs to be managed; a certain level of fatigue is essential for adaptation and conditioning, but the coach needs to recognise when fatigue becomes dangerous. This involves an intimate knowledge of the athlete and usu-ally calls for a supportive team approach using a physiologist and medical team. The coach needs to be able to manage the psychological component of the athlete and the crew and how that team functions.

A crew has to be able to work together, bringing commitment, motiva-tion and trust. The coach needs to recognise the individual's strengths and abilities and how these can be used to make the crew stronger and faster. The coach also needs to manage the emotional energy, helping the athlete learn to cope mentally with the unceasing grind of training and, ultimately, with the race itself. Coaches ensure that the athletes stay emotionally alive, rather than emotionally drained. Good coaches have managerial skills, allowing them to pull the entire process together and ensure that as many needs are met as painlessly as possible.

To be successful in rowing at the highest level, then, requires fine atten-tion to detail to build boat speed and improve technical skill. The goal is deceptively simple but the path extraordinarily demanding. Only a few manage this journey. Ultimate success comes down to how the path is managed, how the road is walked.

In the end, success in rowing always comes down to training. Matthew Pinsent speaks about training in his book *A Lifetime in a Race*: 'Training is the most dependable and consistent part of life in our sport. Through thick and thin, home and abroad, good weather and bad, training is a constant.'

Athletes who train hard and consistently, are open and flexible to change and are able to take responsibility for themselves in this process have a greater chance of becoming champions. 'Excuses change nothing. They only make you feel better for a short time,' says Matthew.

Of course, this is not just about winning in rowing.

This is the key to any success in life.

8

🚣🚣🚣🚣

TEAM DOC

Pretoria, 2011

A doctor should be a clown at heart, a scientist at brain,
and a mother at conscience.

– ABHIJIT NASKAR, *TIME TO SAVE MEDICINE*

October in the province of Gauteng is one of the most beautiful months of the year. It is spring and the countless Jacaranda trees lining the suburban streets flower profusely, creating a breathtaking display of purple. It is nothing short of enchanting and the wonder is always a delight.

In October 2011, Roger identified the need for medical support in his growing squad.

Roger is an ambitious and insightful person who has the cunning ability to see clearly what a system needs. He is equally smart about hunting down a way of meeting these needs. He is ruthless in that regard. He constantly seeks solutions to problems and remains positive and upbeat. He has enormous charisma and charm, and the gift for establishing where a person's strengths lie and then using those strengths in the best possible way to ensure the development of the squad.

Roger recognised that the rowing team had medical problems that could potentially hold them back. There had been a number of health issues over the years that had been poorly managed simply because the team had no one to whom they could easily refer athletes. Ill-health and injury had cost the team heavily at times, with athletes being unable to race at World Championships overseas. Like many, Roger found doctors somewhat inaccessible and difficult to communicate with. He felt he did not have a close rapport with doctors, and needed someone with a good understanding of rowing.

Roger had been working with sports scientist Jimmy Clark for a few years. Jimmy first met Christian Felkel, head coach at the time, in 2004 and had worked sporadically with the team. From 2007, Jimmy became a more permanent team member, and two years later he started working closely with Roger when Roger took over as head coach.

Jimmy was meticulous in his approach and did a considerable amount of work with the team to raise the standard of performance in the entire squad, ensuring that they started to think about their lives and adopt a lifestyle that would support top-level performance. He called it the Performance Lifestyle. But Jimmy realised he was constrained when it came to the clinical problems in the team. He agreed with Roger and felt the team would benefit from the support of a medical doctor.

Roger wanted the squad well-positioned on his high-speed train, and this included a high-functioning support team, moving towards the goal of the London Olympics. The team comprised Roger in the driver's seat with two assistant coaches, AJ and Dustyn, and part-time volunteer coach Paul Jackson. It included sports scientist Jimmy Clark, Nicola Macleod (a biokineticist and strength trainer) and Garreth Bruni (the team physiotherapist, who was occasionally helped by Corli van der Walt and Andri Smit, all three of whom worked in a practice at the High Performance Centre in Pretoria). Garreth treated most of the squad and travelled with them to competitions. Roger felt he needed more medical support as the qualification regattas before Beijing and London had been fraught with health issues.

I had known Roger for a few years as he had coached Matthew and Lawrence, both of whom had close relationships with him. I first met him in 2007 when he coached Matthew and James Thompson to their silver medal at the Under-23 World Championships in Strathclyde. He struck me immediately as a person with enormous energy and resourcefulness.

In November 2010, our family moved from Johannesburg to Pretoria, with a distance of 60 kilometres separating the two cities. Johannesburg is a vast metropolis, the richest city in South Africa, the centre of business in the country. Pretoria is smaller but politically more important, being the administrative capital of the country. Pretoria is also the centre of elite rowing in South Africa. Roger recognised the need for a centralised system and Pretoria had good rowing water nearby, making it an automatic choice.

Matthew and Lawrence were already at the University of Pretoria and were rowing with the national squad based at the High Performance Centre, which was part of the university. James was about to begin his matric year at Parktown Boys' High School and Charles was finishing Grade 7, his final junior year at De La Salle College. In 2008, David made the decision to concentrate his work primarily on bone marrow transplantation. He decided that the best place to do this was at the Pretoria East Hospital with Dr Jackie Thompson. He joined forces with her and, over the next few months, gradually moved himself to Pretoria until he was working full-time in the Transplant Unit. With Jackie, they built a large and successful Bone Marrow Transplant Centre.

Moving to Pretoria was a natural choice for our family, and it made sense in many ways. I was born in Johannesburg and had lived there all my life. Since our marriage, David and I had moved a number of times. With our growing family our needs were constantly changing, but we only moved within the confines of a few areas in the city. Moving out of Johannesburg was a big move for me. I embraced it as best I could, stopping my work at the Witwatersrand Hospice, where I had worked for seventeen years. I have never found change easy, and hard as it was to break from Hospice, I tried to see the move as an opportunity for change. Leaving my work at Hospice freed me up and enabled me to arrange the sale of our home in Johannesburg and the purchase of a new home in Pretoria. It gave me the time to arrange the dreaded packing and subsequent move as well as transporting James to and from school in Johannesburg until he finished, and supporting Charles who would be starting his new school, St Alban's College, in January 2011.

Back in 2005 we had bought a plot in Sable Hills Waterfront Estate, on the southeastern aspect of Roodeplaat Dam just outside Pretoria. We planned to build a weekend house there as the boys were rowing often on the dam and it made sense to us. Unfortunately, we were unable to afford to build the second home. When we made the decision to move to Pretoria, we discussed countless options, one of which was to build and live at Sable Hills. Eventually, however, we decided to buy a slightly smaller property in Pretoria, which would free us up financially to build the long-awaited house at Sable Hills. We moved into a beautiful north-facing home in St Patrick's Road in Muckleneuk, with the most glorious view of Pretoria and the Union Buildings. The annual flowering of the Jacaranda trees in the area was simply breathtaking.

We were able to finish the plans for Sable Hills and started the building project in January 2012. It was completed by the end of the year. It became our own weekend retreat. At that time, Lawrence and James were training with the national squad. Matthew was living in Pretoria and had started working. Lawrence and James decided to move permanently to Sable Hills and lived there for three years, with the rest of us visiting over the weekends. Over time, however, David and I found owning and managing the two properties difficult and time-consuming, and neither of us had much spare time. In 2015 we made the decision to move to Sable Hills permanently. We sold our house in Pretoria, a home I had grown to love and was saddened to leave, and for the eighth time in our married life we packed up our things, and moved to the dam.

We currently still live at Sable Hills, 20 kilometres outside Pretoria. The area is very close to bushveld, with animals roaming freely on the land. When I walk through the estate I see a number of giraffe, zebra, wildebeest, red hartebeest, waterbuck, nyala, kudu, impala and warthog. Ironically, one of the animals ñot at Sable Hills is the magnificent and stately sable antelope itself. The area is a beautiful part of the world with spectacular sunsets and views over the dam and surrounding bushveld.

Moving to Pretoria created a state of limbo for me from a work point of view. I had worked for Hospice for years and my heart was deeply rooted in palliative medicine. During my time at Hospice I saw much suffering and pain associated with illness and death, but at the same time I witnessed joy, hope and courage. It was the work that somehow brought out the best in me and I was able to give what people in that situation needed. I was now effectively unemployed, and it felt strange. Since qualifying, I had always worked. Becoming a mother had not stopped me and I had pushed through, juggling my work with my role as a mother as I thought this was important: for me, for David, for the boys, for the community. I felt a certain inexplicable, deep-seated responsibility to South Africa to work as a doctor. Medicine meant that to me. It was more than a job.

As a doctor, you see people at their most exposed and vulnerable. A doctor has a duty to protect them. Suddenly, after all these years, I felt lost, rudderless. On moving to Pretoria I did a few locum sessions for the Pretoria Sungardens Hospice and travelled back to the Hospice in Johannesburg to help there when needed. I was not sure I would continue with this. Matthew was recovering from his back operation and was well into his rehabilitation when we moved. I was not sure what work I would pursue, and was hoping some other options would present themselves.

At this point, the idea of a doctor helping the team started to gather momentum in Roger's mind and he began talking to Lawrence and Matthew about it.

One day Lawrence asked me, 'Mom, Roger is quite keen that you come and work with the team and be the doctor he refers to. Would you be interested?'

'I would definitely be keen to look at it and see if it could be feasible. I am not qualified in sports medicine, though, so I am not sure it is possible.'

A few days later Roger phoned me to ask if I could meet him. It was a situation of my being in the right place at the right time and being able to meet a need he had identified. He opened a door for me, though not a door I had not considered before. With the boys rowing seriously, I had wondered over the years whether I should do some sort of sports medicine qualification to equip myself to help them. I had even previously enquired about doing a diploma or degree in this field. Matthew's back operation had been traumatic both physically and emotionally, and had made me realise how much there was to learn in this field.

My answer to Roger's request was, 'Yes. Let's give it a try and see how I go. However, I am not qualified in sports medicine, so I hope I will manage.'

He responded, 'Well, you are a doctor, and that is what I am looking for. Someone I can communicate with easily as doctors are usually so hard to talk to. I need someone more involved with the team.'

It was another key moment in my life, although the true reasons for this were not yet clear.

I became the team doctor for the rowing team in November 2011. It was unknown territory for everyone, and although many were relieved to have someone to refer to, there were some who appeared uncomfortable with me and some awkward moments. I had to find a niche for myself as the team was already established, and initially I found it hard to break into the role. I pushed through and the position seemed to work itself out. In the end, it actually came together very easily.

Each day, I became more focused on the team. I tried to make a difference, and what I lacked in experience I made up for with diligence and hard work, good common sense and a deep, natural feeling and understanding of the demands of rowing and high-performance sport. I cared about the programme, the athletes, the support team. I still lacked confidence and belief in myself, but I enjoyed the work.

I worked relatively well with the support team. Teamwork was essential, but we did not always get this right. I forged close relationships with the coaches and we managed the athletes comprehensively and effectively. I worked well with Jimmy, trying to find out everything he had done with the team, using his knowledge and experience and giving my own input where there were gaps. In 2011 I had two sons in the team, and this swelled to three from 2013. As Matthew left after the Olympics and Charles had not yet joined the squad, I never faced the unique position of having all four sons in the team. I do not think the boys have ever been embarrassed or compromised by my being their mother and the team doctor, and for this I am exceedingly grateful. They are mostly generous with my time. I would say they are proud of me and the work I have done and continue to do.

David supported the work. He has always supported whatever work I do. He has never put any pressure on me to work, but always supported my wanting to work as that was not negotiable for me. He never put pressure on me to earn a salary. I am indebted to his generosity in this regard, especially as I was in a volunteer position for some time. His kindness through the years afforded me the freedom to be a mother and a doctor, both of which were important to me. There have been times when I have regretted not being a specialist in some discipline, but when I look at the boys I know I made the right decision. Being a mother far, far exceeded my need to be a specialist doctor.

The path ahead, however, had further complications in store for me. Life seemed to have a way of putting obstacles in my path, especially when the journey appeared to be going smoothly.

Life had settled into a routine for me, working with the athletes. The move to Pretoria finally felt comfortable and I was finding living there a little easier and more familiar.

For some time, I had been concerned about the frightening possibility of finding a lump in my breast. Despite going for a number of tests and check-ups because of this concern, I had been assured and reassured that everything was fine and that I had nothing to worry about. Our family went on holiday in December 2011 but my suspicions continued.

It would not be the first time in my life that my suspicions and instincts would prove accurate.

On return from holiday I insisted on further tests. I had to follow my instincts. Within a day I was having an MRI scan. David came with me as he was worried and knew I was anxious. The fact that he chose to accompany me confirmed how serious we both knew this was likely to be. I lay there waiting for the result. It was not long before the doctor came in to tell me that he was unhappy with what he had seen. He needed a biopsy.

I started to feel really frightened. Until that moment, it had been a nagging doubt. Now I was afraid, really afraid.

There was a reason for the nagging doubt.

Two days later I was diagnosed with breast cancer. I was 49.

It was January 2012, six months before the London Olympics. The radiation treatment I had undergone for the Hodgkin lymphoma in 1978 had compromised the breast cells, causing damage at a molecular level, and 35 years later those malignant changes had finally and irrevocably manifested themselves.

There are some truths in life you never want to face. That day, reality crashed into my world, dislocating me from my life as I knew it. I had to confront the awful truth that I was one of the statistics now; I was the dreaded positive result. That day remains a dismal, painful blur, with David and I trying to be practical and logical, but unable to deal with the emotional trauma. Outwardly, I held myself together; inwardly, I broke apart in despair and deep fear.

For any woman, breast cancer is a shocking and emotionally shattering diagnosis. From a cancer point of view it is not a bad one to have, as the treatment is effective and associated with a high degree of survival. From an emotional point of view, it is a lot worse. Breast cancer is just so painfully out there; losing a part of your body that is associated with your femininity and identity, your appearance and sexuality, is brutal.

Once again I was faced with the extreme brevity and fragility of our human lives, the swiftness with which life can change, the random and indifferent way life dishes out pain and grief and loss.

But the spirit to survive and fight is strong within me, and that is what I did. I just pushed through it with a dogged resolve, despite a profound and aching sense of sorrow and loss.

I was advised to have a double mastectomy and found the surgery brutal in the extreme. The day before the operation, David and I celebrated our 25th wedding anniversary and we took all our boys and Matthew's girlfriend Alicia out for lunch. The boys ordered a Jägerbomb for me – a Red Bull and Jägermeister cocktail. 'You need fortification for tomorrow, Mommy.' I needed more than a Jägerbomb for fortification. The surgery was nothing short of horrifying and I felt hacked apart. Violated. I knew there were support groups for women in this position but no one came to me after surgery, no friendly faces came by to offer supportive services. I too never looked for the support and battled on without the pink ladies, the reach for the sky dream team or whatever they were known as. I relied heavily instead on support from my family and friends. To be frank, I do not feel I have ever fully recovered from the emotional trauma of that surgery. The grief and loss were far, far greater than I could have ever expected. Some wounds never heal. I had no idea how to deal with the changes I was facing.

But despite the damage, I was strong – maybe too strong. I did not let people know how much I suffered. I could not talk about it and would not allow my guard to fall. I was vulnerable, but no one would have known this as I was adept at putting on a brave face. I chose to have the breast reconstruction and underwent five operations in the space of two years, relying on a strong will and boundless courage to push on. Fortunately, I recovered quickly from surgery and each time pushed myself a bit harder to come back faster and stronger. I have never felt that the reconstruction was successful, but I moved ahead because I had to.

The illness altered me physically and mentally. Inevitably, after such trauma, depression set in and the medication I was on precluded me from using antidepressant medication. I asked the oncologist what to do as I was finding myself emotionally low and fatigued. 'The only thing proven to help with fatigue is exercise,' he said. And so I embarked on a long-overdue exercise programme of walking and swimming. Without a doubt, it saved me from falling further into the deepest and blackest of holes. I had to concentrate on just getting through each session, the long ten-kilometre walk, the two-kilometre swim. Every day I pushed on relentlessly, determined to overcome my emotional deterioration.

Fortunately, the disease was contained and localised to the breast alone. There was no local or distant spread. I faced the decision whether to have chemotherapy. David and I arranged for a tissue sample to be analysed in America for the molecular risk of recurrence. This test was unavailable in South Africa. It showed a low risk of recurrence. Together with the oncologist, we decided that chemotherapy would not make enough of a difference in reducing the risk of recurrence, and we opted not to go that route. It was a clear case of the risks, both short and long term, being greater than the benefit of chemotherapy. Surgery had dramatically reduced the risk of recurrence. I was put onto hormone therapy to further reduce this risk.

Effectively, I was in remission. Despite what it had done to me physically and emotionally, the surgery had contained the disease, and I thank God for that. I have to trust that the hormone therapy will keep it that way. Over my years of working at Hospice I had witnessed countless women dying of breast cancer, including David's mother. I knew what a slow and relentless killer it could be.

Working was vital for my recovery. It made me forget myself and my misery, stopped me feeling sorry for myself and brooding on feelings of persecution and victimisation. But the palliative work I had been doing before the illness became impossible for me. I found myself unable to tolerate the level of emotional pain that is so closely connected to that work. I broke down repeatedly with patients suffering from breast cancer who were now dying. The boundary between something that happened to others and to me was no longer clear or contained.

Working closely with death became untenable for me. A few years later it would become even more untenable, but I did not know that yet.

Working in sports medicine took me away from the pain, both my own pain and that of the patients I had worked with in palliation. Being the team doctor gave me a focus outside of myself and my problems and kept the profound feeling of depression at bay. I gratefully walked through the door that had unexpectedly opened for me and found myself working on a totally different spectrum of medicine. Suddenly, I was working with younger people, with the focus on health and wellness and winning. I was keeping them healthy rather than preparing people for death. I was in a completely divergent world.

I immersed myself in the work, throwing myself into the job with all the energy, dedication and commitment that I have come to know are strong traits of mine. That powerful inner voice drove me on, pulling me away from the dark and back into the light.

My role as the team doctor has had its challenges. It has not been easy being the mother to four of the athletes at various times and the doctor to the entire team. I worked hard on being fair and building trust. I gave each athlete the best I could. Each of them. I tried to encourage each and every athlete who sat in front of me to be the best they could be, to expand their potential, to reach higher and further to become an Olympic athlete. I feel that I have succeeded in being fair to everyone. I became known as Doc and to this day that remains my name within the team.

The impact of the work I did and the difference it made were not always clear to see. At times this was demoralising for me. The system I worked in was, and will undoubtedly remain, coach- and athlete-driven, and I am used to being a leader. Doctors like to be in charge. They don't easily take leadership from others. I had to know my place: I was the advocate of the athlete but I also knew what the coaches wanted: athletes who kept on training to build power and speed. The coaches wanted improvement. Slow athletes were problems, and athletes who had stopped improving fell behind. At times I had to pick up the pieces of a broken athlete and try to help him or her make sense of bitter disappointment.

Many wondered whether there was enough work and would ask me, with suspicion in their voices, what I did all day. My feeling remains that they have absolutely no idea. I found plenty of work. There was the usual treatment of various ailments, illnesses and injury. I tried to encourage the athletes to see me as often as possible. I kept very accurate and detailed notes and got to know those I dealt with. I fought against the stereotypical role of a doctor whom you visit when you are ill, and educated the athletes to see me before they got sick, simply to come and talk to me. I developed my interest in promoting health and well-being and preventing illness and injury, which in my opinion were a critical part of the athletes' lives. I loved this aspect of the work. I was available all the time and I think this was one of the most valuable aspects of my work: just being there, in close proximity, available for a quick word.

I watched their ergo sessions, witnessed their ergo trials, watched them training and racing on the water when possible, travelled on camps and tours with them. I enjoyed educating the athletes; I spoke to them as a team every Saturday, highlighting key areas that would help them become elite athletes and live the life that would support that dream, finding the small margins that would enable them to become champions. I researched their diets and promoted healthy eating. I wanted them to be healthier, to train better and more consistently. I monitored them physically and kept on eye on their blood parameters. I built up a complete picture of each athlete to know and understand them better.

I was fastidious about drug-free sport and educated them regularly. The cycling doping debacle had devastated me as Lance Armstrong had been one of my heroes. I was determined to continue the clean record of South African rowing. I would not allow the team to use a single supplement that had not been properly tested in a trusted laboratory in England. I believed in a zero-tolerance approach to doping in sport.

I emphasised full recovery and made it part of the athletes' job. The more they recovered, the more they could train. How many people out there can say that eating and sleeping are part of their daily work? I gave the athletes as much as I could to keep them training, with as little illness or injury as possible along the way. I endeavoured to make decisions based on the best interests of the athlete, with careful thought and clinical judgement, and involved the athletes in the process by educating and informing them of their options.

Matthew's injury gave me insight into the mind of an injured athlete. I knew there was a fine balance, that athletes sometimes ignore the early warning signs of an injury and hope fervently that they can push through the discomfort and row themselves right. I knew that fear and panic followed rapidly when the pain or niggle did not settle and the athlete was unable to train. Things spiralled downwards from that point and morale flagged. If the injury resulted in a formal diagnosis that would lead to an operation or more definitive treatment, that would mark the lowest point. From there, things would only improve; rehabilitation began and there would be a steady upward climb. As the athlete progressed and become able to focus again, morale would rapidly improve. I marvelled at the healing power of the body; given enough time, the injury would heal. I found I was able to be calm with injured athletes, reassuring them that it would come right and they would row again.

In many ways, however, I needed to become tougher and more robust in my role as team doctor. Just as my compassionate side was an asset, it also made me overly sensitive and there were times when I buckled in the harsh environment in which I worked. How strange in life that strengths can also be weaknesses. Sports medicine is a strange branch of medicine, a little removed from what I would call mainstream medicine.

Working with the athletes brought difficulties and obstacles. I could gauge how successful an athlete could be by the number of 'yes, buts' they said to me, how many excuses they gave, how many external factors they said were preventing them from doing what was suggested.

I knew the athletes well. I learnt who could push through, who took themselves too seriously or worried inordinately about themselves, who needed to be pushed and when it was imperative to hold back. Ergometer trials were a challenge. The fear of a trial superseded reality for some athletes and I needed to be clear-thinking when it came to making decisions regarding trials, knowing when to recognise inexpressible fear in the athlete. I had to push hard to get the athletes to consult me as many would prefer not to see a doctor. Traditionally, seeing a doctor meant there was a problem. Athletes do not want to see themselves as sick or having problems, as this immediately puts doubt in their minds about their ability to perform. It was difficult to change this mindset into something more positive and better aligned with high-performance output. I still battle with this issue.

With the work came a loneliness I had not expected. I was neither athlete nor coach and as a result I spent vast amounts of time alone in my office while they were training. I found camps and tours especially lonely. There were times when I wondered what the hell I was doing there. Doctors are trained to be busy, and usually work under high pressure with high volumes. I found myself in a strangely paradoxical situation, where healthy athletes meant that I was doing my work well. I kept myself focused during these quieter periods by immersing myself in the world of the athletes and their needs, constantly researching ways to make them healthier and more resilient. Touring brought its own challenges. It was always difficult to negotiate a comfortable path when nerves were high and anxiety about racing surfaced in the athletes and coaches. I was away from home and family for many weeks.

Strangely and unexpectedly, the palliative work I had pursued for years prepared me for the elite sports world. In palliation, time is of vital importance. There is little time left for the patient. Treatment must be quick and effective to give these patients as much quality of life for their remaining time as possible. In sport, time is equally important to get the athlete back to training. The harder they train, the faster they get, so I pushed hard to get on top of things as quickly as possible and was not inhibited about trying things. In palliative medicine I always believed that there was something more that we could do. I never stopped trying with my palliative patients, and I felt I would never stop trying with the athletes. Terminally ill patients have high levels of pain, and I was expert in treating pain. When the athletes presented with pain I felt confident about treating them with adequate doses of medication to control the pain as quickly and effectively as possible. Palliative medicine taught me how to listen unconditionally and develop effective communication skills. I was not afraid to broach sensitive issues and could handle the emotional side of the work comfortably. This helped me to be encouraging and compassionate when confronting the emotional world of the athlete. But above all, over the years, medicine has taught me the potential strength of the doctor–patient relationship and it is this I hold sacred.

Communication was important to me, both with the athletes and the coaches, creating an environment of building up rather than breaking down. Dealing with the difficulties and facing them actually enhanced the trust within the team.

During the cycle leading up to Rio, I was asked to look after a special group of athletes, the para rowing team. Each of these athletes had either been born with disability or had been through trauma that had resulted in their disability. Once again, I faced a new challenge about which I had much to learn. Their stories showed me how extraordinarily courageous and tenacious they all were, how they had faced the world and moved with their disability. And now they were working towards the Paralympic Games. Sandra Khumalo rowed in the single scull and Lucy Perold, Dieter Rosslee, Shannon Murray and Dylan Trollope made up a four coxed by Willie Morgan. I worked closely with this team and their coach Marco Galeone for the years up to the Games doing what I could to prepare them for their chance to perform.

In so many ways medicine has taught me the meaning of life and the incredible human connection between the world of science and research and the reality of facing the world that comes our way. I have seen much in the way of tears, grief, heartache, anger and breakdown in the offices in which I have worked. But I have also seen extraordinary bravery, courage, tenacity and determination. I have deep and unmitigated respect for both the athletes and the terminally ill patients I have cared for. They have taught me that, no matter how arduous and painful the journey, no matter which obstacles and wrenching disappointments block the way, human beings have the ability to transcend difficulty through courage and determination. We do not always have control of what happens to us but we all have the gift of choosing how we deal with it and the way we handle the direction in which our path takes us. When we are faced with hardship, we have the power to choose how we walk that path.

I was a bit of a mother to the athletes and played a nurturing role to them. They were like my children; I cared about them all and felt their joy and their pain. At times I was a buffer between them and the tough world of the coaches and their expectations. I remained primarily the advocate of the athlete. The athletes lived in a harsh and unforgiving environment with little respite from the pressure of performing well. Compassion was not always in abundance in that world. I felt I added a small degree of empathy. Some of the athletes could talk to me in a way they could not talk to the coaches, and at times this proved valuable within the team. I could reassure and encourage them, endeavouring to see the best in all of them.

From the experience I have built up over years working with the athletes, I feel there are some fundamental qualities that distinguish a world-class rowing athlete. High-level rowers can bear a staggering amount of physical pain. They are hard on themselves and do not let themselves off lightly. They are rarely satisfied and will push for perfection. They are able to look at themselves and consider their role in a situation before they look at others. They do not blame others and make no excuses. They have a strong work ethic and a deep-seated hunger and passion to achieve what many would call impossible, in a world where the margins are so ridiculously tiny it comes down to milliseconds.

When I began working with the team I decided to register for the Sports Medicine degree at the University of Pretoria under Professor Christa Janse van Rensburg. I completed six months of the coursework, as well as my protocol for my research. From that point, breast cancer and my work and travel commitments with the team conspired against my completing the degree. By far the biggest reason for not continuing with it was still to come. Unfortunately, at the beginning of 2016, with overwhelming difficulty I made the decision not to continue with the degree.

At times I have thought of stopping my work with the team, for a myriad of reasons. When I consider this option with serious intent, however, an overwhelming feeling of sadness comes over me. Walking this journey with those who strive to excel and push their bodies to extraordinary levels is both a challenge and a unique privilege. I always return to the familiar feeling that staying immersed and building experience is the only way forward.

Looking back now, I feel that one of the main purposes of my taking on the rowing doctor's job was my son Lawrence.

But I did not know that then. It was still coming.

9

🚣🚣🚣🚣

SLUMP

Pretoria, 2014

Trying to push this problem up the hill
When it's just too heavy to hold.
Think now is the time to let it slide
— JAMES BAY, 'LET IT GO'

It is impossible to pinpoint exactly when the decrease in Lawrence's performance began. It could have been any moment from the World Championships in Bled in August 2011, as that marks the start of a number of humbling disappointments for him.

Lawrence was depressed and frustrated when he and Ramon failed to qualify the men's pair for the London Olympics. He was disillusioned after their disappointing 13th place. He managed to contain his despair, pick himself up out of the blackness and row in the annual Boat Race in Port Alfred later in September 2011. This was his third Boat Race in the Tuks First Eight, and he had won all three. Being in the University Eight A crew is prestigious; this buoyed him up a little and contained his depression. We celebrated his 21st birthday shortly after Boat Race, throwing a thumping party with friends and family, everyone dressed up as characters. Lawrence dressed as The Hulk and was superb: clad in small denim shorts, the rest of him painted green, he looked, quite frankly, pretty close to the character.

After a short break he returned to the start of the final year of training before the Olympics. He was full of energy and resolve to work towards trying to qualify the boat for the Olympics at the Late Qualification Regatta to be held in Lucerne in June 2012.

The ultimate test of performance in rowing is racing at the Olympics. An Olympic medal is the highest award you can receive in rowing. Unlike in rugby, cricket and football, where the World Cup is the highest award, rowing places the Olympics at the pinnacle of its training and achievement. Everything is geared towards that event. Training is divided into four-year cycles, starting after a short three- to four-week break after the Olympics in October and progressing until the next Olympics four years later. The major Olympic Qualification Regatta is held at the World Championships in the year preceding the Olympics. The qualification regatta is without a doubt the most stressful regatta in which an athlete can row, as every athlete in the world is desperate to qualify. Athletes come prepared, knowing they are going to war, that they may need to push themselves and fight harder than they have ever had to, to qualify for one of the few celebrated spots in the Olympics.

After Ramon di Clemente made the impossibly painful and difficult decision to retire from rowing at the end of 2011, his position was left open. Not long into the new season, Lawrence and Shaun Keeling were paired in the men's pair.

Their first race was the Late Qualification Regatta in Lucerne, where they failed to qualify the boat for the London Olympics.

Once again I found myself on opposite ends of the spectrum. A week after Lawrence failed to qualify the pair, the lightweight four raced at the Lucerne World Cup and achieved their stunning second place, losing to the Chinese lightweight four but beating Great Britain and Denmark. I went from despair and pain for Lawrence to joy and elation for Matthew. There were always these mixed emotions as a rowing spectator, and especially a rowing parent. In some of the local rowing events I have had to witness the boys rowing against one another, one brother trying to beat another brother. I have not yet had to witness and experience the hardship of any of the boys fighting it out with their brothers for selection into boats for World Championships or Olympics. I think that would be harrowing for me.

Watching Matthew achieve the ultimate success in rowing at the London Olympics, Lawrence knew what he had to do. Once again, he came back to the start of the new four-year cycle with intent and resolve to train harder, perform better and qualify for Rio in 2016. He wanted to put the crushing disappointment of not being at the London Olympics behind him and push onwards and upwards into the new cycle. He was determined, positive and focused.

However, from the moment I started working with the team in November 2011 I had a subtle but nagging concern about Lawrence. His blood profile was not ideal, but still within normal limits. I was surprised that his haemoglobin (the protein and iron complex in red blood cells that carries oxygen) and haematocrit (the percentage of red blood cells found in the blood plasma) were lower than the average in the group. I measured the group a few times a year so I was able to monitor these parameters, and noted that he remained on the low side. I had a blood result from 2010 and the parameters had dropped since then. I did not like what I saw. But there was no real reason to do further tests as the profile, although low, was still within normal limits. When the subsequent results showed a similar picture, I asked David what he thought about doing a bone marrow test to see why his blood picture was low.

He shook his head. 'There is no reason to check this out. Lawrence is still performing and would be unable to train if there was something seriously wrong. You're overreacting. Don't always think the worst.'

I was reassured. I pushed on, thinking that it must all be related to his training and the well-described effects of endurance training on plasma volume and blood cellular mass.

One of the challenges for me in sports medicine and science is that there are no separate levels of blood parameters for elite athletes. I know the levels and profiles for the average person on the street and assume they are the same for an elite athlete. But are they? Professional elite athletes train for a minimum of 20 to 30 hours a week. It is likely that their profiles are the same as the average sedentary person, but they may not be. I feel we need more information about this. Another challenge is the difficulty of testing elite athletes when they are racing in particular. Most research is done in a simulated laboratory environment. It is rarely done at the time of a real event, when the margins are minute and the athlete pushes themselves to the absolute limit and frequently beyond what they thought was their limit.

There were a few other things that made me worry about Lawrence. I noted over the next few years that he seemed to get sick very often. In previous years, he almost never got sick. Now, he seemed to pick up infections, like upper respiratory and gastric infections, very easily. There were numerous episodes of these upper respiratory infections and he was often on treatment for them, sometimes needing two antibiotics before he got better. When he came down with an infection he really got sick and would be flattened for a week. He also complained of fatigue on a number of occasions. He would come to me and say he felt tired and flat. 'It feels as if I have nothing in my legs,' he would say. On further questioning he was otherwise fine, with no symptoms; he was definitely not classically sick. Athletes are often tired; it is the result of what they do. There was a joke that if they did not feel tired they were not training hard enough. It is well known that continuous, hard training makes athletes prone to infections as the immune system can be compromised by high-level exercise. So it was not inappropriate for him to be having these episodes of fatigue and infection. They could be explained away simply by the nature of his training. He would always recover, telling me he felt so much better and stronger again. He was never sick or fatigued for long enough to warrant further tests.

These questions still play on my mind. At what point is a tired athlete – or anyone else, for that matter – investigated for tiredness?

On a number of occasions, I discussed Lawrence with the support team. Our weekly meetings were usually attended by the full support team. Roger, AJ, Jimmy Clark, Garreth Bruni, Nicola Macleod and Monja

Human, the psychologist to whom we referred athletes, all attended these meetings. There were many reasons and theories put forward as to why his performance was gradually decreasing. Most felt that Lawrence was training too hard and that the cumulative effect was a decrease in performance. By training so hard all the time he was depleting himself, and was not fully recovering between sessions. It was possible his energy tank was being depleted too often and not enough time was being given to refill it. According to the coaches and Jimmy, he needed to train more cleverly, picking his battles more specifically rather than putting everything he could into every session and exhausting himself. Lawrence had a tendency to train harder when things were going badly. And so the cycle continued.

Other possible reasons put forward to explain his diminishing performance and his proneness to infection were that his lifestyle was to blame, that he was not taking sufficient care of himself, eating badly and not sleeping enough. Others thought he had blossomed and peaked too early, a classic case of winning too easily when he was young, and was now suffering a tailing-off of that performance. Some felt he had reached his ceiling, that his current performance was as good as he was going to get. He often got sick while travelling. It was almost expected that on arriving overseas Lawrence would come down with an infection. During the short three-week break in September when he managed to catch up on all the parties and drinking he had missed out on during the year, he was also prone to getting sick. These were all good enough answers to explain why things were not going that well.

To ensure success in rowing, the athlete needs to train hard. Training is the key to winning. To keep training, they need to prevent injury and illness. This was a topic I attacked hard, constantly talking to the squad about ways to keep strong and healthy, and about how to recover from sessions. Recovery in high-level sport is one of the keys to success. It was not surprising that Lawrence's recovery was scrutinised and blamed for his performance levelling off.

Over the next two years there were a few specific times when Lawrence's illness and fatigue pushed me to investigate him further. On two occasions I sat him down in my office, saying, 'Right, Lawrence, I am going to be the doctor now. This is a proper consultation and we are going to go through you from top to bottom. I am going to ask you a lot of questions to see if I can get to the bottom of these episodes of tiredness and why you keep getting sick.' I would take a full systematic history and perform the best possible examination. I specifically looked for enlarged lymph nodes and signs of chronic illness.

The worry and concern continued. I did a battery of blood tests, looking for signs of a chronic infection. As before, these showed a lower-than-expected haemoglobin and haematocrit, and a slightly elevated CRP (C-reactive protein), a marker of an inflammatory or infective process or tissue injury. None of these showed a marked, clear-cut abnormality, so it was easy to say we would watch it. To make it harder, Lawrence always seemed to get better after these episodes. It simply never went beyond that point.

What was of even more concern, however, was when the initially slight but steady flattening of his performance progressed to a more overt decrease. Over a three-year period, there was a definite downward trend in his performance. Many questions were asked and the coaches showed irritation that he was not performing. In 2013 he rowed with Shaun Keeling in the men's pair and Shaun felt something was not right. He told me later, 'I knew something was wrong. Lawrence was not rowing well and I was consistently stronger than him. He always seemed under pressure in the boat and was not really coping that well. I could not understand it.'

They showed promise, coming fourth in the Lucerne World Cup in July 2013. A bit later, in August 2013, Lawrence and Shaun rowed the men's pair at the Senior World Championships in blistering heat and humidity in Korea. As usual, Lawrence was sick from the travelling and only started to improve for the semi-final.

Shaun and Lawrence rowed to an average eighth place at that regatta.

Despite some disappointment about not making an A final, the two were upbeat. Shaun says, 'It was a great year. I loved the training. I was moving on from the disappointments of the Olympics and I was enjoying rowing with Lawrence.'

'We were training well but were trying to sort out some technical difficulties and establishing the crew dynamic in the boat,' adds Lawrence.

But Lawrence's gradual and subtle downward spiral continued.

In 2014 he noticed he was struggling to achieve high-enough splits in his ergometer pieces. The ergometer approximates the pace of rowing in a boat. Coaches use the time it takes to row 500 metres as the 'split' that measures the pace of the athlete. He was having to work much harder to come closer to the splits he wanted, and this was exhausting him. There were a few sessions where his heart rate and his rate of perceived exertion (RPE) were higher than expected for the splits he was getting. The RPE is an athlete's subjective perception of how hard the session was for him or her to complete.

I spoke to Jimmy. 'I am worried about Lawrence. His splits are low but he is calling a higher-than-expected RPE. Do I need to be more concerned?'

Jimmy seemed slightly offhand about it, shaking his head, blaming the fact that Lawrence was not recovering between sessions and was working too hard all the time. 'He needs to work smarter, Danielle. Every time he works harder than he needs to, he will pay the price. It does not come for free.' In fairness to Jimmy, though, this remained the most likely reason for the slump.

Lawrence spent much time discussing his performance and training with Roger, who advised him to train more cleverly. They worked extensively on how he trained and considered ways of getting more output for a more conservative input. It was at this time that Lawrence started to work not harder but smarter, trying to find ways to make up the margins he knew he needed to make it into the A finals and medal level – the position he wanted and knew he could achieve.

I spoke to Roger on the occasions when I was busy checking Lawrence more intensely and he agreed to decrease his workload, at times giving him anything from a few days to a week off. After the annual Selection Regatta in 2014 when Lawrence could not do more than one race due to another upper respiratory illness, Roger told him to go and get better and not to come back until things had improved. The coaches were getting tired of the cycle of ill health and poor performance. At that time, I discovered he had *Helicobacter pylori*, which I thought might be contributing to his ill health. This is one of the bacteria that make up the gut microbiome, and is associated with peptic ulcer disease and gastric cancer. I treated him, and he responded to treatment. Once again the situation settled and he returned to training.

Lawrence and I had many talks on improving his self-management and the possible causes of his deterioration. I devised lists of guidelines of how to manage himself. He worked hard on all the things we discussed. He wanted to get better and faster and would do anything for this. He committed to extreme measures of hygiene and infection prevention, he improved his eating, he slept more and, in general, recovered better. He changed the way he trained, becoming more cautious and less aggressive when it was unnecessary to attack the session. I treated allergies, I looked for asthma and checked repeatedly for a chronic infection. We were striving hard to improve things, but we were working with such small margins and there were few signs pointing to anything more serious.

What was fundamentally difficult for Lawrence was the slight possibility and thought that there could be something wrong. Confidence can be a fragile component. It is critical for ongoing performance that athletes do not lose belief in themselves. Confidence and self-belief in an athlete can be strong but dangerously brittle. This left me with a delicate situation to handle. I had to negotiate the fine line between looking harder and deeper at the problem, which may not have even been a problem, and alarming Lawrence more than necessary, causing negativity and doubt within him.

This was a difficult time for me. As a mother it hurt me to see Lawrence battling his way through insurmountable difficulty and things just seeming to work constantly against him. Watching him was akin to watching someone struggling up the steepest mountain with a heavy load. As a doctor I was worried, but there just was not enough evidence to push me to do further tests. I was afraid of over-medicalising the sporting world in which I worked, so I just kept watching and observing. In many ways I was completely alone in this; my instincts were alerted but all around me were the needs and beliefs of people who wanted Lawrence stronger, or saw him as already strong, or did not want to entertain the thought that he was not strong, or were advising him about how to live differently to become stronger. It was a lonely place for me. As someone who easily doubts herself, it was not a good situation.

On the water, the boat was not going that well. There were many technical problems and both Shaun and Lawrence were working hard to improve the technical aspect of their rowing. Each time I went out on the motorboat with Roger, I sensed that things were not going well. In one of their sessions, they raced three pieces against other crews. The first piece was very good, but the subsequent two were extremely slow and the other crews beat them.

Roger was angry: 'How can you put out one good piece and then dish up that for the others?' Then, turning to me, 'You see what I am faced with? They manage one good piece and the rest is rubbish.'

Lawrence's ergometer pieces and trials were another point of concern. He could not be consistent and would dip seriously in the middle of the trial, just managing to push through in the last 500 metres to keep himself close to his previous best time. Racing on an ergometer is different from racing on the water. A rowing ergometer is a fixed structure. The athlete moves backwards and forwards on a seat, as opposed to rowing a boat, which accelerates and decelerates, making technical ability as important as power. On an ergometer, power is the key.

An ergometer trial is the hardest test a rowing athlete can do. It is a maximal performance test on the rowing machine during which an athlete pulls as hard as he or she can for 2 000 metres. They are performed at regular intervals during the training year. The ergo trial is the single best way of measuring the athlete's performance and speed in almost perfect conditions. Their power output and effort can be accurately measured and the times are used for selection purposes. Ergo trials are the ultimate test of their endurance and ability to sprint. Sheer power, guts and determination enable the athlete to get through such a brutal test.

In South Africa, the athletes colloquially refer to ergometer trials as a Bar-One day, a term coined by Lawrence years ago. A Bar-One is a well-known South African chocolate bar. An advertisement for it, once, referred to it as giving you the ability to manage a 25-hour day. In rowing terms, a Bar-One day refers to three ergometer races within 25 hours. The athletes race a 2-kilometre race, a 5-kilometre race later that same day, and a 17-kilometre race the next day. Athletes are lined up next to one another and perform the tests together. Despite being next to their colleagues, each athlete is virtually alone, eyes fixed on the screen in front of them, racing for themselves. There is no way of seeing the splits of the person next to you. You have to motivate and push yourself.

Athletes fear ergo trials – they are unforgiving and brutally difficult. The athletes suffer in silent and excruciating pain from the moment they start the trial. There is neither a crew member nor the emotion of a water race to help pull them along. An athlete once asked me, 'Doc, can you please shout out to me during the trial that I am not going to die?'

Lawrence seemed able to train well at a steady level and not struggle, but as soon as he raced, it was as if some invisible force was holding him back. Within the first three or four minutes of racing he was exhausted. As he came through the middle of the race he would feel an insurmountable, crushing fatigue, more than he had ever felt before. The middle part of the race always requires the most physical strength. Muscle fatigue has built up by this stage, and only the most conditioned and strongest athletes are able to make a move at this point in the race.

He put the fatigue down to his not being strong or conditioned enough. It frustrated and angered him. But in the spirit of pushing through difficulty, he always showed up and gave what he could. He never gave up. He

182

never blamed anyone or made excuses. He *always* raced.

In June 2014 he had an extremely important ergometer trial. Due to ill health, he had already had some time off from his disastrous Selection Regatta in May and he needed to show the coaches he was still strong. Mentally, he later confessed to me, he was taking some strain. There were cracks in his shield of self-belief but he pushed himself into believing he was strong. The coaches still backed him, but he was clearly running out of chances. He walked into the ergo room after warming up, and looked tense and quiet. He got onto the ergo machine and did a few hard strokes, stopping to slap his thigh muscles as he always did and focus himself on what he had to do in the next six minutes.

I always watch these trials and have to say they are not easy to watch. It is the closest I have ever been to witnessing and fully comprehending the level of pain that comes from the maximal effort of racing for 2 000 metres. When you're watching racing on the water from the bank, it all seems far away. As a supporter on the grandstand or the jetty, you are not as close to the pain. When the ergometer is less than three metres away from where you are standing, you are right inside the athlete's world of pain. You can smell the sweat and the agony. You become part of the elation and the despair. Seeing the athletes collapse afterwards always and without fail brings tears to my eyes and I have to leave the room. It is even more painful for me to see my own son put out that level of effort and be so physically broken afterwards.

The trial started and Lawrence seemed to be holding himself well for the first 500 metres. Things went badly from the second 500 metres and I could tell he was struggling. I can always tell because he seems to lift his shoulders at the end of the drive, a sign of deep physical distress, almost like a deep and desperate groan. I was even more distressed when I heard him grunt in pain as he pushed himself harder. He finished the trial, but was 11 seconds off his personal best time.

This was not good. He got up and left the room. Roger avoided looking at me. All the coaches did.

'Are you okay, Lawrence?' I asked as soon as I had a minute alone with him.

'I had nothing in my legs,' he said, despondent and flat. 'I could do nothing out there. There was nothing in me. That was the worst trial I have ever pulled.'

He later told me he was beginning to think that perhaps he had reached his personal ceiling and was no longer able to improve to the level of which he had once thought he was capable. In fact, he had started to think he needed to give up rowing.

The coaches met immediately after the trial. I saw them going into a private meeting and my heart sank. I knew what was coming. Two hours later the word was out.

Lawrence had been dropped from the men's pair, the top boat in the South African men's squad.

This was a horrible, bleak and humiliating day for Lawrence. But the coaches had to focus on speed and identify the fastest combination of athletes. They move on. They have to. The new pair comprised Vincent Breet and Shaun Keeling. Vince was familiar to the squad but had left South Africa after matriculating to attend Harvard University. He was studying Biomedical Engineering and rowed for the Harvard First Eight. As was the custom for South African athletes training or studying abroad, he had recently returned from Harvard to row for South Africa in the international season. Shaun Keeling remained the top-performing athlete and Vince was paired with him for the World Championships to be held a little later that year in Amsterdam.

Lawrence was devastated. He struggled privately to accept it, although he understood the reasoning behind it. Shaun and Vince went on to win the bronze medal at the World Championships in Amsterdam a few months later. At the moment of that bronze medal finish in Amsterdam, I was standing with Lawrence. He said, somewhat flatly, 'The chances of my getting back in the air have just got a whole lot slimmer.'

For Shaun, the bronze medal was monumental. It gave him hope and validated all the hardships and difficulties he had experienced over the years. He had been waiting a long time for this moment, and believed he should have won more medals along the way. What we think will happen is so often not the way it unfolds.

Lawrence was teamed up with David Hunt to row in the coxed pair, one of the few non-Olympic events in rowing and one that had fallen slightly out of favour with mainstream rowing. The training went well and Lawrence's health seemed to stabilise. He did not get sick or complain of fatigue during this period. David and Lawrence trained well together; the time in this boat was good for Lawrence. In a way, the pressure came off him and he could rethink and gather himself. Lawrence has never been a bitter or resentful person. He naturally sees the best in people and situations, and this time was no exception. He went on a training camp with the squad to Tzaneen in Limpopo and according to the racing data, Lawrence and David were fast. The coaches felt they could medal at the World Championships in Amsterdam.

Lawrence was feeling good. Interestingly, that year, the famous and unbeaten Kiwi men's pair of Hamish Bond and Eric Murray were planning to race the coxed pair event in Amsterdam, as well as the men's pair race, in an attempt to spice up their training and performance. So the event now promised to be a spectacular one as the Kiwis had dominated the men's pair event for five years. David and Lawrence were eager to race and see what they could do. They wanted to be on the podium. The coaches felt their times were good enough.

They did not medal.

They finished in fifth position. Great Britain, Germany and Argentina beat them. The Kiwis won and set a blistering new record for the event.

It was not a bad result for Lawrence and David, but it was below what was expected of them. But Lawrence had got sick on arrival in Amsterdam and David had a skin infection and was not well. After the repechage, it was David who said, as he staggered out of the boat, 'That was a one-man show. Lawrence pulled me down the course as I had nothing in me to row.

I was not feeling strong at all, and Lawrence did all the work.'

Once again, the result could be explained. And really, how could a fifth-place result at World Championships point to there being something wrong with an athlete? Nevertheless, they had not achieved what was expected. Again, I was not happy.

On their return to South Africa, both Lawrence and David went on to train for and row in Boat Race in Port Alfred. It was Lawrence's sixth Boat Race for Tuks. They won, beating a highly motivated and strong UCT crew, but Lawrence he told me afterwards, 'Mom, that was the hardest race I have ever rowed. It was intense. I am not sure why it was so hard. I think UCT were really strong and maybe our crew was not as strong as it has been in years past but I have never rowed a harder race than that.'

The difficulty with interpreting this statement is that Boat Race is *meant* to be hard. It is a gruelling event raced between two crews over 6.5 kilometres of winding river with each crew trying to get ahead of the other to gain the advantage as soon as possible. Crews tend to start with astounding speed and work beyond themselves in the first half, often paying the price in the second half when the overwhelming muscle fatigue and mental sluggishness start to work against them. The race is strategic as the river curves and unleashes obstacles, such as tidal current, wind and sandbanks, which all play havoc with steering. Boat clashes are common and the course a cox steers can make or break the result of the crew. It is almost universally thought that if the race is not considered hard it is likely the athlete did not work hard enough in it. 'The race is so hard, you never question it. It is impossible to quantify the effort in a maximal test like that because it is always hard,' Lawrence explains.

For me, however, the result was another alarm bell. I was starting to worry a lot more. I felt there were enough signs in Lawrence's performance to point to its being well below his capability. I was convinced that he had not reached his ceiling and that something was holding him back. I was moving closer to making a decision to fully investigate Lawrence.

He had a three-week break after Boat Race and returned with the rest of the squad at the beginning of October 2014. On the return of the squad I did some routine blood tests on all the athletes. I was immediately worried about Lawrence's blood results. He had an overt anaemia – a low count of haemoglobin in the blood – and his CRP was now very high. I spoke to Roger and told him I was worried about Lawrence and needed to do further blood tests and some investigations. Roger agreed to put Lawrence on light training for two weeks while I did the tests.

Lawrence was anxious, almost desperate, when I spoke to him and explained what I wanted to do. 'Mom, we need to find something. I cannot believe this is where I am and I am starting to doubt myself. We have looked for things before and all has been clear but I am feeling there must be something. I need to know if I am sick.'

I was amazed that Lawrence had been able to race Boat Race with anaemia, and it explained his comments about hard it had been. More than anything, though, it explains the type of racer Lawrence is and how mentally and physically tough he is to push himself that hard despite feeling weak.

I had a more difficult conversation with David later, suggesting we do a bone marrow investigation and a computerised body scan. He told me, 'I really feel it is not necessary at this stage. He has just performed so well and would never have been able to pull that hard if there was something seriously wrong. Do some blood tests again, repeat some of the tests looking for a chronic infection like TB. None of the patients I see could row to fifth place in World Championships. It is not possible that Lawrence is ill.'

David is a clinical haematologist; he sees patients with blood diseases, mostly malignant ones. The patients he sees are seriously ill. It is understandable that he would have compared Lawrence's situation to that of the patients presenting to him and refused to see that Lawrence could be one of them.

I repeated the blood tests and continued looking for TB and other chronic infections.

At the end of the period of light training, I asked Lawrence, 'How are you doing? How are things feeling?'

He answered, 'I'm feeling okay, but I should be feeling much stronger after doing light training. I don't feel as good as I thought I would.'

This was the final warning for me. I made a decision that I was not going to sit back any longer. I knew without a doubt that we were dealing with something more serious. I needed to follow my instincts and take this further. I contacted a physician friend, Verena Ballhausen, to ask her advice. I felt that David was not capable of stepping back and looking at Lawrence as a patient, rather than as his son and a world-class athlete. Verena looked at the results and I discussed the history with her.

She agreed. 'Danielle, I am not happy with these results. We need to exclude something more serious.'

The investigations were booked for the next day. I did not want to wait another moment. I felt strangely relieved to know we were going to do some conclusive tests. David had a pre-booked conference in Cypress and had left the night before. He was anxious about going, but I encouraged him as I know and understand the work he does and how rapidly the research and knowledge base increases. It is a highly researched field and he needs to keep up with developments as much as possible. The conference he was to attend was a workshop on lymphoma with the European Bone Marrow Transplant Working Group. I also did not want to alarm Lawrence too much, so I just casually mentioned that we needed to do a few more intensive tests to see what was going on. If David had cancelled his trip it would have made Lawrence overly worried.

I told the coaches that things looked concerning and I needed to do further tests, which would involve a scan and a bone marrow biopsy. I was anxious and they knew it.

'It's going to be okay, Doc. Everything will be fine. I am sure they will find nothing,' said AJ, with kindness and reassurance.

'Stay in touch with us, Doc,' Roger said. He always felt I was right in my clinical opinion and always backed me. He was concerned because he knew I was worried.

I knew before the results of any tests that it was not okay.

10

REALITY

Pretoria, 2014

With casual brutality, illness reminds us of the limits of human will [...]
In my body something was afoot; there had been treachery within the
citadel. Quietly an alien force crept in, overwhelming the loyal defenders,
taking and holding the positions of strength.

– ANNA LYNDSEY, *GIRL IN THE DARK*

The next 48 hours happened fast and were a whirlwind of tests as I tried to establish the truth, to chase it down as quickly as possible. I went into full-scale efficiency mode and arranged everything. David had left for Cypress the night before, for the lymphoma conference.

The tests were all scheduled at Pretoria East Hospital, where David works. It was almost with relief that we drove there. I could sense it in Lawrence; he needed to know the truth now and it felt right to be delving fully into this.

He first had the CT scan, and then he went for the bone marrow biopsy. It was to be done in David's rooms by Dr Theo Gerdener, one of David's colleagues.

'Should I give Lawrence Dormicum?' Theo asked. Dormicum is a medication often used for its sedative and amnesic affects during unpleasant procedures. It is known as conscious sedation, and removes the memory of a painful and unpleasant procedure.

'Treat him as if he were any one of your patients. What would you normally do?' I asked.

'I would give the medication.'

'Give it, then. It is the right thing.'

I was struggling to keep perspective and needed to try to remember that Lawrence should not be treated any differently from the thousands of other people who presented to the practice, were worked up, investigated, diagnosed and then treated. Medical staff often make the mistake of treating medically trained patients or their families differently, thinking they know more than they actually do. I have learnt over the years that it is best to treat a medically trained patient in the same way as you would any other patient. In this way, well-devised systems are followed and correct protocols adopted.

I did not want to watch Lawrence have the bone marrow biopsy but I did not want to leave him either. He was remarkably calm and brave. I suppose if it is possible to bear the pain of an ergo trial or race, a bone marrow biopsy is entirely possible and manageable, just different. I could not make it any easier for him. As he went in to have the procedure, I received a telephone call from the radiology department, asking for me to come back to the department. I walked there alone, heavy-hearted and afraid. This was not a good sign. I knew deep within me that they were going to give me bad news. I braced myself to face the pain, ready to hear the worst, but hoping fervently that I was wrong. What else could I do?

'I did not want to just send out a report. I wanted to tell you myself what I am seeing here,' the radiologist said as gently as she could.

I was grateful for her concern and kindness. I sat down in front of the screen and she flashed up Lawrence's scan. I was shaking and scared.

'I am afraid it is not good news. He has massive thoracic and abdominal lymphadenopathy.' Lymphadenopathy means enlarged lymph nodes or glands. 'He is packed with enlarged lymph nodes and I am worried that this is likely to be a lymphoma.' She pointed out the areas of concern.

I was shocked by what I was seeing. 'I don't understand, I examined him

from head to toe repeatedly and there were no lymph nodes.' I faltered in
shock, holding back the tears.

'Well, the strange thing is that there are very few superficial glands,' she
continued. 'It has affected the deep areas and unfortunately the spleen is
also involved.'

She could see I was struggling and she became very compassionate. 'I
am so sorry. This cannot be easy for you, but I know this is not good, this
does not look good. We will need to identify a superficial gland for surgical
removal, so once he has had the bone marrow test please bring Lawrence
back for an ultrasound examination so I can mark a place for the surgeon
to work.'

I could see things were happening fast and I needed to get moving. I
could not fall apart now; I had to be strong for Lawrence and sort out
a plan of action. I had to get back to him and see whether he had managed to get through the bone marrow test. I could not arrive hysterical and
upset. I needed to be as collected and strong as possible, holding my feelings calmly together. All my training in palliative care seemed completely
applicable and vital now. I had learnt how to hold myself together, perfectly calm in the midst of families and patients crashing apart in misery
and grief. In those situations I had to hold back my own private feelings
of distress because those families and patients needed me to be calm and
strong, and to guide them. When you are in that position, you hold the
patient's distress – the patient must not be further burdened with yours. I
managed to contain my rising shock and panic and walked bravely back to
Lawrence, terrified of what he would ask me, not knowing how I was going
to deal with his questions.

I telephoned David as soon as I was outside the radiology department.
He had landed that morning in Cypress ready to attend the working group
meeting on the very illness with which his own son might now be diagnosed. It seemed almost ridiculously ironic.

'David, it is not looking good. The radiologists say that Lawrence is
packed with lymph nodes and it looks like lymphoma. Theo is doing the

bone marrow right now. This is just awful, I cannot believe what they have just told me.' I was in shock and struggling to be coherent and clear.

David was angry that I had been given a likely diagnosis. His mind was working fast. 'What size are those glands? It is not possible for Lawrence to have lymphoma. The guy has just raced at World Champs,' he kept saying. 'They cannot give you a diagnosis based on the scan. It is a tissue diagnosis and we need a biopsy of one of the glands. It could be generalised TB as an infection. This is still the most likely scenario. Please take those scans to Andrew. I want him to have a look at them. I trust what he has to say. I will phone him and tell him you are bringing them.'

He became more businesslike as we spoke. I knew he was extremely stressed and was trying to remain calm and think clearly. It has never been easy being the doctor and the parent. It was awful for him being far away. I knew this would cause him massive worry and distress.

I was numb, trying to keep myself thinking clearly. I did what David asked and took the CT scans to another of his colleagues, Dr Andrew Macdonald, who viewed them calmly.

'Andrew, the radiologists say it is likely to be lymphoma. David is having a fit that they have told me this and he wants you to look at these and give an opinion on them,' I said as he took me into the boardroom away from the busyness of the afternoon practice. 'I do not know what to say except that this is shocking news as Lawrence wants to go to the Olympics and how this will all fit in with his plans I have no idea. He cannot be sick,' I stupidly blurted out, as if that was the most important thing.

Andrew raised his eyebrows at my comment. Later, I wondered what he must have thought at that moment when I was worrying about the Olympic Games while Lawrence might have a life-threatening disease. For anyone not involved in sport at that level, it is illogical, almost ridiculous. But for someone trying to make it to that level, it is exactly the opposite: it is everything.

Andrew probably thought, *What a pushy, overbearing mother.*

Andrew studied the scans and asked me, 'What has been going on with

Lawrence recently? How has he been?'

Looking back, I realise what a position we had put Andrew in at that moment. He had to deal with me on one side, tearful and in shock, looking for immediate answers and almost begging him to tell me it was okay and that this was an infection. On the other side, he was dealing with David wanting confirmation that the radiologists were likely to be mistaken. Andrew had not seen Lawrence, and neither taken a history nor examined him. He had just been presented with a scan and asked to comment.

He took his time, and eventually picked his words carefully. I had the sense that he gathered himself into the moment to try to contain my rising anxiety. 'Look, Danielle, these are fairly significant lymph nodes,' he hedged. 'We will need a biopsy to be sure of what we are dealing with. From the scan it is not possible to say what is causing this. We need to arrange a lymph node biopsy as soon as possible.'

I was devastated, trying to keep control. I found myself pacing up and down, trying to get my head around the possibility that Lawrence was very ill. The pacing calmed me and stopped me from running away.

At that moment, Theo called me as he had finished the bone marrow test. Lawrence came out and fortunately he was doped and laughing. I was relieved. It meant I could avoid speaking about the diagnosis, and could skirt around any questions he might ask. I knew I was unable to tell him the most likely truth at that moment as I would have broken down and upset him terribly. Theo told me he had taken a good specimen of bone marrow, which would be processed as soon as possible.

'So, Mom,' Lawrence giggled. 'What's up? What have they found?'

I joined him, laughing slightly hysterically. He has always had a very good sense of humour and I was happy to use it, along with the medication effect, as a way out of dealing with a difficult conversation. We giggled and laughed at everything we came across, which helped ease the constricting pain in my chest.

'They have found some enlarged lymph glands inside you that need to be checked out. We need to remove one of them so that we can see what is causing them to react in this way,' I explained vaguely to Lawrence. He nodded his head and then roared with laughter. The news was not registering with him.

I was now fairly calm in the crisis and managed to get Lawrence back to the radiologists for a sonar to identify a lymph node for surgical removal. This was rapidly arranged; within an hour he had seen the surgeon, Dr Michael Heyns, and been booked to have the procedure the following day. The medical staff we had dealt with in this short space of time had been incredible to us and I was grateful for their individual input.

I wanted things to happen fast as I could not bear the waiting. We needed answers now.

Back home, I had to let the boys know about the tests. I explained that Lawrence had enlarged lymph nodes but that we needed the biopsy before we could say conclusively what we were dealing with. I did not want to say much more as we really did not have a formal diagnosis. I was emotionally exhausted and finding it distressing to talk to anyone. My mind was racing ahead, trying to imagine what the future held for Lawrence. Calls were coming in, with people asking what had happened, and I was in no position to give answers except to say that we were in the process of making a diagnosis.

I had a difficult and emotional conversation with Roger explaining the various possibilities. I asked him to explain the situation to AJ but not to say anything to the athletes until there was a formal diagnosis.

Lawrence was admitted to hospital early the next morning and had the biopsy of his lymph node. Despite the anxiety, there was an inexplicable sense of relief that we were at last moving closer to the truth. As soon as he was able to walk and had recovered from the anaesthetic, I took him home. He seemed relaxed and comfortable.

David made the decision to come home as soon as he knew the CT scan findings. He had arrived in Cypress in the morning and, after our conversation, he had booked to come straight back that evening. He arrived home at the same time as Lawrence and I drove into our driveway from the hospital. He was upset, but still very much in denial and wanting proof of the disease.

'No one with a malignancy could have rowed to fifth place at World Championships,' he just kept saying. He was afraid and, I could see, puzzled by this possibility.

David was not looking at the reality that Lawrence was supposed to have medalled at that event and that fifth place was a relative underachievement. He was also not fully acknowledging how extraordinarily strong Lawrence is both mentally and physically. It had never been in Lawrence's mental athletic make-up to contemplate illness. Lawrence's entire cognitive programming is to work harder when things do not go well. He has never been one to allow things to slip away from him. Until this point, he had assumed that he was just not working hard enough. There is something admirable and unique in this. It shows his strength of character and an outstanding degree of mental stamina that he did not simply give it all up and walk away. He is a fighter and a warrior of the highest calibre.

Once we had Lawrence home and resting after his operation, David and I could talk more seriously. It was clear that he needed proof of the diagnosis so I suggested we go back to the hospital to review the findings. He agreed. He needed to be more clinical and less emotional in his approach to the diagnosis; more of a doctor and less of a parent.

He went to see the radiologists himself and spent some time with them, going through the scans and assessing the severity. After that, he went to the laboratory with Theo where the pathologists were reviewing the bone marrow and the lymph node biopsy slides. He looked at them himself. Being a clinical haematologist, this process was routine for him. He sees thousands of patients with such conditions. But this time, it was different. This was his son. Lawrence now likely had the same illness as many, many others, and this was profoundly hard for David. At the same time, though, there was the enormous practicality of the situation calling for a diagnosis and a systematic approach to the illness. This process and structured approach was both helpful and calming to us.

I waited patiently for David until he had seen enough to make a diagnosis for himself and finally acknowledge that Lawrence was ill. I was expecting the worst and had been quietly trying to prepare myself. He came out looking exhausted and drawn.

'I know what is happening. I know the truth. It is not good,' he said softly. 'Lawrence has Hodgkin lymphoma. Unfortunately, he has Stage 4 disease as it has attacked the bone marrow and is in the spleen. It is unbelievable to think he has such an advanced illness. I simply cannot believe it. I do not know how this happened.'

Lawrence had cancer.

For the third time in my life I faced that word, that world of shock and fear. This time it was far worse. This was my son.

Even though I had suspected that it was serious and had repeatedly told myself that Lawrence was ill, I still felt unprepared for the truth. I realised later how impossible it is to be emotionally prepared for such grave and chilling words about someone as close as your own child. I could feel the pain and grief welling up like a tidal wave after a terrible earthquake. As David delivered the diagnosis to me, I was acutely aware of a searing pain etching itself onto my soul. I was bleeding. There are some things that remain burned onto your very core, forever. The same illness I had had more than 30 years ago. 'No, please no, please do not allow this to happen. Let this happen to me, rather. Why him?' I moaned out loud to David, to God, to the world, begging and bargaining. 'How is this possible? Why does he have to go through this? Not Lawrence.'

Powerful memories flooded back to me at that moment. Clear images of my parents around me after my staging laparotomy at 15 for exactly the same illness. I was being wheeled back from theatre in a nightmare of sedation and pain. I was crying. I could see my mother in her red coat, deeply distressed at the horrifying level of my pain, walking next to the gurney, trying to calm me. My father was on the other side, begging God to let him take the suffering from me. Now, I was no longer the child, I was the mother. It was me begging God to let me take the suffering from Lawrence.

It has to be one of the most profound, fundamental and natural instincts for a parent to want to protect their children from pain and suffering. It was an equally profound and excruciating reality that I could not take it from him.

He would have to bear it himself. And I would have to stand by and bear witness to it.

It all fell into place, like the last few pieces of a difficult jigsaw puzzle. The long period of unexplained episodes of fatigue, the continual infections, the decrease in performance, the weakening blood picture, Lawrence's comment about the Boat Race being the hardest race of his life, the fact that he did not feel stronger after light training. I thought back to the blood tests taken after Boat Race and how he had managed to work that hard in the boat despite his weak blood parameters. All these facts that had seemed so vague before now made perfect sense. The image of him working harder in the boat and not understanding why it continued to feel so bad evoked my tears. He must have screamed out in silent frustration about why things felt so laboured, despite how hard he was working. This picture will remain with me forever. Despite how painful it is to contemplate, it is the image of a true warrior with the heart of a lion, a magnificent beast who never gives up.

David and I were crying, the two of us sitting in the car not sure how to proceed and where to go but knowing at that moment how unpredictable and fragile life can be. We stopped at a shop to get a few groceries. It seemed such a futile, meaningless and unimportant chore, but it gave us purpose at a moment when nothing around us made any sense at all.

I phoned my sister Claudine and broke down. 'Claud, Lawrence is ill. He has been diagnosed with Hodgkin lymphoma and is in Stage 4.' The shock and grief poured out of me as I tried to explain it to her. Talking about it and answering her questions in an ordered way eased the terrible searing pain slightly, allowing me to breathe.

'What are you telling me? I am so sorry. I cannot believe this. How has this happened? Is it genetic that he has it now after you had it?' she asked, distressed and shocked.

'No, it is not genetic. It is a cruel random blow from somewhere out there. I do not know why this has happened but he must have had it for a few years already. How does it strike a family twice? And how will he go to the Olympics? That is all he has ever wanted. I cannot bear that he has to suffer with this.'

Hodgkin lymphoma's cause is unknown. It is not genetically linked. It peaks in people in their 20s, and again in people over the age of 55. There are geographical clusters of the disease and it has been linked to viruses such as Epstein-Barr (the virus that causes glandular fever) and the human immunodeficiency virus (HIV). Whatever its cause, it results in a DNA change in certain white blood cells known as lymphocytes, resulting in the formation of abnormal cancer cells. These cancerous lymphocytes continue to behave like any other cancer cell, growing and spreading in an uncontrolled way, slowly replacing normal tissue with malignant cells.

I did not want to think about what the cancer was doing and how far it had spread.

I managed to ask Claudine to help me with the painful task of telling the rest of the family. I did not have the energy or strength to tell my father, my siblings, my friends that things had gone horribly and inextricably wrong for Lawrence.

David and I were trying to make sense of the situation.

'Why?' I asked. 'Are you serious that this is Stage 4? How did this happen? How long has he had this?'

'I just do not know. Maybe two years, maybe a little more,' David said, his voice flat.

'I knew there was a problem. I was not happy. I felt something was wrong and now I am told it's Stage 4. This is shocking and inexplicable.' I was starting to rage. Like a river held back, I could feel my anger rising. I wanted to blame someone. I wanted to scream out my frustration and pain at someone, release the hurt and shock, claw my way clear of this. I wanted to scream out to God and space, 'No! Take this from me. Do not give me this. I do not want this. It is not fair! I can bear that I have had cancer twice, but not my child.' It would have been easy to blame someone, anyone – David, telling him he should have listened to me, but in the end I understood him perfectly and what had held him back. I was angry with myself. Why had I not followed my own instincts earlier and pursued the nagging worry? Why did I still not trust myself enough? What was still holding me back, after all these years? I raged on, howling out my despair and fear.

David was quiet.

'What will happen now, David? How do we go on?' I demanded. I was frantic now. I needed a plan, I needed answers, I needed something to guide me during the next few days.

I had worked with dying patients for years and understood what Stage 4 meant. No one survives Stage 4. It is always too late, and the cancer always wins.

David became calmer and more systematic as he settled into a practical approach and could speak as a medical professional who treated this type of cancer on a continuous basis. 'We can cure this, Danielle,' he gently reassured me.

'How can you be so sure? This is Stage 4. I had Stage 1. This is another diagnosis altogether.'

'Hodgkin lymphoma is curable, even Stage 4. I will refer him to Jackie Thompson, as I cannot treat him. It would not be right, I am too emotionally involved to treat him. I know what treatment he needs but I cannot do it. I have already discussed it with her, as well as with Andrew and Theo, and we know what Lawrence needs.'

'Please tell me what is going to happen. Is he going to have a bone marrow transplant?'

'No, he does not need a transplant now. We want to give him high-dose chemotherapy. He is going to be okay, Danielle. We will cure him.'

His words were comforting. I was falling apart but at the same time I knew how resilient I was, how strong David and I were together. We could do this. Our family was good in a crisis; we would manage this.

But before we could get to that stage, we had a far more difficult task ahead of us.

My overwhelming and immediate concern was how we were going to tell Lawrence and witness his dreams smashing around him. I wanted to protect him from this, but I was effectively powerless and knew that we had to follow the path that had opened up in front of us. We had to go through it. Suddenly the memory of the delightful children's book *We're Going on a Bear Hunt* by Michael Rosen came to me and made perfect sense at that moment. It tells a story of the obstacles in a little family's path, and how they could not go over them or under them – they just had to go through them.

We could not avoid what was before us. We had to go through it. Right now we had to tell Lawrence, and explain to him how, in two days, the journey of his life had suddenly become more threatening.

Each day that we live has its own degree of happiness and suffering. It is an internal, private scale that moves according to the events of the day, like a seismometer. That day, the tracing was off the graph paper. It could not capture the extent of the moment that was rocking my world. To tell my own child that he had an advanced disease, that the illness had been secretly growing in him for a few years, was harder and more poignant than any other time I have had to break bad news to someone. Being a palliative care doctor, there had been many of those times. How could we explain that his life would not be the same again – certainly for a while, and maybe forever? We did not know.

Lawrence got up when he heard us return. He had slept off the anaesthetic and was feeling relatively well. The pain was under control and he was eager to talk to us. He knew that we would have information as we had been gone for a long time.

'What's up, parents? Have you got any results?' he asked in his inimitably funny way. We sat down in the lounge, quietly, trying to contain our dread and fear.

I tried to ease our way into the difficult answer. 'We know what is happening now. We've been at the hospital, and Dad has reviewed everything.

They have looked at your bone marrow and the lymph node, and things are quite serious. Unfortunately it is not an infection, it is not TB or anything like that. We are so sorry to have to tell you this, but you have a type of cancer called Hodgkin lymphoma.'

'Cancer!' Lawrence was visibly shocked. This diagnosis had never come up in any of our discussions. 'What are you telling me?'

He started to cry and buried his head in his hands, sinking down, his world crumbling as the word started to register. It was terrible for us to watch his shock. We tried to comfort him. We felt helpless and wretched as we witnessed Lawrence's world breaking apart.

'Cancer,' he repeated. 'What does this mean?'

David began, 'This is treatable, Law. You need special treatment. You need chemotherapy. We can treat this. This cancer can be cured. It responds well to chemotherapy.'

Like a drowning person flung a lifebuoy, Lawrence flipped into action. 'What do I need to do? Tell me what I need to do. I need to get rid of this. I need to kill this thing. I need to be strong again. Tell me what I must do.'

Just as a race requires a race plan, so Lawrence needed a plan for the illness. He wanted to know how to attack the illness with a structured but deadly assault.

'You will be unable to train for a while and will need to give absolutely everything to the process of treatment. The treatment is a specific regimen of high-dose chemotherapy. You will see and be treated by my partner Jackie Thompson. We will see her tomorrow.'

'Am I going to be okay? Can I die from this?' he asked bravely. Brave questions deserve brave answers and they must always be answered.

'If we left the disease alone and did not treat it, yes, you would die from it. But we will not do that, so the answer is no, you are not going to die,' said David gently but firmly. 'Hodgkin lymphoma is 90 per cent curable, and we plan to cure you with chemotherapy. The treatment will more than likely knock you down flat but you will get back up again. We will treat this.' David's words were reassuring and calm.

'How did I get this? How long have I had it? Why have I got the same thing as you had, Mom? Why is this happening?' He was asking a lot of questions, trying to make sense of the shock, trying to sort through and tidy the mess a little, putting it into perspective, into small, manageable pieces to be managed and dealt with separately, little by little.

'How bad is it?' he asked, afraid.

'It has attacked your lymph glands and this has weakened you,' David said calmly. 'The disease has unfortunately spread to other areas of your body and we need to stop this process as soon as possible. It has spread into your bone marrow and spleen. The disease is staged according to how far it has spread and in your case it has spread to distant areas. This makes it Stage 4, which means that the cancer has spread well beyond the area where it originally started. Hodgkin lymphoma usually spreads very contiguously and systematically, and it is a late manifestation that you have it in your spleen and bone marrow. It has been growing quietly in you for a while. We are going to need to do further tests to see if it is anywhere else.'

Lawrence quickly grasped the concept that he would be unable to train during treatment. We were grateful for this. 'If stopping training will help me get rid of this, I am happy to do that. I must get well, I want to be strong again,' he repeated urgently. 'I will do whatever you tell me to do. I have been unwell now for so long that I am happy to have the chance to get better.'

This rapidly became his plan: he pledged his commitment to the process of getting well again. There was never any doubt within him that he would recover and be back to race again.

In a strange, reassuring way, there was relief to have a diagnosis, as there had been many times when I had wondered whether I was imagining a problem. For Lawrence, it was finally some validation of his erratic symptoms. There was now a clear cause of his declining performance and for Lawrence that meant one thing: if the cause could be cured, he could be fast again. He had not reached his ceiling. The treatment plan gave him hope and purpose.

For me it reinforced the fact that my instincts are often correct and I needed to learn to trust them. I let others take the lead too easily, which usually throws me off my instinctive path. It was a strong message to me.

That afternoon David and I spoke to our boys, each one handling the news in a different way, each one trying to swallow the bitterness and make sense of the shock. James was quiet, containing the shockwave by asking many, many questions. Charles was anxious and panicked, worrying what it meant for Lawrence, and trying to find out more about the treatment. Matthew broke down. 'I cannot believe this is happening to Lawrence. Why does he have to go through this?'

The connotations of the word 'cancer' are horrible. Hearing that word close to us, right within the circle of our family, felt like a death sentence handed down in court. The brothers were all afraid, just as we were. They did not want Lawrence to suffer or to have to walk this harrowing path.

Later that evening Lawrence's girlfriend Nicky Mundell arrived from Johannesburg in tears. My heart went out to her, facing a rough path ahead with a partner who was ill, far sicker than any of us had thought. 'That night, the first day of the diagnosis, was the most vulnerable I have ever seen Lawrence,' she told me later.

We huddled together as a family that night, talking and trying to make sense of it, piecing it all together. This was an attack we had not expected. We needed to gather ourselves against the assault, and present a unified strong defence. We would do what we could to protect and defend Lawrence during his battle. As parents, we naturally wanted to protect and defend our child, and so did the brotherhood. They were strong and close. Nicky knew she could be strong for Lawrence, a support without which Lawrence would not be able to manage.

Lawrence became the priority for all of us. In our own ways we knew we would look after him and carry him through this time.

We also all knew that Lawrence himself was strong – stronger than even he knew.

Later, I phoned Roger to clarify the situation. He was anxiously awaiting the confirmation of what we had spoken about the night before. This was shocking news for the coaches and the entire support team. Athletes are fit, strong and healthy. Athletes race and win. Becoming seriously ill is outside the conventional paradigm of an athlete. The coaches all had long-standing relationships with Lawrence, so he was more than an athlete in some ways. They cared. When I called Jimmy Clark, he was shocked and devastated. 'I don't know what to say, Danielle. I cannot imagine what you are going through.'

We were all going through a private hell. But we could not allow ourselves to lie wounded. We needed to defend Lawrence. To stand up and fight.

The next day, we rolled into action.

Lawrence, David and I went in to David's practice to see Jackie Thompson, David's haematologist partner and colleague. David was now on the other side; he wanted Jackie to be the doctor, to take control. She drew the situation together into a logical course of action. She enjoyed seeing Lawrence and was good with him, explaining the chemotherapy, the process, the side effects, all that he could expect. Jackie is quite a quirky doctor with a solid sense of humour and the ability to be thorough and efficient while chatting and getting to the bottom of problems.

She reassured us enormously. 'This disease will be eradicated after two cycles of chemotherapy,' she explained. I found that hard to believe, but she was not joking. It is not something you would joke about.

David had spoken to Jackie before our meeting with Lawrence. 'How can this be happening to my son?'

Her answer: 'You have dedicated your life to knowing and treating these illnesses. Now you can treat your son. Maybe this is the purpose.'

Lawrence had to have a positron emission tomography (PET) scan before he could start treatment. A PET scan is effectively two scans in one. Radiolabelled sugar is injected into the individual. Malignant tissue metabolises rapidly, and the first scan picks up where the radioactive sugar has been used. The second scan is a straight CT scan, giving the anatomical detail of the exact area where the radioactive sugar has been used. Any tissue that is rapidly metabolising will show up on the scan.

Until this point, the bone marrow biopsy had been the worst test and the rest had been manageable. The PET scan changed that. It was one of the hardest tests for Lawrence. It required very specific preparation, making it quite an effort. The preparation included specific dietary changes for 24 hours before the test: no carbohydrates, no caffeine, no alcohol. The latter two were easy; the carbohydrates took a lot more discipline. Lawrence had to drink a contrast solution just before the scan and then lie dead still without moving while the contrast spread through his body.

That sounds relatively manageable. Until you know how long the scan will take.

Two hours.

It was torture for Lawrence, as it is probably torture for most people. We are simply not wired to be that still for so long. Nevertheless, the PET scan is a very accurate way of assessing the extent of active malignant disease. David, Nicky and I waited outside while poor Lawrence was stuck in there. Although we knew that Lawrence had Stage 4 lymphoma, we knew we still needed to assess the full extent of the spread. The PET scan would provide this information. It was a stressful time for us as we sat outside, on edge.

After what seemed like forever, the radiologists called us in. They knew David well as he had referred many patients to them, and between them they had discussed countless patients over the phone. They were anxious and nervous, unsure how much we knew about the extent of the diagnosis. They had the scans displayed for us, and they tentatively approached them to explain the severity of the disease. They were concerned and kind, worried about how to tell us. We put them at ease: 'We know the diagnosis and we have a plan of treatment. The important thing is to see if it has spread anywhere else. This has been a difficult time and devastating for Lawrence to go through this.'

The PET scan showed advanced disease. Even though we knew it had spread significantly, it was a further shock for us to actually see the scans.

There was lymph node involvement in the chest, abdomen, pelvis, neck and axilla. There were multiple lesions in his spleen and the disease had spread into a number of bones, namely three vertebrae, several ribs, the pelvis and the femur.

I felt things could not get worse from this point. I was giving way to fear. Doubt flooded my thoughts. How do you fight such advanced disease? How do you win? It was difficult to see that this was potentially curable, to remember Jackie's words, 'We will eradicate this in two cycles.'

But strength prevailed. It was imperative for me, for David, for our family to keep our spirit and morale buoyant. We needed to believe that curing this was possible. We needed to help Lawrence be a warrior now, to give this his best shot. To don his armour, pick up his shield and weapon, and stand against this onslaught. Somewhere deep in me the familiar thought of having no second chances resonated uncomfortably. Now, more than ever before, I needed to be strong and believe in this one perfectly aimed defensive shot.

Large, matted areas of malignant lymph nodes showed up black on the scan, along with similar areas in the spleen and bones. Being organs that require a constant supply of glucose, the heart and brain also showed up pitch black on the scan. When I showed the pictures of the PET scan to the boys, James's dry and dark sense of humour surfaced and he commented, 'You see, Lawrence has nothing but a black hole where his heart and brain should be.' We roared with laughter; it is always good to see the funny side of grim and painful reality.

Lawrence required a few other baseline investigations before he could start the chemotherapy. He needed full lung diffusion tests to assess his lung function. Some of the chemotherapy could cause lung damage and a deterioration would be important to document, especially as he planned on returning to training. At that stage, we were going along with his firm conviction that he would return to his life of training and racing. In truth, we had no idea how the chemotherapy would affect him and whether it would be possible to even get in a boat and row again, let alone train as an elite athlete. He also needed a cardiac sonar or echocardiogram to assess his heart, as one of the drugs can result in damage to the heart muscle.

He had one other personal thing he needed to do. The chemotherapy drugs he would soon be having work by attacking and killing any cells that divide rapidly. Malignant cancer cells are their main target, but they can attack any rapidly dividing cells, such as hair cells. As a consequence, patients lose their hair. One of the other cells that come under attack are the cells that make sperm. If these are damaged sufficiently, they stop making sperm, which results in permanent sterility. We could not allow this to happen. As was standard practice, Lawrence had to give specimens of semen to freeze for later use if he wanted to have children. These were some of the many issues he had to face at an age when most young people are enjoying their lives, choosing careers, travelling, and searching for themselves and what they want from life. Most of them are not concerned about whether they will be able to have a child in years to come. It was easy to see how much we take for granted in life and how oblivious we are to the fine line between life running smoothly and crashing aground.

On the eve of Lawrence starting chemotherapy, I sat down and wrote a general email to our family and friends as I did not have the reserves of energy to speak to so many people individually. I needed to conserve my energy for Lawrence. Claudine had already spoken to many people, getting the word out, which had been an enormous help to me.

It was moving for me to write the email confirming the situation, and explaining the treatment and how it would affect Lawrence. It was the best I could do.

To our dearest Family and Friends

Following our devastating news last week, we have been touched and overwhelmed by the messages and calls coming through to us from everyone and the concern shown to Lawrence and our family.

At this stage of things, we want to keep you informed of developments as it has not been possible to speak to most of you.

Last week we found out that Lawrence, despite being young and strong and really well, has Hodgkin lymphoma and unfortunately is in an advanced stage. It is a very responsive tumour so there is a strong belief (90%) that this will be completely cured and that is what is being planned.

We are wrestling with this and supporting him through his own process of coming to terms with the diagnosis, its treatment and the implications of these. We are strengthened in this by an incredibly supportive family, close friends and a groundswell of sincere goodwill from our broader work and social community. We are privileged to have enormous resources at our disposal, by which I mean a medical team and community with a wealth of knowledge, expertise and infrastructure. This brings confidence and the reassurance that we are able to offer the best for Lawrence.

Lawrence will start chemotherapy this week in three-week cycles and at this stage is scheduled for six of those cycles. The road ahead will be tough at times especially as Lawrence is unable to do what he loves most for the duration of the treatment and that is to row. He is a very strong person mentally and physically and this will stand him in good stead now as he faces this part of his journey in life. He has shown great strength of character this week and we are extremely proud of him.

We have fought this fight before and with all of your help, we will fight it again. We will fight it in the only way we know, on every front, to win.

We thank you for your sincere support and good wishes and we are sorry we haven't responded to each message directly.

Keep Lawrence in your thoughts and prayers.

It was remarkable that, within five days of the decision to do further investigations, we had a formal, accurate diagnosis, had seen a haematologist, and had a full-blown six-month treatment plan in place. The full armada of machinery for treating Lawrence was warming up. We felt more in control now; the shock had settled into spaces within us where it was slightly more manageable and bearable. We had a plan and could break up the next six months into smaller, more tolerable pieces.

We all knew what needed to be done. We were ready to help our warrior.

Lawrence had committed himself fully to this process. This time, the fight would be on a different battleground. He was armouring up to fight as hard as he needed to: in his mind, with absolute certainty, were the knowledge and belief that he was going to win this battle.

11

TREATMENT

Pretoria, 2014

Everything can be taken from a man but one thing: the last of human
freedoms – to choose one's attitude in any given set of circumstances,
to choose one's own way.

– VIKTOR E FRANKL, *MAN'S SEARCH FOR MEANING*

At the time of his diagnosis, Lawrence was living with James at Sable Hills. I felt it was best for him to move back into our home in Muckleneuk for the duration of his treatment. He needed the security of being closer to us. We all trekked out to Sable Hills for the weekends and he came with us. Nicky visited him as much as possible. She was living and working in Johannesburg so she came through whenever she could, but knowing we were able to care for Lawrence was a big relief for her.

Lawrence's chemotherapy treatment regimen, specifically for Hodgkin lymphoma, was known as escalated BEACOPP, named as an anagram of the drugs used – bleomycin, etoposide, adriamycin, cyclophosphamide, oncovin, procarbazine and prednisone. This regimen was well researched and documented in the medical literature, and both Jackie and David had decided on the escalated regimen as opposed to the standard BEACOPP regimen because Lawrence had characteristics of high-risk illness. He was young, male and at Stage 4. This meant he had a slightly higher risk of recurrence than someone without those risk factors.

Lawrence began his journey into the world of chemotherapy on Tuesday 21 October 2014. It started with a test dose of bleomycin to establish whether he was allergic to it. The allergy could be potentially life-threatening and is associated with worse side effects in the lung. This was a definite concern. That Lawrence was an athlete made it critical to preserve as much lung function as possible. It was important that Lawrence was carefully managed with this in mind. The doctors could plan around him training again because his prognosis was good.

He started his first cycle the following day.

From that moment on he became part of the 'chemo circle', a select, special group of people all sporting intravenous (IV) lines and bags of IV fluids in various colours and sizes, slowly dripping potent, toxic medication into their veins to fight aberrant cancer cells. They were all treated in the Chemo Room, a bright, sunny room with large windows offering beautiful views of the surrounding Pretoria suburbs. Many in this group were bald or wore headscarves. Some looked extremely ill, while others worked on their laptops and had driven themselves there. There was a mix of ages, just as there was varying support from family and friends.

While they waited for the bags of drugs to empty into their veins, the group tried to relax, feet up, on comfortable leather recliners placed all around the room. There was a good atmosphere in the Chemo Room, although it was somewhat subdued, with an underlying anxiety. It was well organised, with competent, friendly nursing staff on duty and a perfect mixture of professionalism and compassion.

I tried to go with Lawrence to all his chemo days. On the days I could not be there, Nicky was able to arrange time off work and be with him. We did not want him alone for these sessions. I sat with him, chatting if he was up to it, or reading and working if he was not.

Lawrence fitted in to his situation easily. He was a pleasant, easy-going patient. The staff warmed to him immediately. He formed bonds easily, and everyone enjoyed him. He also came with some unique characteristics. Firstly, he was the boss's son. The staff were anxious to please and do well.

Secondly, he was an elite athlete. This put him into his own category as most of the patients were far from that – many were holding on as best they could. Thirdly, he was young, and although many haematological malignancies affect younger people it is still relatively unusual to be 23 years old and receiving high-dose chemotherapy. And lastly, he was such a pleasant, good-natured guy. He has always had the enviable trait of giving people the best chance by automatically thinking the best of them. As a result, he is a lot less judgemental than most of us. The staff loved him. The nursing sister who took his blood had a soft spot for him and baked brownies for him every time he came to have blood taken or to have chemotherapy. Being an athlete, he also had magnificent veins, and the nurses appreciated how easy it was to insert IV lines into him. Athletes are always proud of their veins and are delighted when they show up easily in their arms as they become fitter and leaner in their training programme. There is a sort of unwritten competition between athletes about who has the biggest veins. Lawrence never posed difficulties for the staff in this regard.

If all went well, the chemotherapy regimen of six cycles spaced three weeks apart would result in his being treated for four to five months. Days one, two, three and eight of each cycle entailed a trip to the hospital to the Chemo Room. One day we were there for eight hours. He never once complained, despite feeling exhausted after the chemo sessions. He had to take oral treatment from days one to fourteen – fistfuls of cortisone pills, among others. All the drugs were designed to attack his bone marrow, trying to stop the malignant cells from dividing too quickly and outstripping cellular division of normal cells. The chemo would stop the malignant cells from taking over normal bone marrow function.

Malignant cells are anarchists – they do whatever they want, and cannot be controlled. They divide rapidly and effectively. Hodgkin cells divide in a strange and orderly way, causing very specific cellular changes that can be identified under the microscope. The disease was named after the British physician and pathologist Dr Thomas Hodgkin. Hodgkin cells cause an inflammatory reaction in normal cells, causing them to expand in size, resulting in the characteristically enlarged lymph glands. The tumour burden is often all in the lymph nodes, before it spills over into other areas such as the spleen, liver, bone marrow, lungs and brain. It is almost as if the cancer cells are feeding themselves to healthy cells, and so causing a reaction. The drugs try to stop this process by stopping the anarchy and re-establishing some modicum of natural order.

Human bone marrow is responsible for making all the blood cells the body needs: the white and red blood cells, as well as platelets. When these are knocked out, it causes side effects because important blood cells are now in short supply. This is effectively what the chemotherapy was doing. Besides launching an attack on the malignant cells, it was also attacking normal function of the bone marrow, stopping normal blood cells from being produced. If red cells are low, the patient becomes anaemic and may need blood transfusions. If white cells decrease, the patient becomes neutropenic, and therefore highly susceptible and vulnerable to infection. Neutropenia is an abnormally low level of neutrophils, a type of white blood cell that is important for fighting infection. If platelets are low, it causes bleeding problems, which can be dangerous. Lawrence's blood was closely watched. If the cell count dropped too low, he would be unable to have the next cycle of chemotherapy and would have to wait for the blood picture to settle.

He rested without drugs for the last seven days of each cycle while his bone marrow struggled to recover from the onslaught of toxic drugs.

Friends would visit him in the Chemo Room and Lawrence enjoyed seeing them. He wanted people involved. They distracted him, bringing the healthy world back to him. Seeing his friends brought an inkling of normality into his world of sickness. Shaun Keeling, John Smith and Naydene Smith all popped in to see him when they could. They caused a stir in the Chemo Room because they all looked so fit and strong and well, and were all training at an elite level. Family also came in and out to see him; my sister Monique and her husband Steve, as well as the boys, all visited Lawrence when they could.

213

Each of the seven drugs given to him had its own toxic side effect profile. He was educated about these prior to his starting the chemotherapy so he knew exactly what he was about to go through.

One of the first side effects was losing his hair. He had been warned about this, and within the first few days after the start of the first cycle his hair came out in bunches, great big handfuls of hair falling away from their damaged base. Within a few weeks he was completely bald. It reminded me of my own experience of hair loss, so long ago now, when fistfuls of my hair fell out from the deadly radiotherapy beams.

For the first two weeks of each cycle he felt ill – generally, miserably, globally ill. He was drained and weak, mildly nauseous, with horrible headaches and a deep indescribable tiredness, as if he could not move another step. He would come home and collapse on the couch. Fatigue was one of the more potent side effects and he struggled with this for the duration of the chemotherapy. He was fatigued far beyond anything he had ever experienced as an athlete.

He suffered from severe bone pain on the day he was given medication to stimulate the bone marrow. This was a routine method of trying to prevent the bone marrow from failing to produce enough normal cells. Part of his treatment was Neupogen, which stimulated the bone marrow to expand, increasing the blood flow into it for it to continue producing blood cells. The pain would usually hit him in the middle of the night. One morning I got up to find him lying on the couch, looking grey and ill. 'What's wrong, Lawrence? Are you okay?' I gasped, shocked at his appearance.

'I have such pain,' he moaned weakly. 'I have taken medication but it has not helped and I could not sleep from the pain.'

'Why did you not wake me? I would have helped you.' I was upset to see him looking so ill.

'I didn't want to disturb you. I thought I could manage.' That was Lawrence, strong and resourceful, not wanting to be the cause of added stress for others.

Nausea is a common, well-known and almost expected side effect of chemotherapy. Lawrence did not have much nausea; recent medication has managed virtually to eradicate the awful symptom of chemo-induced nausea.

One of the drugs in the regimen was prednisone, which is a glucocorticoid steroid. This is not an anabolic steroid like testosterone but rather a steroid that has powerful anti-inflammatory properties. He was on huge doses of prednisone and one of its side effects is an increased appetite. Well, that was a complete understatement when it came to Lawrence. He simply could not eat enough. His appetite increased voraciously. He felt permanently ravenous and ate everything he could find. No matter how much he ate or how full he felt, he remained hungry and was constantly on the rampage for food. He became a Pac-Man, gobbling his way through the field. He put on a whopping 15 kilograms during the treatment.

After three cycles of chemo, Lawrence started to complain of a burning sensation in his hands and feet, a typical pain caused by irritation of the nerves. In medical terms this is known as a neuropathy. One of the drugs, Oncovin, was attacking his peripheral nerve cells and causing damage. This was a worry; once peripheral neuropathy is present it frequently never improves. Jackie and the team made the decision to stop the Oncovin after the third cycle.

The more serious side effects of the drugs were the damage that the chemotherapy could do to his heart and lungs. Adriamycin and bleomycin were the two drugs that had devastating potential to cause irreparable cardiac and pulmonary damage. One of the advantages of the escalated regimen, besides the obvious one of curing Lawrence, was that the adriamycin and bleomycin, which caused these dangerous side effects, were used in slightly lower doses. We were still worried, however, and I read up on the somewhat scanty information about the cardiac effects of adriamycin in sportspeople. I was trying to build up a picture of Lawrence in the post-chemotherapy phase.

After the second cycle he was scheduled for another PET scan, which was booked for 2 December 2014. Once again, Lawrence prepared himself for this unpleasant test. He braced himself and went through it, keen to find out how well the chemo was doing its job.

Once again I felt familiar feelings of anxiety and irrepressible nervousness. David, Nicky and I went with Lawrence and waited outside. As time passed we became more and more anxious. We waited and paced around for three hours, which felt like an eternity, before the radiologists called us in. I was shaking and I could sense David's anxiety. Nicky was almost in tears. The radiologists flashed up the scans on their big screens. They looked at us and then broke into big smiles.

We could not believe it. The picture was completely different. The old scan was next to the new one for comparison and the ominous dark patches of lymph node clusters in the mediastinum, abdomen and pelvis were gone. They explained that the chemotherapy had eradicated all visible signs of the disease. I broke down with Nicky and David. Somehow seeing the evidence in front of me unleashed a torrent of relief. Until that point I had not dared to hope. We were crying and hugging each other, laughing at the same time.

It was a joyful time, the first in a long time. Suddenly some light appeared in this dark tunnel. The doctors had not been joking: the regimen had eradicated the disease after two cycles. We were ecstatic.

We celebrated that night with the family. For the first time in a few months we felt we could trust that things were going to be all right. Later that night I wrote another email to all those who had held us in their thoughts and prayers.

Dear Family, Friends and Colleagues

A huge thank you to you all for your amazing support of us during this difficult time. We have been touched by the messages from everyone and would like you to know that they have made an enormous difference to us and especially to Lawrence as he goes through this.

Lawrence is through the difficult second cycle of chemo and has managed very well up to this point. We are so proud of the way he has handled himself during this time, with a positive spirit and belief and doing everything necessary to ensure he recovers from this as well as possible.

We had the second PET (positron emission tomography) scan today, which shows that the disease is in remission with no evidence on scan. This indicates that the tumour is highly responsive to chemo and it increases his chances of a cure to around 97%.

This means that things are exactly where the oncologists hoped they would be at this stage. They hit him hard for two cycles in order to eradicate the disease. The regimen they chose was intense and it is quite remarkable how well Lawrence coped with the drugs and the side effects.

However, it is imperative that he continue with the chemo for the remaining four cycles as he needs to 'finish it off properly'.

We are hopeful that the chemo will be completed in another four cycles which brings us to February. His next chemo starts tomorrow and then the next cycle is just before Christmas so we are possibly thinking of going to Knysna after Christmas.

It is quite incredible how the good news has lifted our spirits and given us hope for his full recovery as well as in his return to what he loves best, training and racing.

I think the past few months have shown us the calibre of person Lawrence has become. He has inner strength and resilience and an uncomplaining disposition, which have enabled him to navigate his way calmly through this adversity. Truly he embodies the motto of the Lincoln family, Strength in Adversity. The Brittain genes add tenacity and this is Lawrence.

So for now we continue on this path supporting him as best we can. Please continue your support of him as well as our family during the next few months. We may not speak much but we value each and every one of you.

And so we go on; it is appropriate to use one of the mottos of the rowing team –

Onwards and Upwards.

Messages flooded in. We could not have been happier or asked for anything more at that moment. Of course, the big question came up over and over after that: if the cancer has been eradicated why does he need to continue with chemotherapy?

The answer seemed simple, but needed to be explained. Lawrence had completed two of the six cycles. Two cycles had eradicated the disease visible to the naked eye, but the concern was what was happening on a cellular level. The chances of there still being malignant cells was high. If the chemotherapy stopped now, after only two cycles, he would almost certainly relapse rapidly. The job needed to be completed to get full remission.

He was not even halfway through yet.

And so the chemotherapy continued for another four cycles. We established a good routine and I managed to keep working with the rowing athletes and still be there for Lawrence. Every Saturday I would address the athlete group on various topics and I always included a small update on Lawrence and his progress, pictures of him and messages from him. Generally, he was not able to do much on his off days. The fatigue was overwhelming and he needed the time to rest and recover, his body regenerating and preparing quietly for the next onslaught. I also did not want him exposed to any infection as his immune system was weak and vulnerable.

After the fourth cycle, he became very sick. His bone marrow was now significantly suppressed. He developed an upper respiratory infection and this rapidly developed into pneumonia. We were beginning to think he needed admission to hospital. At 3 am I woke to check on him and found him seriously ill with a fever, coughing and breathing difficulties. David paced around, unsure of himself.

'What would you do if this was one of your patients, phoning you in the middle of the night with these symptoms?' I asked him gently.

'I would admit them,' he said simply. That clarified the situation immediately.

We drove Lawrence to Pretoria East Hospital at 3:30 am and he was admitted into an isolation ward in the Bone Marrow Transplant Unit. He needed high doses of antibiotics as well as oxygen therapy. He stayed in the unit for five days until he was well enough to go home. The doctors and nursing staff treating him were wonderful and we knew he was being cared for well. Anyone visiting him had to change into hospital theatre garb and pull on caps, bootees and masks. No one could infect him in any way. He was vulnerable now, with a depressed immune system. He needed to get through the following weeks with as little chance of serious infection as possible.

Time had rolled into December and we were hoping to get away to Knysna for a ten-day holiday in between his chemotherapy cycles. The lung infection delayed his next cycle by two weeks, so we were unable to take the holiday we desperately wanted. Instead, we stayed at our home in Sable Hills, which, being on the banks of the Roodeplaat Dam, felt a bit like a holiday to us. We loved coming out to 'the bush' as we called it, as the terrain is definitely more like the bushveld than the highveld terrain of Johannesburg and Pretoria. It was an ideal place to go for the break we wanted. About 200 metres from the water's edge, our home has a splendid view of the dam on which the boys had spent so much time. The sunsets are magnificent. There is a peace and tranquillity in Sable Hills I found soothing and therapeutic for our family after the harrowing time. I was disappointed about not going to Knysna, but nothing really mattered any-way except Lawrence's need to stay well and strong to cope with the last few chemo cycles.

I was due to attend a conference on various topics related to rowing medicine in England in late January 2015. It was hosted by British Rowing and I planned to attend the conference with Jimmy Clark. We were both anticipating a high standard of presentation and felt it was perfectly aimed at those of us who had devoted our time and energy to rowing. I was look-ing forward to it – rowing is a relatively small sporting discipline, with specific and unique medical and physiological issues. It was an opportu-nity to meet other support teams and hear what some of the bigger nations were researching. Usually, rowing conferences were aimed at the coaches, so I was looking forward to a more medical angle to the content.

But sadly, it was not to be for me.

When Lawrence became ill with pneumonia I realised that the line between coping with chemotherapy and life-threatening illness was delicate and fragile. I felt I could not leave. I made the difficult decision not to attend the conference as I felt I needed to stay at home with Lawrence. I sobbed bitterly as I explained my decision to Jimmy. I knew that if something were to happen I would want to be there and would not easily forgive myself if I was not.

Lawrence recovered from the pneumonia and his blood counts improved. The last two cycles of chemotherapy were less eventful, although he was suffering from overwhelming fatigue and the drugs were starting to have a cumulatively toxic effect on him. He slept most of the time and could do very little. It was painful to watch him growing weaker and heavier, each day looking less and less like an elite athlete and more and more like a patient with advanced, intractable disease. He was pale, with dark rings around his eyes, and was flabby and lethargic. He no longer had any of those magnificent, healthy-looking veins. He would be at the bottom of that vein competition now. Many of his veins were blackened and thrombosed, as if they had been burnt out and obliterated.

The Chemo Room and oncology practice were on the third floor of the hospital. At the beginning of the first cycle of chemotherapy, Lawrence said he would walk up the stairs. It was a particularly steep and narrow stairway. Each time we got there for his treatment, he stoically climbed the three flights of stairs. On the morning of the start of the fourth cycle, he was unable to climb them. He was just too tired and breathless. He told me he could not do it and caught the lift. For the next three cycles, he used the lift each time. These were the things I witnessed silently and painfully. I had to accept this was part of the journey. I had to believe that, when all this was over, he would heal and his body would regenerate.

And he would climb the stairs again.

As all things inevitably move on, so too did the relentless process of chemotherapy. The end was approaching. On 18 February 2015, he received his last intravenous treatment. To celebrate the day, I baked scones for the staff and patients and we bought gifts for the fabulous support staff. Lawrence had made it. He had completed a long journey, remaining mentally positive. Physically, he had come through it relatively intact. It was a day of victory, marred only by his profound weakness and fatigue.

All that was left now was to finish the last week of oral chemotherapy.

Despite looking weak and ill, Lawrence was in remission. He had become a survivor.

It was not yet possible to speak of a cure. It was too soon. As many as 20 per cent of Hodgkin lymphomas can relapse within the first five years of treatment. The five-year period following the completion of initial chemotherapy is a critical time for cancer patients. Malignant cells could still be lurking in hidden areas, waiting furtively for their chance to refuel and restart their deadly oncological progression to rapid cell division. It is a dangerous time, which needs careful observation. Relapse would certainly mean further treatment and the possibility of a bone marrow transplant. I knew that, in the appalling event of relapse, things would become more serious. Returning to training would become impossible.

But this was now, and we had to focus on the present. The next five years would be a time of high alert and careful observation.

Waiting. For five years.

I had been through it once before, was currently going through it again, and now it was Lawrence's turn too.

For now, we speak only of remission to keep us from daring and hoping too much.

It is simply about the present.

Lawrence emerged from the illness and treatment more grounded than before. The illness had defined his tenacity and courage, and seemed to make him more of who he already was.

As expected, I felt altered by Lawrence's illness. It is impossible not be changed by the experience. A piece of my mother's heart had been squeezed in a cruel vice of fear. There are things that change you in life, things that damage you irreparably and things that strengthen who you already are. I felt strengthened. Despite the devastation I endured at the time of his diagnosis, I was able to deal with it from a position of strength. I believed he would be fine and besides, we had all the expertise and experience we needed readily on hand. For the wisdom and support we received from the team treating Lawrence, I have immense gratitude and respect.

I have always been afraid of change, and the hardship that comes with it. But there always comes a point during that fear when it becomes clear that there can be no going back. With Lawrence's illness, I had to concentrate on moving forward. Despite the pain, the heart does not give up easily; the will to keep going is strong.

In life, we all have to stand up, face the pain and overcome the fear, just as the athlete overcomes the fear and the pain and moves forward, racing to win. Over the years I have come to realise that hidden in pain is immense power. And power begets power. Fear begets fear.

We are all warriors, and these are our battlegrounds. We choose how we fight. We fight to survive and to win.

12

꒦꒦꒦꒦

CLAWING BACK

Pretoria, 2015

*We were out there in the open ocean for a week or more. No food, no water.
I lost count of the days and the nights. By then I didn't know any more who
was alive and who was dead, and what's more I didn't care. I only knew I was
still alive. That was all that mattered to me. I lived on nothing but hope, and
a dream. I had a dream and I clung on to it [...] I thought if I dreamt it hard
enough, hoped for it hard enough, it must come true.*

– MICHAEL MORPURGO, *HALF A MAN*

By the end of March 2015, Lawrence had completed all his chemotherapy, both oral and intravenous. It had been an exhausting six
months and he looked ill. It was impossible to see that he had once been
an athlete.

Following the chemotherapy, he entered a phase of recovery and regen-
eration. It was pointless doing tests immediately as his body needed time
to recover or the tests would simply show the ravaging effects of chemotherapy, rather than actual disease.

He had reached a milestone but he was not well. He continued to suffer from repeated upper respiratory infections, abscesses and boils, and
was constantly on antibiotics as his immune system struggled. I had to
accept that it would take time to rebuild an immune system that had been
destroyed by the inexorably slow-growing cancer itself, followed by a

regimen of toxic drugs. He needed time to heal and regenerate.

It was a period of waiting. He needed to trust that time would heal him physically. He needed to be patient.

I needed to mark the moment, to step back and acknowledge all that had happened. We threw a huge party at Sable Hills to celebrate his completing chemotherapy and going into remission. Lawrence called it his Fuck Cancer party. One of David's patients had given David a black beanie with the words 'Fuck Cancer' embroidered in green on the front. David gave this to Lawrence, and he wore it at his party. We invited everyone we knew and I catered large cheese platters, breads, hummus, two large lambs on the spit, salad and pita breads, followed by ice cream and toppings. Champagne flowed and our spirits were high. We made speeches, I put together a slide show of the journey and we really celebrated to mark the event. It was a momentous and special day, the first step on a long road back to full recovery.

Once Lawrence knew he was safely in remission, he became desperate for one thing, and one thing only.

He wanted to start training again.

There had never been any doubt in his mind that he would commit fully to the treatment but after that he wanted to get back to what he loved doing most.

He began almost immediately with a light gym programme. Nicola Macleod, the strength and conditioning coach at the time, bought him a T-shirt with words on it that were funny and apt: 'Installing muscle, please wait'. She devised a light programme for him and he began the slow and progressive building phase. Jimmy and I drew up some guidelines for him to slowly claw his way back to being some semblance of an athlete. There were no protocols out there, no research about elite athletes coming back to training after high-dose chemotherapy. We set goals and rules for him, but this was not easy for him. He was used to training hard, not holding back. Even though he knew the dangers, and he knew what we were unsure of, he wanted to train harder and was impatient. He was tired of waiting but he needed to be patient and give it time.

The rowing squad was travelling to Lesotho for a training camp in the mountains during March 2015. Lawrence wanted to go and asked me what I thought. Or to put it a little more accurately, he said, 'I want to go with the team to Lesotho to train. There is no reason why I cannot be with them.'

I approached Roger. 'I think we should consider bringing Lawrence on camp. It will do him good to be with the squad. I can keep a strict eye on his training. Leaving him behind when he has been excluded from so much will be mentally tough for him. He has been crushed enough; let's build him up.'

Roger could see the benefits. He can be flexible and open to different ideas and suggestions; he is gifted with an ability to see the bigger picture clearly. He agreed.

But being on camp did not prove easy for Lawrence. He was clearly frustrated. I was insisting he keep his sessions shorter, lighter and at a very low work rate. He had to maintain his heart rate at 120 beats per minute (bpm), slowly building up over weeks to 140, 150 and then 160. This was torture for him. He was not allowed to run as he was too heavy. The danger of loading his musculoskeletal system would be too great at this time, when he had the mind of a champion but the body of a poorly conditioned, overweight and recently ill person. Jimmy and I set the weight cap at 98 kg. More than that, and he was not allowed to run.

It was during this time that his good nature was tested and he became impatient and irritable. I was adamant he would not train harder until he had been assessed from a cardiology point of view. He begged, 'I may as well not be training. It feels as if I am doing nothing.' Despite capping his efforts, the progress was evident and by the end of the camp he was doing close to 20 kilometres of light work in the single scull, a light gym programme, and light ergometer or Wattbike workout.

I kept at it with him. 'You have to be patient. Give it time. You need to wait for healing and recovery.'

I knew Lawrence was coming right. Things were looking good, but he needed to have tests to determine the extent to which chemotherapy had damaged him. He had some blood tests, which showed improvements, and his full lung function tests showed some expected compromise, but the doctors were confident that would improve.

On 1 April 2015 he had an important scheduled cardiology assessment. I went with him to the assessment. A team of two cardiologists reviewed him. One of the hardest moments for me was watching Lawrence bravely attempt the stress electrocardiogram (ECG) test. They used a standard testing protocol called the Bruce Protocol, where the patient begins the run at a ten per cent incline for three minutes. The incline then continues to increase by two per cent every three minutes. As if that is not hard enough, the speed of the treadmill increases at a predetermined rate and the patient runs until they cannot any more. It is a maximal effort test. Lawrence huffed and puffed and sweated his way through this test, looking nothing like an elite athlete.

Watching him made me ache for him. It was heartbreaking to see how far away he was from who he had been and who he desperately wanted to become again. But the mentality of the athlete prevailed. Even in this state, and at this level, Lawrence asked the technician if anyone they had seen in the practice had ever beaten what he had just managed to do. She said simply, 'No, no one.'

He was satisfied. He had won. These were small victories, but they showed how determined and competitive he actually was. His heart was then examined under a special sonar called an echocardiogram and, after quietly studying the images and assessing the function of the heart for some time, the doctor turned to Lawrence and said, 'Your heart is fine, Lawrence. There is nothing wrong with you. Go and win medals.'

It was a key moment on the journey, a turning point. Lawrence felt like a bird soaring free from captivity. He could spread those wings, now, knowing absolutely and conclusively that his heart was not going to hold him back.

There was no way he would allow us to hold him back any longer.

He was physically ready. He had never stopped being mentally ready.

His next goal was to commit to losing the weight he had gained from the chemotherapy. He set his mind to it from that point onwards and lost weight rapidly over the next few weeks. He reduced junk food, and cut back significantly on portion size. He was determined. He reached his 98 kg target within a few weeks and was allowed to start running again. It was another significant milestone on his journey.

He was now training for longer and at a higher intensity in the scull, and the movements were starting to flow more easily as the weight came down. He no longer had an enormous stomach impeding each stroke. He was starting to look like an athlete again. By May 2015 he was weighing 92 kg, having lost the 15 kg he put on during the treatment. He was driven and determined to get back into proper training and form.

Another PET scan investigation was looming and on 28 April 2015 he underwent his third scan. This was a nervous, anxious time for all of us and will, unfortunately, always be a test associated with significant tension: the outcome determines the future. We knew Lawrence would need regular check-ups and blood tests in the first five years following his treatment. The PET scan was the ultimate test of whether everything was under control. Brooding questions dominated my thoughts. I struggled to contain the fear. Would everything be okay? Had he remained clear? Was the scan going to be as good as it had been the last time?

The scan was predominantly clear except for a slight shadow over an area in his chest known as the anterior mediastinum. The concern was the possibility of relapsed disease. We needed a biopsy of that area to be sure, but the area was too small and seemed insignificant. Relapsed disease would be very serious. But it was too soon and too small to be of real concern. After a discussion with the medical team and the cardiothoracic surgeons, we decided not to do anything and to repeat the scan towards the end of the year. Jackie felt the most likely explanation was that the area was regenerating thymus tissue. The thymus, between the sternum and the lungs, stimulates production of T-lymphocytes.

I decided not to talk to Lawrence about this as he was starting to train hard. I knew there was a chance he could make the selection for a crew for the 2015 World Championships later that year. If he knew there was a possible problem, no matter how small, the doubt would compromise him mentally. He had been through enough for the moment.

This was an uncharacteristic decision on my part. As a palliative care doctor I have always believed the patient should know as much as they want to. I have never felt comfortable holding anything back from a patient, yet here I was not giving Lawrence the full picture. I was protecting him. But I feel I made the right decision and would do the same thing again if faced with a similar situation.

We pushed on, carrying the concern in ourselves. It reminded me of the scene in the movie *The Lion King* when young Simba asks his father, King Mufasa, 'But what's that shadowy bit over there?' and Mufasa answers, 'That is beyond our borders. You must never go there, Simba.'

It had been two months since his last chemotherapy cycle. Lawrence was doing well. He had been taken out of the scull and given the chance to start training in the men's pair and men's four. He was training with more intent, clearly showing the rest of the squad he was back. It was a special time watching him return, slowly but surely, so focused and determined, clawing his way back to where he wanted to be. He was a long way off, but he never tired or wavered or stumbled.

He just kept moving onwards and upwards.

The next big test for him was whether he could do an ergo trial. The squad was preparing for a trial just before the major selection for the 2015 World Championships. Lawrence wanted to do the trial. He was feeling strong and keen and determined. I discussed it with David, questioning whether he should do it. There was no medical reason to hold Lawrence back. His last ergo trial in May 2014 had been disastrous and he had been dropped from the men's pair as a result. I knew he was eager to see what he could do. I agreed that he could proceed with the ergo trial.

No one really knew what to expect – not even Lawrence himself. Most people, including the coaches, thought he would get in the region of 6:20, or possibly closer to 6:25. It was not realistic to expect more from someone who had finished high-dose chemotherapy two months before that.

After the trial, Lawrence told me knew he was strong. Unbeknown to all of us, he could feel something within himself. Like a closely guarded secret and personal revelation, Lawrence could feel he was gaining strength daily. All the training he had done in those years and months before the diagnosis that had felt so difficult, as if there had been some invisible force holding him back, causing serious self-doubt, now somehow had the effect of making him stronger and much more powerful. It was as if the resistance had been released and he felt a freedom he had not felt for years. He felt stronger than he had for a long, long time. It unleashed a strength in him of which he always knew he was capable. He was only just beginning to feel this.

On 20 May 2015 Lawrence walked into the ergo room after his warm-up and sat down, taking a deep breath. He did a few hard bursts on the machine, stopping to slap his thighs as he always did and focusing his mind on what he wanted to do that day. He had nothing to lose.

He was no longer defending. He was attacking.

His time? 6:14.5.

It was unbelievable. He had flexed his muscles and showed his lion heart and strength.

One of his fellow rowers, David Hunt, later asked what time Lawrence had got. His response was, 'What a beast!'

That result showed clear intention. Lawrence was coming back with a furious drive and determination. If his health withstood the strain, nothing would stop him now.

13

🚣🚣🚣🚣

THE LONG, HARD CLIMB

Pretoria, 2015

There are few opportunities in life to know how deep you can go.
— TIAGO LOUREIRO, SOUTH AFRICAN ROWING COACH

With the go-ahead to train properly and an ergo trial result to show that he was coming back, Lawrence threw everything at it. He threw off the shackles Jimmy and I had placed on him and committed to the training relentlessly. He was flexing his muscles and wanted to see how far he could push them, to test himself. He was at rock bottom and had nothing to lose.

In JK Rowling's *Harry Potter* book series, each wizard has a Patronus, which is the magical embodiment of his or her positive energy that protects against evil. According to the book, a Patronus projects hope, happiness and the desire to survive. It does not feel despair; the force is positive. For me, Lawrence's Patronus would be a lion. Strong, powerful, huge in stature and mentality, ruthless when necessary, but also patient enough to wait for the perfect timing. But it is not just about waiting. The lion is a hunter. It waits to attack – the moment when the lion becomes the warrior.

His training pieces improved steadily. After the usual selection races, endless hours poring over spreadsheets of racing times and watching crews race on the water and the ergo, the coaches selected crews for the upcoming international season and the all-important Olympic Qualification

Regatta to be held in France in 2015. Lawrence was selected into the bow of the men's heavyweight four. Shaun Keeling and David Hunt were the top-performing men's pair and were to race in that combination. Lawrence's crew comprised Sizwe Ndlovu, Vincent Breet and Jonty Smith. Sizwe had become a heavyweight since the London Olympics and was determined to try to make another Olympic Games. Vincent Breet had returned from Harvard to row for South Africa and make the selection for the Olympics. Jonty Smith was a relative newcomer to rowing, having only started at university. The coaches were hoping to qualify two heavyweight boats for the Rio Olympics. It was a lot to ask from a brand-new crew combination, with various issues in the boat. Lawrence was returning from high-dose chemotherapy, Sizwe was transitioning from lightweight to heavyweight, Vince was disappointed not to have made it into the heavyweight pair and Jonty, although strong, lacked racing experience.

Four months after completing chemotherapy, Lawrence had made it back to high-level racing. It was extraordinary. David told me, 'Many patients go into remission quickly, but not many return that quickly to physical peak and strength.'

Shaun Keeling had not found the start of 2015 promising. He had come back after the December break with a number of problems to face. Lawrence was out of contention as he was still having chemotherapy. Vince Breet had returned from Harvard University out of shape and condition. He had not trained enough back in the United States. David Hunt was having some health issues. Shaun himself was recovering from shoulder surgery and had suffered a bout of a severe upper respiratory infection in December, which had spilled over into January. He returned to full training in January and wondered, *Who on earth am I going to row with?* As the training season rolled ahead and international racing approached, things settled down for him and he was teamed with David Hunt in the heavyweight men's pair.

The first semi-international regatta was the annual prestigious Henley Royal Regatta. The heavyweight four, with Lawrence, drew a top British four and lost in the first round. The heavyweight pair with Shaun and David lost in the semi-final to a British pair.

The second regatta was the Lucerne World Cup, held in July 2015. I always accompany the squad to this regatta. It is an important regatta as it is close to the World Championships, and most top international teams race at Lucerne. The results at Lucerne allow teams and coaches to assess fairly accurately their standing in world rankings.

The men's four was disappointing. They raced the heat and came fourth, placing them into the repechage. I watched the repechage from the grandstand at the finish line. It was a grey, misty day, cold and bleak. I was virtually alone as it was early in the regatta and most spectators are not particularly interested in the repechage.

The South African four came fourth, not making it into the A/B semi-final.

As I watched them bravely trying to race to second place, I willed them on, silently praying and hoping they could make the cut-off. My fervent pleading was in vain. The loss I witnessed induced in me a flood of tears and I wept alone at the finish. I kept saying to myself, *When will things get a little easier? When will they start working out?* But I also knew we needed to be patient and keep working. I knew Lawrence had a way to go before he had fully recovered.

The rest of the South African results were good. Both the men's lightweight double with James Thompson and John Smith and the women's lightweight double with Ursula Grobler and Kirsten McCann came second, claiming the silver medals. The women's heavyweight pair with Lee-Ann Persse and Naydene Smith placed fifth overall, and the men's heavyweight pair with Shaun and David came sixth.

Lawrence felt this race was too soon for the heavyweight four to achieve a better result. They needed more time and a lot more training, refining their technique and building the rhythm and speed a winning crew needs.

The final and most important regatta of the year was the intimidating pre-Olympic World Championships. It was to be held on the stunningly beautiful Lake Aiguebelette in France in August 2015. Our team knew we had a serious regatta ahead of us as every athlete in the world pushes themselves beyond their limits to qualify their boat for the Olympic Games. I had been at the Olympic Qualification Regatta in Bled four years ago and I knew the extraordinary level of stress and pressure the team would be facing.

Under Roger, the team was well prepared. In addition to Roger as the head coach, the support comprised two experienced coaches, AJ and Jacko, as well as newcomer to senior rowing, Tiago Loureiro. The South African results showed consistent improvement. We easily qualified a men's lightweight double with Olympic gold medallists James Thompson and John Smith, a women's lightweight double with Kirsten McCann and Ursula Grobler, who achieved a bronze medal in their final, as well as a women's heavyweight pair, Lee-Ann Persse and Naydene Smith. Shaun Keeling and David Hunt qualified the men's heavyweight pair, coming eighth overall. It was thrilling to see South Africa manage those four results so easily. Shaun was disappointed not to make the A final, but David was just starting to respond to new medication and, in his own opinion, raced suboptimally.

The heavyweight men's four did not manage as easily. They did not qualify.

For his sixth consecutive international race since 2011, Lawrence had another disappointing result. The four came 13th overall. They needed to come in the top 11 to qualify. For the third time, Lawrence was in a boat that did not qualify for the Olympic Games. For the second time, Lawrence faced being part of a crew that would try to qualify through the Late Qualification Regatta in Lucerne the following year.

It was another grim disappointment for him. Another setback. One more slump. The mountain he was on seemed insurmountably steep. Maybe we had all just expected too much of Lawrence, of all of them. Lawrence felt the four did not expect enough of themselves. 'We did not expect to win; our expectation shot the other way and as a result we did not race hard enough to beat the USA, who beat us in the repechage. We needed to expect more of ourselves.'

233

I watched the race, alone at the finish line, waiting, afraid to look, afraid to hope. It was my job to give out the recovery drinks at the jetty after the finish. Over the years I have spent many hours of anguish waiting for crews to come down the course to meet them at the jetty, either delighting in their joy at a good result or dreading their devastating disappointment at a loss. It can be either the best or the worst of times.

Once again Lawrence had to face himself honestly, knowing that he had not made the qualification. He returned to South Africa with the disappointment still thick and bitter, forcing him to acknowledge how far he still had to go. Somehow, though, of all the losses, this one felt more manageable. He knew he had only completed chemotherapy five months ago and was still regaining form. From a contextual point of view, he was alive and well and really, nothing could be worse than being told you had a fourth stage malignancy.

Lawrence joined his brother James in the Tuks eight to race the annual Boat Race. This was his seventh consecutive Boat Race for Tuks and the crew won. Winning Boat Race always felt good to Lawrence, and even more so to have James in the crew with him.

The disappointment of Aiguebelette sharpened the hunger in Lawrence. His passion added fuel to the fire, forging a potent energy of resolve and determination. *I know I can do better, and I will*, he swore to himself.

But there were other things to focus on before he could train again. During the ensuing break, he had his fourth PET scan. We had to check out that shadowy place in his chest; we needed to be sure now. It was time to see what was happening. Once again Lawrence resolutely faced the procedure and lay dead still for two hours while the scanner lined his body up, focused itself, and took the photographs that could potentially change the course of events in a few minutes.

There was no change.

The shadowy place remained exactly the same. It had not grown or changed in any way.

The radiologists confirmed the belief that it was regenerating thymic tissue. The haematologists agreed with this. Tissue decimated by disease and chemotherapy was now regrowing, and causing a slight uptake in that area. Did we need to worry? Not according to David or Jackie or Andrew or Theo. They felt things were fine. The trajectory of Lawrence's progress remained favourable and would not change drastically.

We could breathe again.

I immediately felt the freedom that comes when a worry is lifted.

Lawrence came back from the September break in even better condition. He had made a mental shift. He no longer thought of himself as a recovering cancer patient. Now he saw himself as a fighter, dangerous, even deadly. He had become the warrior on the attack.

And that is exactly what he did: he attacked.

From the beginning of the final year of the four-year Olympic cycle, Lawrence ruthlessly hunted as a warrior would hunt, climbing to the top and refusing to accept the impossible.

Everything was better. He was stronger, fitter, faster, hungrier. All the restriction he had felt as he pushed himself to train while being held back by invisible disease and illness had been released, enabling him to train with a potent blend of power and conviction. He felt almost limitless strength. He thrived on it. Over and over he would tell me, 'I am feeling so strong, Mom.' He felt exhilarated as his body opened up to the training, absorbed the load and surged onwards.

In a strange sense, the illness gave him confidence. Prior to the diagnosis, he was in a dark place mentally. The illness and treatment put everything in perspective. Now, he found training so much easier. He was recovering better again, realising just how bad things had been before the diagnosis.

His performance seemed to accelerate from that point. Each trial, each race, each training piece seemed easier; he felt lighter, stronger and faster. The squad was at full momentum, facing an intense year with final crew selection pressures, five training camps away from home and three international tours.

It is a blunt and almost callous fact that, even if athletes qualify boats the year before, it does not guarantee their selection for the Olympic crew. After qualification, selection begins afresh, with the entire squad trying to be fast enough to make one of the highly sought-after spots. The athletes were training hard, each focused on their individual private dreams they were hoping to turn into reality. It was a tense, competitive time for all the athletes.

Becoming a world-class rowing athlete takes years and the group spends much time together. The wolf pack merges. They train together, travel together, live together. They know one another well, forging these relationships through both the toughest and the best of times. They drift towards and away from one another as time goes by. The most difficult relationships are competitive. How do you learn to attack your friend in a race and beat them? Conversely, how do you row with someone you may not choose as a friend? It requires a single-minded approach, a focus beyond what many can understand. Some of these relationships go on to become lasting friendships and marriages; others are wrecked.

By April 2016, the coaches were ready to select those who would be racing at the Olympics. Selection is never straightforward; there is always a degree of subjectivity, a certain quality the coaches are hunting for that is not measurable. Fortunately, I am not involved in the selection process and I stay as far away from the work of selection as possible.

At that stage, Shaun Keeling was the clear stroke side oarsman (on the port side of the boat) for the men's heavyweight pair. There were two options for the bow side oarsman (on the starboard side of the boat) who would partner Shaun. Lawrence and David Hunt would fight it out for that sought-after position. They were both strong and fit, and ready for the battle. Lawrence had surpassed his previous form and was the strongest he had felt in years. There were now three people fighting for two places, but it really came down to the battle between David and Lawrence. The tension leading up to the decision was endless, for the athletes, for the coaches, for me, for the families.

After reviewing the huge database of performances, the coaches finally selected Lawrence into the heavyweight pair to row with Shaun.

Lawrence wanted to be in the top boat and felt he had reached a major personal goal. It was a tremendous achievement and, as his family, we were delighted for him. I knew the coaches had made a good decision. Lawrence was ready to race and see how he could position himself against the rest of the world.

But this marked a low point in David's rowing career. He was gutted. The disappointment was deep and bitter. When he was able to look at it rationally with his clear-thinking, logical engineering brain, he knew he had come on form too late. Despite David's being strong and fast towards the end, Lawrence had been fast from the beginning. Knowing that made the decision slightly more bearable. David's father, Dr Ian Hunt, a colleague of mine, later told me, 'Lawrence is a true inspiration. I told David that if he had to lose his place to someone he would rather lose it to Lawrence, who has been such an inspiration and done so well.'

David was selected into the heavyweight four with Jake Green, Vince Breet and Jonty Smith. In his methodical, calm style, he committed to his position in the four and immediately set about building that crew to make the late qualification for the Rio Olympics.

Jake and Sizwe fought it out for the stroke position in the four. The selection went in Jake's favour; Sizwe was out. This was a crushing blow, his hopes for another Olympics decimated. 'It was the worst time for me. The disappointment was massive and bitter, equalled only by the loss of not making the Beijing Games in 2008,' he recalled when I spoke to him.

Sizwe withdrew from the programme and an injury to his hip flared up, requiring surgery. This was followed by a long period of rehabilitation. He was out of the system for the moment, not yet ready to stop rowing but knowing that his dreams for rowing in Rio were over.

At the same time, the other South African Olympic boats were finally selected. Ursula Grobler and Kirsten McCann were selected for the lightweight women's double, with Kate Johnstone not making it. Lee-Ann Persse made the selection for the women's heavyweight pair and the choice of her partner went in Kate Christowitz's favour, leaving Naydene Smith out of the boat.

Selection will always bring great joy and profound agony. There is a deep well of grief to cope with being dropped, but those athletes know they gave it their all, leaving nothing untried. Without them the selected boat would never have been as fast. Kate Johnstone left rowing immediately and started working. Naydene Smith felt her pride stripped from her; she left camp shattered. Two days later she got on the ergo and pulled a PB (personal best), restoring some of her self-confidence.

Sizwe, Naydene and Kate had no choice but to pick up the pieces and move on courageously with the change. Naydene told me later, 'I knew I would never go through that again in my life. Selection gave me the opportunity to know what it was like to train and push myself that hard, to exert maximal effort in trying to achieve something. It is unlikely that I will be pushed that hard again in my life. I am grateful for that, and feel blessed to know I could do that and was part of that level of perseverance.'

For the selected athletes, there was a mountain of work ahead. They were back on the high-speed train and there was no slowing down. The tension surrounding the selection process disappeared and the crews could now train in a less strained but more focused and determined way.

For the fourth time since 2012, Lawrence and Shaun trained together in the pair, coached by Roger Barrow. Shaun says, 'I had started the journey a long time ago with Lawrence and it felt good to have the chance to finish it with him.' They have been close friends since they met. Shaun is like another son to me in many ways. He is a kind-hearted, polite and concerned person. I have known him since his school days at King Edward VII School in Johannesburg. He knew Matthew before meeting Lawrence, and the two of them used to race each other in the single scull during their school rowing careers. Shaun always beat Matthew. They have remained good friends and Shaun was one of Matthew's best men at his wedding.

Shaun himself had had a difficult journey to this point. His huge, burly body was prone to injury and illness. At the same time, though, he was physically strong, and always seemed to deliver a top result despite his health issues. I worked hard with Shaun, helping to get him ready for what was coming. Many believed he could not do it, that he had too many physical problems that interrupted his training. But I had seen the racer in him, the hunger and passion to win, and the belief in himself that he could achieve a world-class result. I knew he had it. Roger knew he had it. We backed him. He was always strong when it came to performing at World Championships and World Cups. He had suffered many disappointments and frustrations on his journey, but always believed he was good enough to win. Not qualifying for the London Olympics had almost ended his career.

But now it was possible for things to change for Shaun.

He felt his time had come.

He had a partner who was strong and, even more importantly, was rowing well. Shaun always believed that training was vital but that the real key to winning was rowing well.

Things were falling into place for Shaun and Lawrence. The technical problems they had struggled with in 2014 were no longer an issue. Shaun was happy with the level of technical skill in the boat. Lawrence was strong. Both of them had managed huge blocks of training without injury or illness. They were communicating well and there was a positive energy between them. Roger worked hard with them and witnessed the change in Lawrence. 'It was like chalk and cheese. Lawrence was now matching Shaun and they became more successful.'

The entire squad was putting in hours of training and completing long miles. They were often away on camp, either in the mountain kingdom of Lesotho, rowing on the spectacular Katse Dam, or training on Ebenezer Dam or in Tzaneen in Limpopo. Camps away are vital for training. They give the athletes the chance to train harder and recover better. They allow the athlete to focus on training, with fewer outside distractions. It is not easy being away from friends and family, but all the athletes and coaches feel that the difference the camp makes to the speed of the boat outweighs any negative aspects of camp life.

Training was one thing, though. Racing was the other. They trained to race.

In March 2016, I travelled with the team to Varese, Italy for the first

World Cup. Lawrence and Shaun came third. The rest of the squad did well, with gold medals for the heavyweight women's pair of Lee-Ann Persse and newly selected Kate Christowitz and the men's lightweight double with James Thompson and John Smith. The women's lightweight double comprising Kirsten McCann and Ursula Grobler came second. The men's heavyweight four managed sixth place. Not what they wanted, but the racing showed promise.

Four months later, we flew back to Europe for the second World Cup in Lucerne. Lawrence and Shaun faced a tougher line-up here and raced to fourth place, beaten by New Zealand, Great Britain and the Netherlands. The unbeaten and exceptional Kiwi pair, Hamish Bond and Eric Murray, won outright, but second and third place were so closely contested by the three crews that it took the judges a few minutes to decide the winners. South Africa came fourth, 0.2 seconds behind the Dutch in second place and the British in third. Lawrence and Shaun were not happy with this race; they knew they had underperformed. There was more work ahead.

South Africa's results at Lucerne continued to show promise. The men's heavyweight four needed to qualify for the Olympics. They had some great racing, qualifying in first place in the Late Qualification Regatta. Jake Green, Vince Breet, Jonty Smith and David Hunt realised their dream by winning and, in so doing, booked their place at the Rio Olympics.

The women's lightweight double won silver and the men's lightweight double came third.

The results were good, but needed to be better.

So, for the team, it was back to hard, focused work on the upcoming training camps in Limpopo. Lawrence and Shaun needed to build more speed and confidence in the boat. They had to refine their technique. They knew they could do better.

After Lucerne, their rowing just seemed to get better and better. Every training session brought an improvement to the movement of the boat. They were developing real speed. They trained against the lightweight men's double, which made them fast as they constantly tried to stay with them. They were good pacing boats for each other. The lightweight double of James Thompson and John Smith were faster than the pair, and the work done to stay with them was invaluable. They could feel themselves exceeding what had gone before. Their pieces, their ergo times and their prognostic times were fast.

Roger had managed and coached Lawrence and Shaun for four years in various crew combinations, and the three of them formed a close unit. The working relationship between the pair and Roger was very good, professional but also friendly. The hierarchy with Roger at the apex and the pair at the base of the triangle worked well. Their approach was simply to remember that all they wanted was to make the boat go faster. Whatever the problem, the solution had to make the boat faster. Everything always came down to the speed of the boat. They kept emotions out of the dynamics in the boat and placed boat speed ahead of personal issues. They were able to approach it in this way because of their personalities. Lawrence was very positive, Shaun was good-natured and patient in his drive for perfection, and Roger was entirely solution-driven. But all three of them were driven by a tenacious inner spirit that was hungry to win. The teamwork between them worked. They knew they needed to find the middle ground where similarities and differences glue a relationship together, rather than rip it apart. But always, fundamentally to them both, the boat always came first. It was their business. Lawrence and Shaun were fortunate also to have a close friendship. This undoubtedly gave them an edge. There have been crews whose relationships have broken down completely under pressure, which made performance more difficult.

As they trained day after day, week after week on the beautiful waters of Ebenezer Dam and Tzaneen Dam, the vast and endless stretches of water and sky around them, time moved on.

It brought them closer to the dream, the hope.

Rio was approaching.

14

OLYMPIC DREAM

Pretoria, 2016

Faster, Higher, Stronger – Citius, Altius, Fortius
– PIERRE DE COUBERTIN,
FOUNDER OF THE MODERN OLYMPIC MOVEMENT

There are many who dream of going to the Olympic Games, but so few who actually achieve it. Being the best in the country, and then one of the best in the world, requires something unique: talent, dedication, courage and long hours of hard work.

Working in this area, I quickly realised that, in rowing, the level of the Olympics is so much higher than that of the annual World Championships. Getting to World Championships in rowing is hard. Getting to the Olympics is much, much harder. The criteria for qualification are tougher and more stringent.

I have asked myself and the athletes the question, What is an Olympic dream? It means different things to people. For some, it is simply to participate at the Olympics, to represent their country. It is a huge achievement just to have got there and to have made it through the severe qualification process. But for others, it is a burning need to stand on the podium and declare to the world they are the best. Fastest, highest, strongest. Lawrence committed himself to this. He had seen Matthew do it; he knew he could do it too.

242

For four years leading up to Rio, the rowing squad prepared, the dream real and vibrant; they could see it, taste it, feel it.

A week after the London Olympics in 2012, I travelled to Ireland with my family. I came across a billboard in Dublin with the powerful slogan, 'Only the strongest shoulders can carry the hopes of a nation.' The billboard was dedicated to Katie Taylor, the Irish boxing gold medallist at the London Olympics. It resonated with me. The Olympics is not only about the athlete. It is about people and nations. Entire countries get behind their athletes. Just as the Olympics embodies the athlete's dream, so it embodies the country's hope for glory. The athletes are the inspiration. They carry the hope of the nation.

Being an elite athlete requires certain qualities. Being a medal-winning elite athlete needs a few extra. Standing on the podium is a testament not only to outstanding talent, but also to an inner toughness and resilience, an inborn killer instinct that drives their ambition to perform. Winning athletes are resilient – they have the ability to survive disappointment. Along the way, the losses far outnumber the wins. Fundamentally, they have to believe it is possible. The athlete needs the strength of a warrior to face the fight and endure the pain. Warriors believe in their strength but they also know they might die fighting. But they cannot be afraid of losing.

'To win at the Olympics is a serious business,' says Matthew. 'It takes great discipline to take it that seriously. You have to be focused and hungry to make it work.'

People talk of this life being a sacrifice. It is not a sacrifice. It is a way of life that is freely chosen. No one can force an athlete to train and perform in this way. If athletes see it as a sacrifice, their performance will be compromised. They cannot pity themselves and mourn all they regard as having been given up. They must love it, breathe it; it must come from a deep, passionate space within them. Everyone chooses to do things for different reasons, but it is important to make the choice and to recognise that you are doing so. Choices create possibilities, but they also bring loss.

No one ever gets it all.

South Africa qualified two boats for London, the men's lightweight four and a women's heavyweight pair. This time, it was different. South Africa qualified five boats for Rio. A total of 12 South African rowing athletes would fight it out. South Africa was sending an impressive team to the Olympics. James Thompson and John Smith were racing in the men's lightweight double. In addition to their gold medal at the London Olympic Games, they had won a gold medal at the Amsterdam World Championships in 2014 and broken the world record at that event; a fourth place at the 2015 Aiguebelette World Championships; and silver and bronze medals at the Lucerne World Cup Regattas in 2015 and 2016. Ursula Grobler and Kirsten McCann were racing in the women's lightweight double and had achieved fourth place in the 2014 Amsterdam World Championships, the bronze medal in the 2015 Aiguebelette World Championships, and silver medals in both the 2015 and 2016 Lucerne World Cup Regattas. Both doubles were hoping to medal at the Olympics.

Lee-Ann Persse and her new racing partner, Kate Christowitz, would be racing the women's heavyweight pair. They had won a gold medal at the first World Cup Regatta in Varese in April 2016, and were hoping for a solid A final result.

The men's heavyweight four, Jake Green, Vincent Breet, Jonty Smith and David Hunt, had qualified for the Olympics via the Late Qualification Regatta in Lucerne earlier that year, winning the race, which put them in a strong position for Rio. The individual crew members had fared well in the international arena. David Hunt and Vincent Breet had achieved gold and silver medals at previous Under-23 World Championships, and Vince had won a bronze medal at the 2014 Amsterdam World Championships when he had raced with Shaun Keeling in the men's heavyweight pair.

Shaun and Lawrence were doing well in their preparation for the Olympics. Lawrence later described their training prior to leaving for Rio: 'Shaun and I had very good training. The camps at Ebenezer and Tzaneen set us up well. We were rowing well. We had a consistent block of training and did not miss any sessions. We were starting to believe we had speed.

We were getting better and better all the time. We felt stronger as well as getting faster.'

There was a close bond in the entire rowing team as they prepared for the Olympics. The energy and excitement was tangible, and special to witness. Each of the athletes' dreams were about to be realised. The team was well prepared in terms of their training preparation and their approach to the Olympics. In the months prior to the Olympics, the coaches and I spent time preparing and dealing with the athletes' expectations to avoid the danger of allowing the Games to become more than they are. Four people within the group had raced at previous Olympics and this experience was invaluable. The group knew what to expect. Roger and AJ had taken most of the squad to Rio the year before on a reconnaissance visit to experience the venue.

Like a storm approaching, the Olympics drew closer until it was time for the squad to leave. They were swept into the passion and intensity of the storm. From that point, it became survival: who could cope best with the flight, the jetlag, the Olympic Village, the extraordinary food hall, the media and the considerable hype that surrounds the Olympics. The enormity of the event is astonishing and can easily throw an athlete off the path. Those who can tolerate the distractions, the discomforts, the changes in routine, will fare the best. Those who can simply take it in their stride. Those who remember to focus on the basics and keep the goal in mind. Those who remember they are there to do a job, to accomplish what they set out to do many years before. These are the athletes who show the dogged resilience and stamina that enable them to perform under great pressure. In the end, it is just another race. Those who allow it to be more than just another race can get lost in the excitement and stress of the event.

I had also prepared the athletes for the travelling, vaccinating them, educating them and discussing ways of preventing illness and injury, as well as local issues, especially the dreaded Zika virus. They would travel to the Olympics in the best possible condition.

Someone once asked me, 'How do they do it for four years?'

I laughed. 'We are not talking about four years. We are really talking about much, much longer than that. It takes anything between four and sixteen years to make it to the top in senior rowing.' I used to say to the younger athletes, 'You are not in for the sprint. You are in for the marathon.'

In the meantime, my own position in the team had changed dramatically in the space of a few weeks before the Olympics. I was always going to be travelling to Rio with the rowing squad, but not as part of the South African Olympic team. Jimmy Clark and I would be travelling to Rio, but not staying at the Olympic Village. We had arranged a flat close to the rowing venue and my family was going to join us there. David, Lawrence's girlfriend Nicky, Matthew and Alicia were all coming to watch. Jimmy and I would get a daily pass into the rowing venue to see the athletes and help where we could. I had discussed the situation with the Chief Medical Officer of the South African Olympic team, Dr Kevin Subban, who had briefed me about how it would work with the rowing team. I would be seen as an 'extra doctor' for the Olympic Team and work within the confines and protocols demanded of that situation.

But that had all changed. Two weeks before the team left for Rio, Dr Subban called me to ask if I would be available to travel with the medical support team for the entire Olympic team. They had unexpectedly lost one of the four doctors scheduled to travel with the team: he had left to take up the highly sought-after position of Springbok Rugby team doctor.

I said yes – of course I said yes. It was an unprecedented opportunity for me and I was honoured to have been asked. Privately, though, I had misgivings, and was immediately anxious and nervous. I knew this was taking me out of that familiar place, the proverbial comfort zone most people love, pushing me into a far less comfortable and more challenging place. Old feelings of inadequacy and poor self-esteem surfaced and a deep fear of the unknown settled on me like a prickly and scratchy jersey. I knew I would need to rely on tenacity and courage as the day of departure drew closer.

I felt intimidated by the medical team: most of them had worked their way up to Olympic-level medical support, working at Commonwealth and Africa

Games. I knew no one and the heavy feeling of anxiety continued. I recognised that I would need to contain my fear. I had somehow landed at the top by default, without looking or asking for it. It was a surprise situation and I was anxious.

But there was little time for anxiety. I was caught up in frantic preparation. The time before leaving was taken up with checking on the rowing team, as I usually did, and with the formalities and planning for the Olympic tour.

I left with the South African Olympic team on 23 July 2016, flying directly to São Paulo and then across to Rio de Janeiro. There was a feeling of excitement and anticipation as we got to the Olympic Village built in a sprawling area of Rio called Barra da Tijuca. We were accompanied by mountains of medical luggage, and it took some effort moving into the space allocated to Team South Africa. The medical and physiotherapy teams set about organising the support structures, and setting up the clinics and treatment spaces required by the team at the Olympic Village.

The Olympic Village was a large area of 31 apartment buildings allocated to all the teams of the world. Each building had 17 floors of accommodation, the entire area housing a staggering 11 000 athletes, 6 000 coaches and a large number of support staff for each team. Some countries had entire buildings to themselves, and decorated the buildings with their flags. Smaller countries like South Africa shared their building with other smaller countries. Set around the buildings were curved walking and cycling pathways, pools, gardens, tennis courts and a few shops. There was the biggest eating facility I had ever seen, offering a wide variety of foods from all over the world. The refrigerators were the most astounding spectacle, rows and rows of fridges crammed with literally hundreds of thousands of soft drinks and all the water anyone could possibly want. There was a medical facility, which was really a mini hospital, complete with a casualty area, X-ray facilities including an MRI machine, and a number of treatment areas. The medical facility had a large physiotherapy and massage area. The village also housed a large gym and a conference room for meetings held during this time.

South Africa took a team of 137 athletes to the Rio Olympics. This was the largest group selected since South Africa had been readmitted to the Olympics in 1992.

I had left with the team on 23 July and returned to South Africa on 22 August. I spent 32 days in the Olympic Village. It was the longest time I had ever been away from home. I caught a viral upper respiratory infection on the flight over, which hit me a few days later, knocking me flat. I spent two days in bed, feeling ghastly. I shared an apartment with members of the physiotherapy team and I am grateful to my special roommates, Grace Hughes, Sandhya Silal and Ashleigh Hansen, who made living in close confines so much easier than it could have been.

The medical team had four doctors and ten physiotherapists. Kevin Subban was the Chief Medical Officer, with me, Paul Maphoto and Karen Schwabe being the other three doctors. Karen spent the first week away from the village travelling with the soccer team, Bafana Bafana, to Brasília, where their competition was held. When she joined us at the Olympic Village a week later, she made a big difference. Her energy, drive and experience were invaluable to me. I learnt a considerable amount from the entire medical team and the other sporting codes to which I was exposed. I especially liked chief physiotherapist Grace Hughes's approach to managing her team of physios and felt she brought a remarkable calmness and structure to her team. Initially I definitely felt awkward, very much like the new kid on the block. We had one room between the doctors, which served as the medical room. At times I felt I hovered around, not sure where best to fit myself. But it was not my show, and I needed to fit in under someone else's leadership. My friend Nici sent me a comforting message: 'There is a purpose in your being there.'

But as with many difficult things, my anxiety settled eventually and I worked where I was needed, bringing myself and what I could to each situation. It was a privilege working with the high-calibre athletes who made up the South African team and very special to meet many of them.

Looking back now, I feel I could have learnt more and delved deeper into the experience, and regret that my anxiety and lack of self-belief held me back in this way. In many ways, I feel I fell into the very situation I had worked hard at preventing with the rowing athletes. I made the Games bigger than they were. I was overawed and shy, whereas I needed to relax and do what I always do: listen, look, make decisions and treat.

The South African media department also made a difference to me. They were friendly, relaxed and experienced, and I spent some good times talking to them, building up an understanding of SASCOC, the Olympics, the entire experience. Mark Etheridge, Gary Lemke and Bronwyn Roets were all part of the media team, and they helped in building my experience of the Games.

But this was Rio de Janeiro and the start of the Olympics edged closer, the tension and excitement becoming more palpable each day. The teams started arriving according to the timing of their own competitions. South Africa had a policy for teams only to arrive before their individual competitions and depart as soon as their competitions were over. The days of athletes staying in the village for the length of the Olympics no longer existed.

The South African rowing team arrived in Rio on 29 July. They were ready to fight for their place in the world.

One of the main advantages of my being part of the greater team was the superb access I would now have to the rowing team.

My family started arriving. Matthew and Alicia arrived, David arrived, Nicky arrived. They moved into their flat in the vibrant suburb of Ipanema in Rio de Janeiro, very close to the rowing course. The Olympic Village was over an hour and a half by car or bus from the rowing course, so I did not see much of them except at the regatta venue.

It was a very different family experience from the London Games, four years previously. James and Charles were unable to be there because of their own training commitments for their respective World Championships. I was staying in the Olympic Village with the team. Matthew was a now a supporter, not an athlete. My father was not there. Things felt strange and incomplete, perhaps even slightly surreal.

The regatta was held on Rodrigo de Freitas Lagoon and had been set up by an ex-South African rower, Colleen Orsmond, who had put together an impressive venue in the four years leading up to the Olympics. It was one of the most unique rowing venues in the world, situated within the heart of the pumping city of Rio de Janeiro, its glamorous and famous beaches close by, its magnificent suburbs contrasting with poverty-stricken favelas, and the ever-majestic and watchful statue of Christ the Redeemer gazing down over the entire area. The city of Rio thronged the lagoon; as a result, the regatta would be part of the everyday crowds and noise of Rio, which gave the location a vibe that added considerably to the event. One of the problems with the course was the wind. There was a crosswind that blew in from the sea, usually from mid-morning, and affected the middle and the second 1 000 metres of the course.

'Usually, international rowing courses are set outside and some distance from the host city, often requiring extensive transport to access,' Roger Barrow said after he had visited the venue the year before. 'As a result, international rowing events are often far away from the crowds and energy of big events, with spectators being made up predominantly of people who are involved with rowing. This event will give many people, who know nothing about rowing but will converge on the lake and hang from balconies and rooftops, the chance to see the best in the world racing on lake de Freitas. The vibrancy of Rio with its noise and traffic and throngs of people surrounding the lake will make the rowing athletes the centre of this vibe during the Olympic Regatta, rather than set away from the rest of the Games. The rowing athletes will feel part of the greater games as a result, and not feel they are out of the main village or main thrust of the Olympic Games. They will be very much part of the momentum of the Olympic Games.'

Rio was ready. It was gathering itself, building up momentum to unleash the crescendo.

Everything was ready.

The 2016 Olympic Games opened on 5 August with a vibrant and colourful Opening Ceremony. Only six of the South African rowing athletes attended this. The remainder of the team were racing the next day and their recovery and preparation were more important. I stayed to cover the clinic and any athletes who may have needed help.

The Rowing Regatta was one of the first events, and began the next day, 6 August.

The time had come.

15

🚣🚣🚣🚣

BELIEVE

Rio de Janeiro, 2016

Never give in, never give in, never, never, never, never –
in nothing, great or small, large or petty …
– WINSTON S. CHURCHILL

The day after the rowing team arrived in Rio, it was down to business immediately. They had a week to get themselves into the best condition for racing. The coaches left for the rowing venue to start the lengthy and painstaking process of rigging the boats. The athletes settled in and completed a light session that day. The following day, they rowed for the first time. Having been to Rio the year before to look at the venue, they knew their way around and felt relaxed.

Lawrence and Shaun were happy with their boat. It was rigged perfectly. They were rowing well and feeling strong. They felt positive.

But the path ahead seldom runs smoothly.

The week before the racing started, as had always been a common occurrence with travelling, Lawrence came down with an upper respiratory infection. I suppose I should have expected it, but I had remained hopeful. *How much harder does this have to be?* I asked myself, not for the first time. *Why are there always so many obstacles?*

We were out of time. He told me he felt sick. I could tell by the sound of his voice that he was going down. I had to treat him aggressively as he tends to get really sick and he needed to recover quickly. I started treatment and prescribed rest for him. There was no other way. He took two days off training and rested. We needed to be patient and allow him to settle down.

Travelling always places additional and significant stress on athletes. Their training already puts them at greater risk of injury and illness than the average person, and travelling just compounds this. The athletes travelling to Rio had crossed six time zones and this shift in circadian rhythm affected them, increasing their risk. I had covered them with as many precautions as possible in general healthcare and prevention of illness. Despite this, they remained vulnerable.

As if this was not enough, Lawrence had added risks. He had an immune system that struggled to fight the attack. But this time it did not sink him completely. With rest and treatment, he recovered.

It was time to race the heat. Lawrence had to push through.

The men's pair faced some tough opposition. The reigning World and Olympic Champions were in this event, the New Zealand pair of Hamish Bond and Eric Murray, the outstanding duo who had dominated this event since 2009. Great Britain, the Netherlands, Italy, Australia, France, Serbia, Spain, the USA, Hungary, the Czech Republic and Romania were all in the line-up. Apart from the Kiwi pair, who were almost assured of a win, all the other crews were of a high standard, so the race for silver and bronze would be close and very competitive. Based on their two previous races at the World Cup events in Varese and Lucerne, Lawrence and Shaun were seeded fourth.

Lawrence and Shaun drew the Australians, Czech Republic, USA and Spain for their heat. Lawrence was just coming through the infection and raced as best he could. He was feeling a lot better, but nowhere near his best. The weather was rough. It was windy, and waves broke over and into the boats. In the space of the week of the regatta, the weather dished up every possibility: cold, heat, rain, wind. When the squad had travelled to Rio the year before to do their reconnaissance, they had realised the wind needed to be factored into their racing. Despite its magical and idyllic beauty, Rio is a coastal city after all, with all the unpredictability and variability that coastal weather brings. The rough water in the heat actually suited Lawrence and Shaun as it would require more technical prowess, and they had undeniably good technical skill. They took the race in their stride, and the pressure Lawrence felt by being ill was swallowed up in the progression of the event.

The pair came second to Australia in the heat, which meant they did not have to go through the repechage. This gave Lawrence an invaluable extra day of recovery before racing the semi-final. He improved daily, returning rapidly to good health. I was relieved and felt that things were finally falling into place, lining up favourably for the subsequent racing.

The rest of South Africa's results were good. Both lightweight doubles won their heats and the women's pair came second. They all progressed straight through to the semi-finals. The men's four came fourth, sending them in to the repechage. 'We had a disastrous heat,' said Jake. 'I went into the race feeling too relaxed and was not in the right mindset.' They went on to win the repechage the following day and felt they had rectified the situation and gained momentum.

Despite my best efforts to isolate Lawrence and protect Shaun from the infection, he came to me the day before the semi-final and appeared ill. He had similar symptoms to Lawrence and was off-colour and symptomatic. I started treatment immediately. Fortunately, he did not go down badly, and after two days of treatment and rest, he was a lot better. Shaun himself felt that no matter what happened, he would race.

When a crew lines up for a race, especially a race of this importance, each member of that crew wants complete trust and belief that the other crew members will give everything they can to the race and, like warriors, fight to win. The squad has coined a few phrases over the years. One of them is 'trust is earned'. One learns to trust someone and, conversely, one earns trust from colleagues. It is not automatically given. Shaun and Lawrence had a special bond, built over the years. They enjoyed rowing together and were constantly focused on getting faster. As Lawrence says, 'Shaun is exceptional. He does not lose and always delivers a good race when it counts.'

Lawrence and Shaun focused their attention on getting themselves physically better and preparing themselves mentally for the semi-final.

As expected, the semi-final proved an intense and stressful race. I find semi-final racing even more stressful than the final, as it really is the make-or-break race. If the boat places in the top three positions, it goes through to the A final, where six boats will fight it out for medal positions. If the boat places in the bottom three positions, the race to be the best is effectively over as the boat cannot do better than seventh place. Coach Paul Jackson always says, 'The purpose of the semi is to make the final. Nothing else.'

The South African pair raced against New Zealand, Great Britain, Hungary, Serbia and the Czech Republic in their semi-final. They came third. Although it was a good race, and one in which they rowed well, it was nowhere close to their best effort. They faced both the Kiwi pair and the British pair, both of whom beat them. Lawrence felt stronger in the race but knew Shaun was still sick and not at his best. During the race, Lawrence was aware of Great Britain calling a sprint and push, after which they pulled away from South Africa. He made a snap, calculated and clever decision not to go with them, not to fight it out at this stage. He felt they did not need to empty themselves of valuable reserves by racing to maximum effort and beating the British pair. At the same time, he knew they were strong enough to prevent an attack from another crew trying to beat them out of third place. It was undoubtedly a critical and mature decision. For us watching from the grandstand, it was stressful as we knew that a B final would have mentally broken not only the pair, but the rest of the South African rowing team. We had no idea how they were feeling. We were just relieved when they made it into the A final. Shaun told me at the jetty after the race, 'I felt horrific in that race, Doc. I didn't know if I was going to make it.'

Lawrence, at this stage, was regaining his strength and form. 'I felt so strong in that race, Mom. When I saw the British go I looked and made a decision not to chase them as I knew Shaun was not feeling that great and it would take too much from us both to chase them. The cost would have been too great. But we could have taken them. We can beat the British pair, I know we can. I am feeling really strong.'

This was especially good news. I knew Lawrence was firing again. The best was still to come from him. They had the day between the semi-final and the final to recover. Shaun rested that day and did not train. He always responded well to rest. I told Roger, 'At this stage, less is more.' Holding back slightly at this time could make a significant difference to Shaun's recovery and ultimately the ability of the pair to perform in the final.

Lawrence and Shaun felt relieved after the semi-final; they had achieved the second step and made it safely into the A final. They could relax for the rest of that day, with a sense of accomplishment and relief. But that relaxed feeling did not last long as the race ahead began to dominate their thoughts. It was time to prepare for the final. I was doing all I could to get Shaun into the best condition to race. They spent the next day and a half talking about their race plan.

As they moved closer to the final, so their fears grew. Lawrence says, 'It is like being on a roller coaster of emotion, but you have to manage the anxiety and nerves.' Their race preparation entailed looking at different racing scenarios and how they would execute the race, taking into account their preparation, training, all their previous races and how they had raced those races, and all they had learnt from other crews during the season and especially during this regatta. Their race plan had evolved; it was almost a summary of the entire season, reaching a point at which they could plan this race. The knowledge that they were approaching the biggest race of their lives was difficult to keep in some form of perspective. It was easy for panic to set in. They needed to hold on to the belief that, despite the enormity of the event, it was still just another race and they were well trained and conditioned. The race plan gave them confidence and helped to keep their motivation up.

On the morning of the race I awoke from a restless night, tense and anxious. I knew Lawrence was strong. I was more worried about how Shaun was feeling. However, the moment I saw him at breakfast in the massive food hall, I knew things were good. He said, 'I feel good, Doc. This is the best I have felt all week.' He was smiling and looked happy. There seemed to be an aura of excitement and hunger to race, and seeing this excitement in him was one of the most memorable moments of the competition for me. I knew at that moment, without a doubt, that they were both strong and that, if there was ever a day they could perform, it was that day. I felt a great comforting sense of relief come over me and suddenly I was a lot more relaxed.

Lawrence reaffirmed how strong he was feeling. It was hard to know how strong they actually were, because normally the squad pushes through to race under very heavy loads. They are more often than not fatigued from pieces and trials, and it becomes difficult to gauge their strength. They do not taper much and they never rest before ergo trials. For this race, Shaun and Lawrence tapered more than normal as a result of them both being sick.

James sent me a message from his training camp in Tzaneen, asking me how they were feeling. I answered simply, 'They are strong.' He was relieved to hear that; based on that comment, he later told me, he knew they could deliver something special that day.

The pre-race routine is something of a ritual for many athletes. They all tend to have their own personal drills and idiosyncrasies, things that help them relax a little, take their mind off the rapidly growing fear of what lies ahead. They often listen to music on their headphones, trying to still the noise of fear in their heads and withdraw into a private space. They try to relax and switch their anxiety off, tapping into a zone of calmness. 'Zoning in', the athletes call it. They are preparing for war. The two to three hours before the race are filled with an unshakeable nervousness and a deep, gnawing fear. The mind of the athlete has to be bigger and stronger than this fear.

Lawrence and Shaun quietly prepared for their racing. They arrived at the course two hours before the race and spent the next hour on their pre-race routine, which comprised the mundane activities of eating, drinking, making their racing drinks, headphones on, lying down with their eyes closed, stretching and warming up, making toilet visits. As Lawrence explains it, 'This is the most nervous I feel in the build-up as the race is pending and there is no going back.' They knew more than anyone that they were about to put their bodies under maximal strain.

They were ready.

They walked to the boat and had a short pep talk with Roger. Lawrence says, 'It was so reassuring to meet Roger, who was relaxed and confident and appeared calm and on top of things. This made a big difference to us as a nervous coach makes us more anxious. He really helped relax us and even joked with us.'

Before the meeting, Roger had spent a few hours checking the boat meticulously. Each aspect of every component was checked for possible breakages and any slight loosening of parts. The careful checking, tightening and replacing is the best the coaches can do to prevent breakages and parts coming loose during the race. Footboards, slides, gates, blades. All are checked and then checked again. They wash, dry and polish the boat to perfection. It is part of their ritual as they want the athletes to take a spotless boat to war. These rituals contain the coaches' own anxieties and nervousness, and keep them away from the preparation of the athletes.

The time before the race is one of the most stressful and tense times for the entire team. I try to be as inconspicuous as possible, sitting quietly and unobtrusively in the background, close to the athletes, keeping an eye on things and being available if they need anything. It is always a delicate time where the sacred preparation zone and quiet mental focus of the athlete needs to be respected.

It is a relief for everyone including themselves when the athletes leave the boating area, carrying their boat down to the jetty accompanied by the coach who carries their blades, settles them into the boat, gives a few last-minute words of encouragement and then finally pushes them off. The waiting is over. They are on their own; they go to battle alone. Everything is ready. No further preparation can change the events that are about to unfold.

The quality of the preparation over the past four years will decide how they fight. No coach, trainer, scientist, doctor or therapist can help them now. They have to believe and trust that the training has set them up to race. Over and over they will say to themselves, *This is just another race. We have raced so many times before.*

Lawrence and Shaun were relaxed as they pushed off from the jetty and started their first few strokes. The warm-up was a standard programme they always followed, and offered them some respite from the tension. It felt familiar, almost comforting, allowing the subconscious to take over.

They did not have their best warm-up that day. The conditions were deteriorating, with the wind picking up, and things did not feel particularly good. The fact that other crews were struggling with the same conditions helped them. But as the time approached for them to head to the start line, the tension built rapidly once again. Lawrence and Shaun were setting themselves up to race, knowing that they would give 100 per cent of their effort in the next six minutes.

The start line is the most terrifying place for a rowing athlete. The overwhelming thought at that moment is the fear of how hard the race is going to be and how much pain they are facing. Like many rowers, Lawrence loves racing, but no one likes the inevitable pain that accompanies racing. There is no way around the pain. Within 300–400 metres every muscle fibre starts to burn. In normal sedentary life, a person breathes about 20 litres per minute. In a race, the athlete breathes about 200 litres per minute. Everything hurts at that intensity. The harder the athlete pulls, the greater the pain. Being fitter or stronger does not lessen the pain. The desire to perform well, to win, helps the athlete tolerate it. The worst thing about racing is the pain. The best thing about racing is winning.

The battle of the warrior comes down to how much pain can be tolerated. Fear comes from knowing the pain, and the fight is against the fear. Lawrence explains the strange paradox: 'The greater the pain, the better the race.'

The body starts to panic and thinks it is going to die. The brain wants to protect the body. The body and the mind have to control it. There are few rowing athletes who do not hear that placatory, silky, inner voice asking, *Why are you doing this? You can stop. You do not have to go through this.* My son James explains it to me: 'The mind is struggling with two voices opposing each other. It is a brutal conversation that starts in your mind as the race begins and the voices are screaming inside your head. One voice is telling you not to worry, you can do it next time, it is okay to lose and allow your opponent to beat you. This is the rational voice, trying to hold you back, accepting mediocrity. It is trying to convince you that next time will be easier to push harder. This can be dangerous. It is important to train the rational voice to say the right things. The other voice is the one that wants to win.'

This is the fight. These are the warriors. They must remain calm and ruthless in battle, they must be deadly.

It comes down to choice. It always comes down to choice.

Racing to win brings out those who have the soul of a warrior, the temperament to remain calm and ruthless in the rage of battle, when the fear is overpowering. A warrior needs to be able to win on any day, in any conditions.

Lawrence's journey to the start line could not have been harder. It toughened his resolve and brought out the true warrior in him.

Lawrence and Shaun moved their boat to their lane at the start. The start line is always deathly quiet. The battle is imminent. Not a word is spoken: it is eerily quiet, except for the slight touch of blades on the water and the wavelets lapping against the boats. The six boats straighten up and move into position. Every athlete is aware of each of their opponents. This is not a friendly space. There is no compassion and empathy in battle. Not a glance passes between them. Each athlete is trying to deal with the storm raging in his mind; outwardly, each one is going through the familiar motions of preparation but inwardly working to calm the threatening chaos. All the preparation comes together at this point.

Lawrence says, 'We are like racehorses in the starting pen. We are ready to go, anxious and jittery and actually just wishing it would start and we can go.'

The starting umpire called the boats by the name of their country to line up, announcing one minute to go. Under the gaze of the magnificent Christ the Redeemer – Cristo Redentor – on Mount Corcovado above the regatta course, the six boats completed their preparations for racing and lining up. The red light is on for the duration of the one minute called by the umpire, but the start is announced randomly to avoid the possibility of boats jumping the start. Out of the deep silence came the monotone voice: 'South Africa, Great Britain, Italy, New Zealand, Australia, France.' The umpire called each country in order of their lanes, the standard way of calling them to attention.

He continued, 'Attention.'

The bell rang and the green light flashed.

Six boats hauled themselves out of the starting blocks. Lawrence and Shaun exploded out the start, maintaining the lead for the first 500 metres. 'Nice and quick out the start, South Africa,' the commentator said, but barely mentioned them again. The South African pair were known to be powerful, with a swift, strong start. They had practised that start many, many times at home and knew that, when the green light flashed, they would be first out.

Throughout the race, the commentators were convinced that Italy and Great Britain would medal. They knew the New Zealanders would win. Everybody knew that. Hamish Bond and Eric Murray were the two Kiwis who had raced in the pair since 2009, winning every race since then. They were the current World Champions, Olympic Champions and record holders. Everyone knew it would be almost impossible to beat them.

Mentally, Shaun and Lawrence felt good in the first 500 metres. They were in the lead, which gave them an edge over the rest of the field. Shaun, the stroke, set the rhythm and tempo of the boat. He also steered to ensure the straightest line to the finish. Lawrence sat in the bow, established the race plan and made the calls. Calling instructions is the coxswain's job in bigger boats, but in coxless boats one of the athletes is assigned this role. Lawrence explains, 'The purpose of calling is to remind the crew of certain key points or plans that have been previously discussed or worked on. The calls tweak the race plan, and ensure that the crew are all on the same page at that moment of calling. It focuses the crew. Calling is important in racing but it is more important during training. It is during training that racing becomes second nature and calling can remind crew members what needs to be done.'

In the first 500 metres of the race Lawrence called out to find the speed they wanted and to remind them to use their legs. The second 500 metres saw the South Africans slip into third place, with Italy taking the lead. After that, the mighty New Zealanders pushed through into first place, which they held until the end. Great Britain started to move and came past South Africa, pushing them back into fourth position.

Things were not going so well for Shaun and Lawrence in the second 500 metres. Lawrence says, 'We were struggling. It was really starting to hurt. We felt stiff in our shoulders and our rowing strokes were short. Everyone seemed to be moving past us. We were in a dark place. We had lost our position and were struggling to get the rhythm flowing smoothly in our boat.'

This is a dangerous place for athletes. They lose their confidence and start doubting themselves. They lose the belief that it is possible to win. The inner voices are telling them not to fight and consoling them that is acceptable to settle for losing. Lawrence and Shaun went through the 1 000-metre mark, halfway, in fourth place. The commentators were happy they were right: 'South Africa is paying for their first 500 metres,' they glibly announced.

At the 1 000-metre line, Shaun looked out of the boat. He was under pressure and felt things were not going well. In general, athletes should not look out of the boat. It disrupts their focus and the rhythm. One athlete in the crew, or the cox if there is one, is usually given the responsibility of looking out to see where the boat is in relation to everyone else. The disruption can be costly to the speed, and can increase the risk of mistakes.

Lawrence also looked out at that moment, a desperate feeling of panic rising in both of them that the other boats were moving away from them. He sensed they were under pressure and their rhythm felt brittle. He knew he had to do something to save the race. He called out, 'Believe,' a word that resonated from the victory in Belarus six years before when Ramon di Clemente had sent AJ, Lawrence and John a message that said only that.

That call proved to be the turning point of the race for the South Africans. It changed their attitude instantly. They began to fight back. They took a few good strokes and the rhythm immediately felt better. They felt freer, less stiff; their strokes lengthened. It shot them out of the dark hole straight back into the light. It was a powerful, emotional call to fight. Suddenly they were racing, the boat working with them. In that moment it became less about defending a fragile position and more about attacking the rest of the field.

Within a few seconds, it became all about having a good race and doing what they had trained to do. In a few strokes, they were holding the other crews. They were rowing well. The speed they knew they had was coming. It was building, stroke by stroke. The Italians and the British had used a lot of energy in the second 500 metres and probably believed that the South Africans had spent themselves in their first 500 metres. But Lawrence and Shaun were gaining momentum. They used the belief they had in themselves now. They had done the training and could be fast, even deadly, in the second half of the race. They could trust themselves.

The third 500-metre split saw New Zealand devour the course and establish themselves as clear leaders. They were unbeatable. The race was on for second and third. Lawrence and Shaun were feeling the improvement in their rhythm and the boat was moving cleanly and perfectly, slicing its way through the water. At the 1 250-metre mark, Lawrence called, 'Breathe', a reminder to start to think about the finish and the sprint they would need to end the race. They needed to begin the winding-up process, the final attack.

At the 1 500-metre mark, he looked across and saw that they were in fourth position and although he did not like this, he could see they had held the other crews. As he felt the rhythm of the boat improve, he called for a push: 'Zero point two never again!' This had enormous significance for Lawrence and Shaun as it was the distance that had separated the Dutch, the British and the South Africans at Lucerne earlier that year, when the Dutch and the British had narrowly beaten South Africa into fourth place. They had both vowed never to allow this to happen again.

This call was staggeringly powerful and enough to unleash the fury in a massive surge of power. They shifted into a higher gear, powering the boat through the water. They were rowing in perfect unison and had never been more focused or more deadly. From the 1 500-metre mark they started to move back on the Italians and British, cleaving the boat through the water. They had purpose and speed and were moving faster than the other crews. The bow ball began to edge forward and slowly, unequivocally, obliterate the chances of the Italians and the British beating them. Neither crew was able to respond.

As they moved into the last 400 metres of the race, Lawrence was shouting, 'The silver is ours, let's end this race, let's close this door!' They were dimly aware of the roar of the crowd, a deep, bloodthirsty war cry, overwhelmed only by the noise of their own blood pumping in their ears. They were in agony. It was the hardest part of the race, but they were focused on the result.

'Brittain and Keeling, coming through!' the commentator shouted.

South Africa crossed the finish line in second place behind the Kiwi pair. They wanted to beat the Kiwis, but the Kiwis would not allow them to make contact. The Italians finished third. The British were fourth.

Silver.

They had done it.

Shaun let out a shriek of joy and relief, hitting the water with his arms and then falling back in the boat in utter exhaustion. They both saluted themselves, acknowledging the fact they had given everything they had to each other. It was a massive acknowledgment of the bond of trust between them. Shaun sat up and raised his arms in victory. Lawrence raised his left arm in a salute. It was a euphoric moment of triumph.

Eric Murray looked across to the South African pair and acknowledged them, clapping his hands, pointing at them and giving the thumbs up.

Roger watched the race on the big screen in a crowd of coaches. I watched the race on the grandstand with David, Nicky, Matthew and Alicia, and the rest of the South African supporters. My dad had stayed behind as we were worried about the availability of tickets and, with him being an elderly man now, I was concerned about how he would manage. Looking back, this was not the best decision; he would have loved to have seen Lawrence win the silver medal and he should have been there. I had come to the grandstand to be with my family as I could not be with the coaches. The stress of being with them would have been too great, but I could not bear to be on my own either.

It is hard to describe the level of emotion a supporter goes through during a race. Watching a race is as close to racing as you can get. Stroke for stroke, you feel it. It does not let up. Fear and hope juggle for position in the hearts of the supporters just as the boats fight for their place in the race.

The South African supporters were excited when the pair were first out the start and looked strong in the first 500 metres. But I knew that 2 000 metres was a very long way to lead and the Kiwis were notoriously slow out the start. When they moved into fourth place I was worried. Had we been wrong to dream and hope? I buried my head in my hands, overwhelmed by anxiety. Jonty Smith's family was standing in front of us and his brother David was incredible. He looked at me and said, 'Doc, it's okay – they are going to do it. They will do it. Believe.'

The moment they started to move up on the Italians and British, my despair vanished. I knew they could do it. We were all screaming – there

265

is nothing else to do except scream, willing them on. I could barely watch. The memory of the final 300 metres of the lightweight four, when they won the gold in London, came flooding back. As I watched them cross the finish line, somewhere inside me a wall broke. I turned to David and burst into tears, deep, uncontrollable sobs of joy, relief and pride, in a moment that was the culmination and acknowledgement of all the pain, hardship and difficulty that had gone before. Such a momentous moment triggered an equally momentous response in me.

It is not often that things work out as perfectly as they did on the morning of 12 August 2016. Almost to the day four years ago, they had worked out perfectly for the lightweight four. Technically, Lawrence and Shaun rowed better than ever before. They won the silver medal 'Because we rowed well,' says Shaun. Their silver medal almost felt like the gold medal as the Kiwi pair had dominated the event for so long.

David watched the pair cross the finish line and felt an overwhelming relief at the result, a feeling that it was finally over, the cancer, the chemotherapy. Lawrence was better. 'Before this moment I could not trust it, I dared not hope. When they fell back into fourth place I lost my belief, I doubted it was possible. But as soon as they moved through the British and the Italians I knew they would come second. No crew fights back into second place and then loses. That was the moment I knew that Lawrence was healed, the cancer was gone,' he told me. This was a profound moment for David, a final release of the crippling anxiety of the past few years.

Happiness and uncontrollable relief flooded through Nicky Mundell as she witnessed the pair cross the finish line. During the race she had felt deep, conflicting emotion, excitement, worry, despair that they might not manage it and what that would do to Lawrence. She struggled to keep calm, as doubt and fear raged through her head. 'As they moved into silver position, a crazed feeling of unreality swept through me. Suddenly, everything was worth it,' she recalls. All the aching despair of Lawrence's illness, everything was suddenly gathered together, delivering sense and meaning to the journey.

Nicky and Lawrence had been together seriously since 2013, but had known each other since 2010. They had met at university. She was studying property management, successfully completing an honours degree. Not only had she faced the Olympic dream with him, but she had also walked the journey of his illness. Her family were not sportspeople but they were hardworking and driven; she understood what it meant to strive against hardship. She had a farming background. Her family came from KwaZulu-Natal and the Eastern Cape. They understood ups and downs, the true meaning of taking life in their stride. Petite, attractive and brimming with energy, nothing was an obstacle to Nicky. She embraced everything with a positive spirit. During their time together, she had learnt what the Olympics meant to Lawrence and she knew that he thrived under pressure, bringing an unparalleled positivity to everything he did. In this, they were perfectly matched. She had pledged her support to him, embracing the all-encompassing lifestyle and focus demanded by the Olympics. Her joy was overwhelming as she watched Lawrence and Shaun stand together on the podium receiving their medals.

Roger was delighted. 'The stars aligned for us that day. Lawrence and Shaun showed enormous self-belief. They coped with the conditions and remained calm. They stuck to what they knew and executed a well-prepared plan.'

Matthew stood with Alicia and Nicky on the grandstand just behind David and me. Back home in South Africa, James and Charles were watching in Tzaneen from their own training camps preparing for the Under-23 World Championships.

My father watched the race with my sister Claudine, Julian and their family and friends in a restaurant in Johannesburg. The excitement built rapidly as the pair came out the start and took the lead. But as they slipped back to fourth place, a nervous silence settled on the group and my father held his breath. Not for long, though. As they saw the pair pull themselves back into the race and move into third, the group exploded out of their chairs, jumping and shouting, willing them on stroke by stroke to the finish line.

'Standing on the podium, despite feeling paralysing fatigue from the physical effort we had just put out there; it does not get better than that,' Lawrence tells me.

South Africa continued to have an unforgettable day, with all four boats making the A finals. Both lightweight pairs won their semi-finals. The women's pair came third to Great Britain and the USA, narrowly making it into the A final. After their shaky start to the regatta, the men's four produced a solid performance, coming second to Australia but beating the world champions, Italy. This placed them in the A final.

We were watching some spectacular racing unfold in front of us. Excitement was building in the team, and the entire South African support contingent. We were stepping forward. All our crews had made it into the A finals.

That day was South Africa's best performance ever as a rowing nation.

South Africa, with France, Poland and the Netherlands, all had five crews that made A finals. The only teams to beat this were the bigger, more powerful teams of the USA, with seven crews, and New Zealand and Great Britain, each with eight crews in A finals.

We had achieved beyond expectation.

But nothing lasts forever.

The elements conspired against Rio that week. Due to dreadful and dramatic weather conditions, which were judged by the Regatta Fairness Committee and Jury to be unrowable, two of the eight racing days were cancelled. Teams lost valuable days for their preparation and recovery. Effectively, they lost strategically placed recovery days. Everyone faced the same situation, but some crews managed better than others. There is no doubt in my mind that this affected our lightweight crews, as it threw them off their trusted method of making weight.

Despite these difficulties, South Africa prepared for its final day of racing. There was a high level of excitement, tension and expectation from everyone: families, coaches, the support team, the press, the entire Olympic team, and South Africans back home.

The women's pair of Kate Christowitz and Lee-Ann Persse came fifth, a big step up from the eighth place at the London Olympics that Lee-Ann and Naydene Smith had achieved. Kate and Lee-Ann came into the Rio Games well prepared, feeling strong and putting out some of their best rowing in the weeks leading up to the Olympics. After solid racing in the heat and semi-final, Lee-Ann was euphoric to have made the A final. Memories of the heartbreak four years before in London, where Naydene and Lee-Ann had missed making it into the A final, still hovered around her, and this result gave her confidence. She felt she had made a breakthrough. Kate and Lee-Ann prepared for the final, focused but also realistic. They raced hard, giving everything they had, crossing the line in fifth place. They were happy with their result and celebrated it. They felt that they had raced to their potential.

The men's four faced their final with the realisation that, based on their performance in the semi-final, a medal was possible. Coming through the repechage, they had not expected to be in this position. 'The night before, sleep was impossible,' Jake recalls. 'Every emotion seemed heightened; I was nervous, excited, energetic, every sensation was scaled up. It was uncontrollable.'

Blistering out the start, the four maintained their third position until the last 300 metres, when Italy made a move, a turn of speed that South Africa simply could not match. They came fourth, narrowly missing out on the bronze medal to Italy. Great Britain won gold and Australia silver. They were gutted. It had been a roller coaster. A horrible heat, a superb repechage and semi-final, and then crushing disappointment. They knew they had achieved beyond their original expectation, but that was not enough to console them.

Unexpectedly and unfathomably, neither of the lightweight doubles made the podium. The lightweight women's double came fifth. Despite a superb build-up through the heat and semi-final, which poised them perfectly to fight for a medal in the final, the lightweight women lacked rhythm and connection during the final. They could not bring on the speed they knew they had in the last 1 000 metres. Speaking to Ursula Grobler a long while later, when she could talk more easily about the loss, she told me, 'I feel Kirsten [McCann] and I were too distanced from the Games. We tried to control too much and this proved impossible. We were nervous before the final, edgy and irritable. The weather threw us, the extra weigh-ins were tough on us. We did not warm up as sharply as usual, we rowed into the buoys. We were doing everything we could in the race but somehow our focus and connection were not together.'

Likewise, the lightweight men won their heat and semi-final, and sailed into the A final. They lined up for the race feeling confident; they had seen the men's pair win silver and they were ready to take on the world. What happened was the opposite. The world took them on, and ripped the race from them. They came fourth, losing to France, Ireland and Norway. John Smith and James Thompson raced to their capacity, racing the first 1 600 metres as hard as they could, in the pack, fighting it out. They thought they could do it, that it would come down to the last quarter. As the other crews started to wind up and pull away, an awful, brutal realisation descended on them that they had nothing left for the last 400 metres. They could not sprint. Despite rowing the hardest they could, it was not enough. They crossed the line in fourth place, their dreams crashing around them. Speaking of it much, much later, John said, 'I did everything in my power, but I had nothing left in the last 400 metres. It took a long time to process it as it did not make sense. We were a great crew, we had worked hard, we felt our recipe was right. It still hurts but it does not burn as much.'

These were profound disappointments for the crews, their coaches, the entire team, their families. All the hard years of training and preparation, the dreams, the purpose, all lay broken in a paralysing sense of grief and loss. At the post-race drug testing I saw harrowing distress from our athletes. Their Olympic hopes and dreams for 2016 had shattered. Seeing them in their rawest moment of grief nearly broke my heart. I knew how much it meant to them and how long they would take to make some sort of sense of it all.

Ursula Grobler later described the heartbreak of that day. 'With 700 metres to go I am not sure what happened, but we did not happen and we finished a disappointing fifth. It felt like someone had come and robbed my house. Did I fly too close to the sun and instead of gold I came home with burnt wings?'

The events leading up to that day did not line up perfectly for their final performances. The weather, the preparation for the finals, inevitable light-weight issues, race conditions – these all played some role in the racing.

The Rio results were disappointing. As the South African rowing team, we felt we had the ability to bring home more than one medal. It brought home to me just how impossibly hard it is to win a medal. It put into per-spective what an outstanding achievement the gold medal had been four years ago. This time, as a team we had achieved massive success: five boats into Olympic A finals. A silver medal. Two fourth places and two fifth places. The women's pair was a great result; they were celebrating their achievement. The men's four was also a great result, but they had sniffed the medal and were disappointed not to have grabbed it. The achieve-ments of the pair and the four were overshadowed by the heartbreaking outcome suffered by the two lightweight doubles. It was a time of conflict. The results were outstanding but there was agonising disappointment not to have achieved more than one medal.

The South African supporters and coaches gathered for a lunch after the racing. I joined my family and we took photographs and toasted the team. The celebration was edged with sadness and disappointment. Once again, I found myself in a conflicted position, this time in my role as the team doctor. I was elated for Lawrence and Shaun but felt devastated for the doubles. I wanted to celebrate but could not escape from the need to hide and process the loss.

The next day, the team scattered. The coaches flew home, the athletes left with their families to travel or return to South Africa. The sense of loss was deepened as I said goodbye to those who had not already left.

I continued at the Olympic Village in my role as a doctor for the rest of the South African team. There was still another two weeks of competition. I witnessed some heroic racing in the mountain bike events as well as the BMX competition, and was privileged to watch the spectacular performances of Wade van Niekerk, Caster Semenya, Luvo Manyonga and Sunette Viljoen as they medalled in athletics and became part of an unforgettable experience for me.

But from the rowing perspective, the competition was over. The aftermath needed time. As in all sports, and in life, you have to get up again after the gut-wrenching disappointments that block our paths, and start over. And when the machine warms up again and starts to pound away at the daily grind of training, a previous win means nothing. You start again from the bottom and work your way up, step by step.

Never backwards.

Onwards. Upwards. Always.

16

AFTER RIO

Pretoria, 2016

Roads go ever ever on,
Over rock and under tree,
By caves where never sun has shone,
By streams that never find the sea:
Over snow by winter sown,
And through the merry flowers of June,
Over grass and over stone,
And under mountains in the moon.

− JRR TOLKIEN, *THE HOBBIT*

Matthew's winning the gold medal was a big story.
Lawrence's story was even bigger.

Not only was he part of the ten South African teams or individuals who had brought medals home from the Rio Olympics, but his personal story caught the imagination of the public. It was as if he had won a gold medal. His success made people feel good. That he had overcome illness and difficulty gave hope to people in similar circumstances. Success in sport has the unique gift of keeping dreams alive. It allows hope to grow. Hope is that immensely powerful feeling of possibility.

Lawrence and Shaun were caught up in the post-Olympic hype and attention. They gave talks, visited schools, motivated people, gave interviews, and attended functions and awards ceremonies.

Would it have mattered had Lawrence not won the silver, and come fourth or fifth or stone last? To me and to our family, his position would have made no difference at all. Could anything ever be as bad as what Lawrence had gone through with his illness? Losing a race would be nothing compared to the pain of the terrible possibility of his relapsing or dying. His illness and our deep gratitude for his health put everything into clear and logical perspective for me.

But to Lawrence, not winning the silver would have mattered very much. It would have burned him inside. It would have built his resolve to fight harder and more fiercely. It would have fuelled the will to go back to the battlefield. To try again and again.

Some interesting outcomes followed the Rio Olympics. It was the first time in South Africa that two brothers had won Olympic medals. It was the first time in South African rowing history that five boats made A finals in an Olympic regatta. It was the first time that a South African rowing coach had been singled out in world rowing – Roger Barrow was nominated for World Rowing Coach of 2016 and went on to win that award, an outstanding achievement for a young coach in a highly competitive environment.

Despite the disappointment of not winning more medals at the Olympics, the rowing results were extraordinary and anyone who understood the intensity and difficulty of rowing knew what those results meant. The London medal had made it possible; the Rio results confirmed that the base was strong and there were dedicated people working towards good results.

The London and Rio successes were the culmination of years of hard work and dedication. Those events needed to be marked and celebrated each year. I planned to celebrate those victories and acknowledge those who had made them happen.

After Rio I asked myself, *Where to from this point?*

As expected, there was a sense of emptiness and flatness after the Olympics. It was inevitable; it is not possible to sustain that level of intensity. The rowing squad disbanded after the Olympics; the wolf pack broke up. The break and subsequent disengagement were important for the team. Everyone needed time away to gather themselves and reconsider their positions.

The gold medal was an unbelievable achievement, unsurpassed by anything in rowing. The silver medal represented tenacity and determination. But despite these medals and the indefatigable resolve they represent, all athletes begin again at the bottom when the new Olympic cycle starts up. It is a fresh start, a clean slate. New chances. Hopes and dreams once again come alive. Places in crews have to be earned again. There is often only one chance.

It was time to consider how we could become stronger and faster. The machine needed work. There is always more to be done.

The squad system is gaining momentum as South Africans see that it is possible to medal at Olympic level. It has been an issue for South African athletes that they lack belief in themselves and what they are capable of. South African rowing has become better known. The media is more interested in the sport, and both medals initiated more coverage than ever before. But hardships continue. Ironically, the year after the Olympics is often the most difficult as funding is short and people grapple with the intensity required to build up to Olympic level. The squad remains on the path of building towards more professional athletes. There is little doubt in my mind that it would be better to have full-time athletes committed to training hard and recovering equally hard.

When the next cycle began and the wolf pack gathered again, not all of them returned. Some new athletes and some old ones showed up to prepare for the four-year cycle leading up to the Tokyo Olympics in 2020.

Shaun Keeling announced his retirement and began working. He didn't feel he could train for another four years without more financial support. He and his long-time partner, former South African rower Kate Johnstone, married in May 2019. Shaun remains an outstanding athlete, going on to complete the Iron Man and a number of running marathons, including two Comrades Marathons.

James Thompson stepped away from rowing. He got married and took a year to travel through Africa with his wife, Carolyn Smith. He does not plan to return to rowing. Later in 2019, James and Carolyn had their first baby, Hayden Thompson. James remains involved with rowing on a number of levels and he has considerable experience and insight to offer.

Ursula Grobler came back when the squad reconvened in 2017, but following advice from her coaches took time off. She needed time to consider whether her body could handle another four years of intensive training. She got married in 2018 and moved to Cape Town, trying to distance herself from rowing. She remained ambivalent in the two years following the Olympics and, despite the break, she realised that the dream still burned deeply within her. She made the decision to re-join the squad at the end of 2018 to push herself to the limit and test whether she would be able to race in the Olympics again. A year later, however, she hung up her oars, declaring that she was retiring.

Lee-Ann Persse took up a position as head rowing coach at a leading girls' school in Johannesburg and, later, head coach for the University of Cape Town Rowing Club. For a long time, she remained undecided whether she would return to the squad after an extended break. She subsequently made the difficult decision not to return. Following that decision, she suffered from a profound depression that sadly, yet understandably, often accompanies leaving high-level sport. After such immersion it seems impossibly tough to move on, move away, build another life. Lee-Ann researched the subject and realised how prevalent depression can be after a career in elite sport.

Kate Christowitz announced her retirement from rowing and moved on.

Jonty Smith had graduated as an engineer prior to training for the Olympics. He stopped rowing and started working as an engineer, keen to pay back his bursary and build his career.

Vincent Breet returned to Harvard University to complete his Biomedical

Engineering degree. It is not clear whether he will ever return to elite rowing.

Sizwe Ndlovu returned from injury in the new season but was ambivalent about returning to high-level rowing. He eventually decided on a coaching role. He married his partner Liyanda and had a son, Lizwe, born in 2017.

When the squad gathered again, Lawrence, John Smith, Kirsten McCann, David Hunt and Jake Green returned to training. They were ready to see what they could do in Tokyo. They wanted another chance to achieve what they know is possible.

Roger Barrow returned to continue as national coach, once again leading the squad to the next Olympics to be held in Tokyo. He remains energetic and passionate about coaching rowing. He is always one step ahead of everyone. His organisational skills and extraordinary ability to think of everything undoubtedly make him the key to the future of South African rowing. Marco Galeone, previous South African para-rowing coach, became Roger's assistant coach.

Andrew Grant returned to the squad to coach for the next cycle, but later moved to become the head coach and development officer for junior rowing in South Africa.

Paul Jackson has taken a break from the squad and the demands of coaching. He longs to retire to his sheep farm near Springfontein in the Karoo.

Tiago Loureiro moved from being a part-time coach of the national squad to a full-time assistant position.

Jimmy Clark decided to move further into the academic world, but remains connected to the team on a consultant basis.

Garreth Bruni and his wife Corli continue to treat the squad; their experience and calm, pragmatic approach are so valuable in this pressurised environment. They remain excellent physiotherapists. The team relies heavily on them.

Nicola Macleod moved on from the squad before the Rio Olympics. She took on a position with the Chinese rowing team and moved to China as a strength and conditioning coach.

I feel some sadness for the loss of the people with whom I had worked closely since joining the squad.

And me? After a period of introspection and consideration, I decided to continue being the rowing team doctor for the next cycle. This was not an easy decision; I was ambivalent for a long time. In the end the pros outweighed the cons and, despite it being a large commitment, I value what I can bring to the team and would like the chance to see how much of a difference I can make, especially since we have a large group of under-23 athletes who need support and education in high-performance sport.

We have choices to make. We have to follow our hearts.

Our journeys require us to make constant decisions. Every decision has its own unique losses and gains. Both co-exist with each decision. We keep pushing on, using whichever gifts have been given to us in the best way we can.

I know how the future stretches ahead of us. Like a river, it bends and twists as it flows and we move onwards on our journeys, following the current of our lives.

No one ever gets it all.

17

BLOOD BROTHERS

Pretoria, 2017

We came into the world like brother and brother;
And now let's go hand in hand, not one before another.
– WILLIAM SHAKESPEARE, *THE COMEDY OF ERRORS*

And what of the brothers?

After Rio, there were other things. For a start, rowing continued.

It was the first time that three brothers would row in a university crew at the annual Boat Race in 2016, after the Rio Olympics. Lawrence, Charles and James rowed together in the tenth Boat Race. In each race, one or more of the brothers had participated. It was Lawrence's eighth consecutive Boat Race and eighth consecutive win. It was also the last time he rowed Boat Race. Matthew was part of the establishment of an independent Tuks University Boat Club, and rowed the first one and subsequently rowed in three more. James rowed in four, and 2016 was his last Boat Race. It was Charles's first Boat Race, and he has gone on to row each year, clocking up four.

Matthew stopped rowing after London, he felt his back would not handle the intensity of the training required to win another gold medal. He completed his studies, married Alicia, started working and moved to London to build his career and academic dreams.

But despite his leaving rowing, there was one more thing he – they, the brothers – needed to do.

They began to plan how they could row together, to realise a dream. They needed to take to completion their long-time ambition of rowing the Buffalo Grand Challenge as a foursome, a brotherhood.

When Charles had decided to take up rowing, the boys dreamed of rowing together one day as a foursome. They waited patiently for the right time. Matthew had to row at the Olympics. James had to finish school and then row for Tuks before joining the squad. Charles had to finish school. Lawrence had been ill, and had then been training for the Olympics.

But before they could do this, there was a heavier thing to face. Lawrence had been well since the chemo but we needed to check. His blood picture was good and he had just performed to the highest level at the Olympics. Lawrence's blood profile had returned to his 2010 level and I was happy. All markers of disease were normal and the future looked promising. On further discussion with the oncologist, however, we made the decision to scan him. Just to make sure. That shadowy bit in his chest was at the back of our minds, a nagging doubt.

Waiting for a scan is a time of nervous anxiety for me. I want reassurance that all is good. I wait with my family as a pack, all coming together, David, myself, Nicky, the brothers.

I was more upbeat this time, knowing how strong Lawrence was.

After the interminable period of scanning, Lawrence came out desperate to eat something and have a coffee.

I knew there was something up when the doctor did not come and speak to us, but left the rooms in a rush without saying anything. Shortly after that they called David up to the scan to talk to him. I was now concerned that there was a problem. David came down after a while and looked distracted and nervous.

There was a problem.

The shadowy bit in Lawrence's chest, the area we had watched for a year, was bigger. It had got to a point where a biopsy might be necessary. Lawrence took it calmly and seemed to internalise it quickly and efficiently.

He said, 'Let's not get bent out of shape until we know the diagnosis and I have had the biopsy.' What a man he is!

Our family can make jokes about anything. When we left the hospital, we met James and Charles, and James immediately said, 'Looks like we might be racing the single sculls at Buffalo next year.' Humour always helps to lighten the burden of anxiety.

After a long day of further scans, comparisons with previous PET scans and numerous discussions with specialists, strong opinions emerged. This was unlikely to be relapsed disease and the shadow was almost certainly regenerating thymus tissue. It was impossible to perform a biopsy as the area in question was out of reach. With this information, the team made a decision to do nothing, simply to watch Lawrence. It sounds simple, but a lot of people gave input and the decision was not made lightly. I felt relieved and calm; he was well, and that's all that mattered.

I told him the decision. He needed to put it out of his mind, and follow his instinctive feeling that he was well and strong. He could train as hard and with as much conviction as he wanted. Lawrence does not need much encouragement to push hard.

When walking the streets of London on a short holiday in January 2017, David and I passed University College in Strand Street and looked up to see a large photo of British physician and pathologist Dr Thomas Hodgkin, who had been affiliated to the university during his life (1798–1866). It was Dr Hodgkin who originally put the pieces together of a unique malignant disease of the lymphatic system. How strange and coincidental that two members of our family have suffered from this condition. We stopped and silently acknowledged the man, his intellect and skill. It was also of interest to me that he published a book in 1841 called *The Means of Promoting and Preserving Health*, a topic I spend much of my time on with the athletes.

For now, though, Lawrence was clear and we did not need to hold back.

The boys jumped on it and set about getting ready for the prestigious 140-year-old Grand Challenge on the Buffalo River.

The trophy is a magnificent solid-silver goblet standing a metre tall.

Clubs and universities put their best oarsmen into coxless fours to race this event. David raced it in 1986 when he rowed for Wits University and won the trophy with Rob McCall, Stephen Leigh and Craig Fussel. Over the years, top South African oarsmen have won the trophy, many of them representing South Africa in the international arena.

Both Matthew and Lawrence had raced it and won in previous years.

The boys knew they had one chance to carry out their dream.

They spent a week together in the four in December, just before Christmas, and another week together six weeks later, just before the regatta. They squabbled and argued as brothers do, but they knew there was something special in the boat. They believed they could win. Matthew had been training in London, mostly cycling, running, ergometer work and gym training. When he got back into the boat in December, after four years of not rowing at all, it was as if he had never left. It was wonderful to see him row again.

Roger helped them with the setup and order in the boat. He needed to take control and advise them because each of them felt that they were the best person to stroke the boat. He put them into a superb formation that played to their strengths. Lawrence stroked the boat and brought to this his aggressive racing experience and power. Charles rowed behind Lawrence in position three, supporting Lawrence and keeping the length in the boat. Roger put Charles and Matthew rowing a tandem in position two and three, which tied them together and took the technical pressure off Matthew, who had not rowed in four years. It allowed Matthew to concentrate on calling in the boat, a vital role to which he brought precision and intelligence. That left James somewhat alone in the bow of the boat, but this was the perfect place for him because he is technically very competent but lacks some of the power needed in the middle of the boat.

Finally, on 11 February 2017, the four brothers carried out their long-time dream of rowing together as a foursome.

There was a lot of excitement. We made it a special weekend, with David, my father, and Alicia and Nicky there to support the brothers.

I warned them before the race, 'Whatever you do, please do not fight on the jetty. You can kill each other up the river, but please, not in front of everyone.'

They laughed, but the race was serious for them. They wanted to win.

They came out ahead from the start and responded to each push from the other crew comprising Jake Green and David Hunt, both of whom had raced at the Rio Olympics in the heavyweight four, as well as John Smith, three-times gold medallist at World and Olympic level, and Leo Davis, who had represented South Africa a number of times at World level. The boys held their rate and pushed through the other crew, putting them under pressure between 1 000 and 1 500 metres. The boys all have very strong finishes, so they knew they could take it in the last 500 metres.

That is exactly what they did, to win by half a boat length.

It was an extraordinary achievement, a dream come true. I knew they could win. I know them, who they are and how powerful their bond is. I know how strong and determined they are and what each of them can bring to the boat. It was a historical moment when they crossed the line ahead of a competent and experienced crew who had fought every metre of the course to beat them. They raised their arms to salute the win and collapsed onto each other.

A few hours before the Grand Challenge, Lawrence had raced the second-most prestigious race on the Buffalo River, the Silver Sculls. He won it. He told me just afterwards, 'I am feeling so strong, Mom. I feel that I could have gone faster if I had needed to.' To hear those words from Lawrence, words which, for so long, he could not say, was magic. It makes me confident that all is well. I know he is well. Lawrence has more to offer. He is becoming the world-class athlete he always wanted to be.

There are only a few rowers who have managed to win both the Silver Sculls and the Grand Challenge on the same day. Gareth Costa, Andy Maclachlan, John Smith and Pete Lambert are a select group of four oarsmen who have achieved this in the past 25 years. Lawrence has joined that group.

Four brothers winning the Grand Challenge is unlikely ever to happen again. It was a unique moment in South African rowing history, possibly even in the world.

After the Grand, there were inevitable changes.

Two days later, James announced to the squad and the coaches that he was leaving rowing. He felt he was not making enough progress and was simply not fast enough. He no longer believed he could make the huge step up that was required to enter the realm of senior elite-level rowing. James made his own decision to stop, just as he made his own decision to row. He rowed for himself, never because of his brothers or his parents.

A short while after that, he announced that he was becoming a father. He and Stacey Patrick are now the proud parents of our first beloved grand-child, Nathan Alec Brittain.

Matthew's life changed direction again when he accepted a position in an international investment company, and he and Alicia packed their bags once again and moved from London to Singapore in the middle of 2018. I do not have the slightest doubt that he will be an enormous asset wherever he works. He plans to return to South Africa in the future.

Charles has followed the path of his brothers, Matthew and Lawrence. He wants to row and believes he can make it. He shows many of the characteristics that could make him the winner he wants to be. Can it be easy following his brothers? Not at all. But he has enough grit and tenacity to help him through the hard times and balance any insecurity and anxiety he feels.

Towards the end of 2017, Lawrence suffered from severe fatigue. We were concerned. We will always be concerned. He had tests, lots of tests. He saw doctors, lots of doctors. But the findings, the tests, the clinical picture, all were clear. This was fatigue, not cancer. Fatigue from what we could not be sure. Fatigue from chemotherapy, fatigue from recurrent illness, fatigue from viral illness, fatigue from training? Just fatigue. He took four months off training to rest his body and recover, reassessing whether it was possible to continue.

284

But he was not ready to retire from rowing.

From April 2018, he slowly returned to training and, in his inimitable style, he managed to make a fast combination with Jake Green in the men's heavyweight pair and race at the 2018 World Championships in Plovdiv, Bulgaria. They came tenth overall, nowhere near where he wanted to be but a result that spoke more of his resilience, grit and determination than his placing in the world rankings.

He was back in the game.

For now, Lawrence is well and I thank God for his current health and good fortune. We stick with the decision to watch and wait until remission passes and we can speak of cure. We take nothing for granted.

Time will tell.

Lawrence will always be a warrior with the heart of a lion. He has no intention of stopping. He wants more and will hunt relentlessly for it. He is committed to the next cycle, building up to Tokyo. He wants to see how far he can take it.

At the end of 2018, he married Nicola Mundell in a glorious wedding overlooking the magnificent land that seems to stretch on forever in the Eastern Cape.

The brotherhood will continue. My fervent hope is that it remains strong forever and withstands the ravages that life throws at it.

叒叒叒叒

EPILOGUE

Poland, 2018

He who conquers himself is the mightiest warrior.
– CONFUCIUS

On 28 July 2018, 8 775 kilometres away from Johannesburg, on the waters of Lake Malta in the middle of the city of Poznań, Poland, a young South African heavyweight men's pair nervously lined up their boat at the start of the final at the Under-23 World Championships.

In that boat was my youngest son, Charles Brittain.

Together with stroke man James Mitchell, a powerful and remarkably tall young man, they faced the race that they had worked for and dreamed of in the preceding months of training.

The pair had suffered a stormy build-up to the regatta. Despite the clear speed they had demonstrated throughout the season, they had been plagued with injury and pushed doggedly through the hard times as they prepared for the World Championships under the watchful eye of their coach Marco Galeone.

James and Charles had come through their heat, winning with ease and racing just hard enough to get themselves moving. The semi-final was a bit tougher. They pushed themselves hard to the 1 500-metre mark and then held their speed, cruising through in first place and securing a top position in the A final.

286

Their result in the semi-final set them up firmly as one of the favourites to win. The commentator, Martin Cross, singled them out: 'The crew to watch are the South Africans.'

They had raced the heat and semi-final just hard enough to awaken their bodies and minds, reminding themselves physically and emotionally about how much pain they would face in the final. This reassured them physically and prepared them mentally for the final.

From the moment they had been put into a boat together, they had been fast. All their training and prognostic speeds throughout the season supported this. Their wins in the heat and semi-final supported this too, but Charles still felt that they had not secured their position enough. They could not dare think that it was possible to win. They faced Greece, Romania, France and Italy in the final. They had beaten the Greeks and the Romanians in the semi-final, but now faced the world-record holders, France, whom they feared – and the Italians, who were unknown entities. With Marco they prepared for the final, going into the race with inevitable anxiety and nervousness.

As they took off out of the start in the final, they dropped immediately into third place. It was not a good start. At the 500-metre mark Charles thought, *Flip, things are going so badly. We are having our worst race.* He was trying to console himself that, despite it all, they were in bronze position and he bargained with himself that bronze was okay. At the 1 000-metre mark they were still in third place, behind by a massive 4.6 seconds. The Romanian and Greek pair had surged out in front and were leading the pack. Both those crews looked unbeatable.

Standing with David, James, my father, and James Mitchell's parents, my heart bursting with anxiety and tension, I screamed them on from the grandstand, stroke by agonising stroke.

My heart sank as we witnessed the Greeks and Romanians surge ahead. But not for long.

With 500 metres to go, the South African pair started to edge up on the Greek pair. Charles looked across and thought, *Let's get through the Greeks and into silver.*

They did.

Charles saw the Italian pair go with them when they overtook Greece. He immediately thought, *Let's get away from them. I am not going to give them the silver.* The moment they passed the Greeks, they put themselves back in the race. James and Charles were now in second place behind Romania. They thought Romania looked unassailable; Charles was surprised by how far ahead they were. The South African pair thought the Romanians would win, as they had such a lead on them.

'I can't see anyone doing anything to the Romanian lead,' said the commentator.

But James and Charles did not give up.

They were coming, moving steadily towards the gutsy and determined Romanian pair. James and Charles were even more gutsy and determined. They had a secret weapon they could use, a weapon they had not yet had to use at this event. They had won their heat and semi-final races relatively easily, and had simply held or even reduced speed as they had finished. They needed something different here if they were going to win.

This required a sprint finish to the line, in the last 300 metres of the race. A massive increase in speed and power through the water. And they could sprint.

Like demons.

At 350 metres to go, Charles could hear the Romanians close by. He yelled out a powerful call to James: 'I can hear them. Gold.'

At 100 metres to go, they knew they would win.

The commentary said it all. 'The charge from the South Africans goes up over 41 [strokes per minute]! They've got contact, they've got overlap. It's a stunning sprint finish from the Saffers! South Africa move out into the lead. They've moved up through the Romanians. I can't believe it! Just immaculate strength there to the line.'

James and Charles powered past the Romanians and crossed the finish line in first place to win gold. They raised their arms to acknowledge the win and each other, before smashing them down into the water as the joy of the achievement began to overpower the pain and the staggering effort it had taken to win.

Charles had come through a tough few years. Despite this, our family knew he had the spirit and temperament of a warrior. A racer with the perseverance and determination never to give up. This was the first time in his career he had dominated to this extent. He had won. His words, 'Winning is the only reason I carry on rowing,' resonated deeply. It is always about winning.

This was a big win, but it was only the beginning.

There are many, many battles ahead. The road stretching out into the future marks a long, hard struggle. That struggle needs courage, fearlessness, hard work, discipline and extraordinary mental and physical strength.

It is the life, the battle, of the fighters.

Warriors.

* * *

Pretoria, 2021

On 30 June 2021, a group of six South African rowing athletes, accompanied by two coaches and myself, will leave OR Tambo Airport bound for Japan.

Our purpose?

Tokyo 2020.

In May 2020, the COVID-19 pandemic that has swept the world stopped Olympic preparation dead in its tracks. Athletes and coaches from every corner of the world reeled under the shockwave, trying to make sense of the unprecedented decision to cancel the Tokyo 2020 Olympics.

Even more unprecedented was the decision to hold the Olympics a year later in 2021, but still with the name of Tokyo 2020.

With enormous difficulty and under the constant threat of COVID-19, the team trained on resolutely. Some athletes contracted the illness. Some recovered from it and some were forced to take a break. Some had other problems and left, some were not selected, some did not qualify.

In late 2021, Charles decided to take a break from rowing and stepped away from the intense world of Olympic preparation. It was one of those difficult decisions that feel perfectly right, but also feel so incredibly wrong.

Eventually, after a gruelling selection and qualification process, two boats emerged, ready to take on the world: a heavyweight men's pair and men's four. Jake Green and Luc Daffarn make up the pair, and three of the four are Sandro Torrente, John Smith and Kyle Schoonbee.

Sitting in the bow of the men's four is my son, Lawrence Brittain.

The games will continue, racing will happen, medals will be won. No spectators will attend. It will be a very different experience. But for those who want to fight for a place, it will be an Olympics just like all the others.

Different, but the same.

Tokyo 2020.

* * *

Writing this story, I have come to realise that, in this world of rowing, everything is interconnected. I see how the same people, the same hope, the same dream, the same struggle connects us in a vast, intricate web.

Rowing runs deep. It is absorbed into your core, it flows in your blood, you breathe it, you live it. It is a continuous cycle, connected on many levels. It brings its own great rhythm of struggle and reward. It demands tenacity and endurance. The rhythm, the flow, is a continuous forward movement.

Our lives and our choices, and the people we become, are connected.

The river of life flows forward. The current takes you onwards; you do not return.

I look back at the journey and expanses of my life up to this point and mixed with the inevitable pain of seeing the boys grow up and move slowly away is a fierce love and immense pride in them, in the men and the warriors they have become. Like anyone, I have had my own lifetime of problems. I have been through some of the worst things, but I have also been through some of the best things. The river of my life has brought suffering. My mother's death, one of my children becoming seriously ill, my own illnesses, and other things about which I cannot speak. These things could have flattened me, and in many ways they did. It is inevitable that we will suffer and suffer again. Did I blame God? Not at all. I have never believed that what happens to us on earth is God's will. He gave us freedom, and we have choices to make what we can of our lives. It is pointless to ask, 'Why me?' because the simplest answer would be, 'Why not you?'

But one cannot stay broken. In the darkest hours, courage leads us on, and life calls us to healing and gratitude. There is always joy and spirit. Life flows forward with the passage of time and presents us with everything we need to grow into ourselves. Do I thank God? Most definitely. I believe in his powerful presence and meaning, the ultimate support.

Between Lawrence and me we have survived three cancers. Being survivors allowed us to use difficulty to become stronger and braver. In many ways, these experiences helped me to become more understanding of others.

I thank my parents and family most profoundly for setting me up as best they could to handle the river of my life. Marrying David, having my children and seeing them grow up has been the best time of my life. I could not have asked for more joy. Witnessing the boys win gold and silver has been spectacular, but they could have come last and it would have made no difference to me.

My greatest joy is the deep and strong brotherly bond that cements the boys together. I pray that this will last for all their lives.

Having four sons has finally brought girls into my life, and I am proud that the boys have chosen dynamic, strong and independent women. It gives me joy to see the boys happy, but even more joy to see them working at relationships and making their partners happy.

The stories of my family have common threads of survivorship, courage and perseverance. These threads weave the fabric of my family.

Life calls us on.

It is what we do: we keep pushing on, and heading for battle, as warriors.

Warriors with the hearts of lions.

REFERENCES

Allers, R & Minkoff, R. *The Lion King*. California, Walt Disney Pictures & Walt Disney Feature Animation, 1994.

Bay, J. 'Let it Go'. Single track release, Concord Music Publishing, 2014.

Bond, H & Murray, E. *The Kiwi Pair*. New Zealand, Penguin Random House, 2016.

Chin, J & Vasarhelyi, EC. *Free Solo*. California, National Geographic Documentary Films, 2018.

Churchill, WS. *The Unrelenting Struggle*. London, Cassell, 1942.

Dahl, R. *Matilda*. London, Jonathan Cape, 1988.

De Couberton, P. 'The Olympic Motto'. Accessed at https://olympics.com/ioc/olympic-motto, 18 June 2021.

Frankl, VE. *Man's Search for Meaning*. London, Rider (an imprint of Penguin Random House), 2008.

Gibran, K. *The Prophet*. New York, Alfred A. Knopf, 1923.

Hand, D. *Bambi*. California, Walt Disney Productions, 1942.

Kass, AA & Kass, EH. *Perfecting the World: The Life and Times of Dr Thomas Hodgkin 1798–1866*. Harcourt Brace Jovanovich, New York, 1988.

King, S. *On Writing: A Memoir of the Craft*. New York, Scribner (an imprint of Simon & Schuster, Inc.) © 2000 by Stephen King. All rights reserved. Used with permission.

Kipling, R. *The Jungle Book*. London, Macmillan, 1894.

Lewis, CS. *Prince Caspian: The Return to Narnia*. Great Britain, Collins, 1988.

Lyndsey, A. *Girl in the Dark*. London, Bloomsbury Circus, an imprint of Bloomsbury Publishing Plc, 2015. © Reproduced with permission.

Mayle, P. *Encore Provence: New Adventures in the South of France*. London, Vintage (an imprint of Penguin Random House), 2000.

McBratney, S. *Guess How Much I Love You*. London, Walker Books Ltd, 1994.

Morpurgo, M. *Half a Man*. London, Walker Books Ltd, 2005.

Naskar, A. *Time to Save Medicine*. Independently published, 2018.

Noakes, T with Vlismas, M. *Challenging Beliefs: Memoirs of a Career*. Cape Town, Zebra Press, 2012.

Pinsent, M. *A Lifetime in a Race*. London, Ebury Press (an imprint of Penguin Random House), 2004.

Roberts, GR. *The Mountain Shadow*. New York, Zola Books, 2015.

Rosen, M. *We're Going on a Bear Hunt*. London, Walker Books Ltd, 1989.

Scott, R. *Gladiator*. California, Scott Free Productions & Red Wagon Entertainment, 2000.

Seuss, Dr. *The Sneetches and Other Stories*. Great Britain, Random House, 1953.

Shakespeare, W. *The Comedy of Errors*. Oxford World Classics, 5:1. Oxford, Oxford University Press, 2002.

Tobias, PV & Arnold, M. *Man's Anatomy – A Study in Dissection, Vol 1*. Johannesburg, Witwatersrand University Press, 1964.

Tolkien, JRR. *The Hobbit*. London, George Allen and Unwin, 1937.

Van Kets, P. *The Eighth Summit*. Cape Town, Mercury (an imprint of Burnet Media), 2014. Reproduced with permission.

Weiner, J. *His Brother's Keeper: A Story from the Edge of Medicine*. London, 4th Estate (an imprint of HarperCollins), 2004. Reprinted by permission of HarperCollins Publishers Ltd. © 2004, Jonathan Wiener.

Wilton, DC. 'Cover Your Tracks', performed by Boy with a Kite, *The Twilight Saga: Breaking Dawn, Part 2*, 2012. Reproduced with permission.

ACKNOWLEDGEMENTS

During the years of putting this book together, I received much encouragement and help from many people.

To *all* the rowers and coaches, and some who are neither athlete nor coach but are involved with rowing, too many to mention by name, all who spent time with me telling me their stories, filling the gaps, explaining rowing and the pain. I have the deepest and utmost respect for all of you.

To some special people who encouraged me during the journey of writing all this: my husband David, my father Bertie, my sister Claudine, and friends Nici Verriest, Sue Tyser, Cheryl Liepner, Sandy Persse, Verena Ballhausen and Ursula Grobler.

To Carel Nolte and Laura Goldsworthy for getting this off the ground, and Julia and Paolo Cavalieri, especially you, Julia, going through your own difficulty.

To RMB for the ongoing and valuable support to Rowing South Africa.

To the incredible editing and publishing team at Bookstorm who managed to make it all come together despite Covid and working remotely. Louise Grantham, Russell Clarke, Angela Voges – you guided me patiently and skilfully through a world of which I knew nothing.

To my entire extended family, whom I love dearly.

And finally, to my family of warriors, who over and over have showed bravery and fearlessness, the warrior mentality. Despite what you think, you are all my favourites.

David – for your constant love and generosity, your unbelievable ability to take everything in your stride, you have been my rock.

Matthew – for your ferocious mental strength and focus, you are a true inspiration and leader.

Alicia – for loving my son and for being so hardworking, organised and dedicated; supporting the move to London and Singapore.

Lawrence – your story inspired this book, your honesty, bravery and good nature, for taking what life throws at you in your stride.

Nicky – for loving my son and sticking by him when the going got rough, for your amazing bright and positive outlook on life.

James – for being the courageous and warm-hearted spirit that you are, choosing your own destiny despite the ground.

Stacey – for choosing my son and committing when all things happened, for your energy, incredible warmth and deep sense of family.

Charles – for showing unwavering strength, courage and honesty as you face the challenge of deep footprints already ahead of you, making your way and showing us who you are.

And last but certainly not least, Nathan – for being the darling grandson that you are and bringing more joy than I ever thought possible.

Thank you.

Made in United States
Orlando, FL
06 February 2022

14534985R00183